Instructor's Manual

THE WORLD OF LITERATURE

Louise Westling
Stephen Durrant
James W. Earl
Stephen Kohl
Anne Laskaya
Steven Shankman
Louis Orsini
Brian Whaley

of the University of Oregon

PRENTICE HALL, Upper Saddle River, New Jersey 07458

©1999 by PRENTICE-HALL, INC.
Upper Saddle River, New Jersey 07458

All rights reserved

10 9 8 7 6 5 4 3 2 1

ISBN 0-13-645193-4

Printed in the United States of America

Contents

Introduction 1
The Hymns to Inanna 3
The Epic of Gilgamesh 4
Poetry of Ancient Egypt 5
Genesis 7
Exodus 8
The Book of Ruth 9
The Book of Job 11
The Psalms 12
Ecclesiastes 13
The Song of Songs 15
The Rig Veda and the Upanishads 16
The Rāmāyana of Vālmikī 17
The Mahābhārata 18
The Vimalakīrti Sutra 19
Asvaghosha 21
Book of Songs 22
Confucius: The Analects 23
Laozi: Dao de jing 25
Zhuangzi: On the Equality of Things 27
Mozi: "Shedding Light on Ghosts" 28
Qu Yuan: "On Encountering Sorrow" 30
Rhyme-Prose (Fu) and Han Dynasty Poetry 32
Sima Qian: Records of the Historian 33
Hesiod: Theogony 35
The Homeric Hymn to Demeter 36
Homer: The Odyssey 37
Sappho 38
Pindar: "Olympian 14" and "Pythian 3" 39
Thucydides: The Peloponnesian War 41
Euripides: The Bacchae 42
Plato: The Apology, The Republic ["The Allegory of the Cave"], The Symposium 44
Catullus: Poems 46
Virgil: The Aeneid 47
Horace: Odes 48
Ovid: Metamorphoses and Heroides 51
The Gospel of Mark 52
Three Qasīdas 54
The Qur'ān 56
Muhammad Ibn Ishāq: The Life of the Prophet 58
Abol-Qasem Ferdowsi: The Tragedy of Sohráb and Rostám (from The Shāh-nāmah) 60
Farid al-Dīn Attar: The Conference of Birds and "The Life and Teachings of Rābi`ah al-
    `Adawiyya" (from The Memorial of Saints) 62
Usāmah Ibn Munqidh: The Book of Reflections 64
Abu 'Abdallah Ibn Battutah: The Travels 65
The Thousand and One Nights 67
The Book of Dede Korkut 69

Arabic and Persian Poetry 71
Kālidāsa: Śakuntalā and the Ring of Recollection 73
Vidyakara: Treasury of Well-Turned Verse 75
Two Bhakti Poets, Ravidas and Mīrābāī 77
Gan Bao: In Search of the Supernatural 89
Tao Qian: Poems 80
The Lotus Sutra 82
Four Tang Poets: Wang Wei, Li Bai, Du Fu, Bai Juyi 83
Yuan Zhen: The Story of Ying-ying 85
Two Song Poets: Su Dongpo, Li Qingzhao 87
Wu Cheng'en: Monkey 88
The Kojiki 90
Manyōshū 91
Japanese Court Poetry 93
Izumi Shikibu: The Diary of Lady Izumi Shikibu 94
Murasaki Shikibu: The Tale of the Genji 96
Kamo no Chōmei: An Account of My Hermitage 98
Tales of the Heike 99
Nō Theatre: Atsumori and Aoi no Ue 100
Korea in the Middle Period: Hyangga, Cho'oe Ch'i-Won, Songs of Flying Dragons, Hwang
    Chin-I, Hŏ Nansŏrhŏn 101
Augustine: Confessions 103
Bede: "[The Parable of the Sparrow]" and "[The Story of Cædmon]" 105
Abelard and Heloise: The Letters 106
Thomas More: Utopia 108
Old Norse Literature 109
Provençal Poetry 111
Marie de France 113
Two Middle English Lyrics: "Quia Amore Langueo" and "The Corpus Christi Carol" ... 114
Marco Polo: The Travels 116
Dante Alighieri: The Inferno 117
Francis Petrarch: Rime 120
Geoffrey Chaucer: The Canterbury Tales 122
Christine de Pizan: The Book of the City of Ladies 124
Michel de Montaigne: "Of Cannibals" 126
William Shakespeare: King Lear 127
Miguel de Cervantes: Don Quixote 131
Naguib Mahfouz: "Zaabalawi" 132
Salwa Bakr: "That Beautiful Undiscovered Voice" 134
Fadwa Tuqan: Poems 135
Yehuda Amichai: "Jerusalem, 1967" and "Tourists" 137
Léopold Sédar Senghor: Poems 138
Grace Ogot: "The Bamboo Hut" 140
Chinua Achebe: Things Fall Apart 141
Wole Soyinka: A Scourge of Hyacinths 143
Rabindranath Tagore: "The Hungry Stones" 144
Rajee Seth: "Just a Simple Bridge" 145
Salman Rushdie: "The Courter" 146
Angkarn Kalayaanaphong: "Grandma" 148
Nguyen Huy Thiep: "Salt of the Jungle" 149

Cao Xueqin: Dream of the Red Chamber ... 150
Shen Fu: Six Records of a Floating Life ... 152
Lu Xun: "Ah Q—The Real Story" ... 154
Ding Ling: "When I Was in Xia Village" ... 155
Matsuo Bashō: Narrow Road to the Interior ... 157
Natsume Sōseki: The Wayfarer ... 158
Kawabata Yasunari: "The Pomegranate," "Snow," "Cereus" ... 160
Abe Kōbō: "Stick" and "Red Cocoon" ... 161
Ōba Minako: "The Three Crabs" ... 162
Sonu Hwi: "Thoughts of Home" ... 164
John Milton: Paradise Lost ... 164
Alexander Pope: Eloisa to Abelard ... 166
Jane Austen: Pride and Prejudice ... 167
James Joyce: "Araby," "Eveline," Ulysses, Finnegans Wake ... 169
Virginia Woolf: To the Lighthouse ... 171
Samuel Beckett: Happy Days ... 173
Madame de Sévigné: Letters ... 174
Jean-Jacques Rousseau: The Confessions ... 175
Charles Baudelaire: The Flowers of Evil ... 176
Marcel Proust: In Search of Lost Time ... 178
Friedrich Hölderlin: "Patmos" ... 180
Rainer Maria Rilke: Duino Elegies ... 181
Franz Kafka: "A Country Doctor" and "An Imperial Message" ... 183
Fyodor Dostoyevsky: Notes from Underground ... 185
Anna Akhmatova: Poems ... 187
Wislawa Szymborska ... 188
The Popul Vuh ... 190
Jorge Luis Borges: Stories ... 191
Pablo Neruda: "The Heights of Macchu Picchu," "The Word," The Book of Questions .. 193
Gabriel García Márquez: "The Handsomest Drowned Man in the World" ... 195
Ángela Hernández: "How to Gather the Shadows of the Flowers" ... 196
Walt Whitman: "Memories of President Lincoln: When Lilacs Last in the Dooryard
   Bloom'd" ... 197
Emily Dickinson ... 199
Ezra Pound ... 201
T. S. Eliot: "The Waste Land" ... 201
William Faulkner: "That Evening Sun" ... 203
Elizabeth Bishop ... 204
Toni Morrison: Sula ... 206
Irena Klepfisz: "Bashert" ... 208
Louise Erdrich: "Saint Marie" (from Love Medicine) ... 209

Introduction

This teacher's manual was written by the six editors of <u>The World of Literature</u>, with the invaluable editorial and writing help of Brian Whaley. We also owe a debt to Louis Orsini, who wrote a number of entries dealing with Hebrew, Greek and Roman, and modern European literature. Our writing styles and suggested approaches to texts are naturally varied. We hope they will stimulate teachers' ideas, help where a text is completely unfamiliar, and offer practical suggestions for the classroom. We think of our manual as a work in progress that will grow and change as <u>The World of Literature</u> finds its way into various educational settings with differing kinds of readers. We welcome suggestions from other teachers, and we know that our own experiences with the book in our classes will show us new ways to explore the feast of poetry and prose from all over the globe that the anthology brings together.

Always a major problem with the use of anthologies is the uncertainty each of us brings to unfamiliar materials. Most teachers are too busy to work up large bodies of new materials every time they teach a course, and the use of works in translation from so many different cultures makes interpretation especially daunting because of the difficulty of contextualizing and because of uncertainty about how clear a sense of literary style one can achieve. Nevertheless, we urge teachers to take the risk, using our suggestions for classroom approaches and letting students take an active part in a group effort to enter the world of the writer. Virginia Woolf challenged readers to think of themselves as fellow-workers and accomplices of writers, banishing preconceptions and opening their minds as widely as possible to what they encounter on the page. We have all found that this kind of approach brings enormous rewards—surprises, unexpected pleasures, new ways of understanding our lives, and glimpses into new worlds. The secondary sources we have recommended are for the most part introductory ones that provide historical, cultural, and biographical backgrounds, as well as surveying basic critical approaches. At the freshman and sophomore university level, highly specialized scholarship can intimidate and obfuscate classroom discussion, but for the teacher's own understanding scholarly surveys may be helpful. We have sought to provide sources that will also orient teachers to the range of scholarship available for individual works. In some cases, however, particularly with recent fiction and poetry from developing countries where there is not yet a well-established publishing tradition, or in cultures whose literatures have not been much translated in English, we have not been able to find adequate secondary materials to recommend. In those cases, for example Ángela Hernández's "How to Gather the Shadows of Flowers" or Nguyen Huy Thiep's "Salt of the Jungle," we can only encourage teachers to take the plunge and trust their students to find ways of making sense of the stories. When there is genuine opportunity for such explorations, students always come through; in fact such situations can provide some of the most exciting teaching experiences.

We owe far too many debts to colleagues for advice and scholarly expertise to be able to acknowledge them individually here. It is sufficient to say that without the support of our lively university community, no project of this kind could ever be accomplished.

The Hymns to Inanna

These narrative poems were shaped by folklorist Diane Wolkstein from shorter hymns and fragmentary poems to the goddess that were translated and gathered together by the eminent Sumerologist Samuel Noah Kramer. Wolkstein is a professional storyteller whose collaboration with Kramer was an unusual example of cooperation between specialists in the two different fields of humanistic research. Kramer was a pioneer in recovering the literature of ancient Sumer for modern readers, and he found Wolkstein's knowledge of stories from around the world and her skill in communicating them helpful in making these 4,000-year-old stories accessible for modern readers. Wolkstein eliminated cluttering repetitions, added occasional explanatory lines, and restored some broken passages with Kramer's scholarly help. The result is a strange, powerful love story told in incantatory, ritualistic form that contrasts with more familiar treatments of love such as Egyptian lyrics, the Biblical Song of Songs or story of Ruth, or poems from the Chinese Book of Songs. The relationship between Inanna and Gilgamesh reflects at its beginning some of the tension between farmers and shepherds that we find in the Genesis stories of Cain and Abel and Jacob and Esau, but its resolution is more peaceable. Inanna's power in the relationship is starkly different from Sita's dependence on her husband Rama's will in the Indian Ramayana. Both began in oral traditions long predating their written forms, but clearly the Indian value system placed women in passive positions in which they could be stolen and fought over by men whose honor was defined by the "purity" of these possessions. Inanna's vigorous behavior both in courtship and in her underworld adventure offers opportunities for discussion as a contrast to these other traditions.

An important first step in making students comfortable with these materials is discussion of their form, particularly the highly ritualized, repetitious way the love story and the story of the descent are told. Asking students to look for patterns of repetition helps them begin to see where the emphasis of the religious belief might lie. Attention should be paid to Inanna's costume in preparing for marriage and in readying herself for her journey below. Students can be directed to identify symbolic elements such as the plants related to Dumuzi, the dead meat into which Inanna is transformed by Ereshkigal, and the progressive undressing that leads up to this horrifying defeat.

For "The Courtship of Inanna and Dumuzi" the progressive stages of courtship can be identified, with discussion of the significance of each one. Inanna's resistance to her suitor relaxes as he sings to her of his devotion and the gifts he brings, and she then engages with him in an eager dialogue of physical union described in terms of the landscape's fertility. Students should be urged to look closely at the pledges the lovers make to each other after their union, for many qualities of their sacred relationship are defined in the final stanzas. This hieratic, semi-divine marriage is very different from concepts of marriage or amorous partnership students are likely to have, and lively debate could result from questions about these cultural differences. Could it be, for example, that the glossy fold-outs in Playboy function in similar ways to ideas about the reproductive power of Inanna? Have we merely secularized these ancient impulses and debased what were once sacred attitudes?

"The Descent of Inanna" is such a strange narrative that class time can productively be spent discussing what makes it so, and how modern readers might explain its spooky power. The story can be seen as a counterpart to such tales as the rape of Persephone or the death of American Indian corn deities. All relate human lives to the lives of plants, but the stories differ in the causes of death for the human personification of plants or grain.

For further information about these poems, the best place to start is <u>Inanna: Queen of Heaven and Earth</u> (New York, 1983), by Diane Wolkstein and Samuel Noah Kramer. This volume is the source of our selections and contains excellent introductory materials and appendices by both authors. Kramer provides invaluable background information about Sumerian history, culture and literature. Kramer's <u>History Begins at Sumer</u> (Garden City, New York, 1959) is an earlier introduction to Sumerian literature containing both very accessible scholarship and translations of major works. Thorkild Jacobsen's <u>The Treasures of Darkness: A History of Mesopotamian Religion</u> (New Haven, 1976) is a major study of the religious traditions of the region.

Questions for Study and Discussion:

1. How are modern American attitudes about love and sexuality different from Sumerian ones as you infer them from these poems? Do we see our reproductive lives as linked to the seasonal rhythms of the landscape?

2. Is it possible to understand the motivations of these Sumerian divine beings? How is the depiction of character and soul different from those of our own culture?

3. Do we share religious values with the people of ancient Sumer? What relationships are there between contemporary religions and these ancient ones?

4. What finally brings Inanna and Dumuzi together? How does he convince her that he is the appropriate bridegroom?

5. What does the young king receive from his divine queen? How can we understand Sumerian values as mirrored in this sacred marriage?

6. How is Inanna's journey to the underworld shaped for dramatic effect? What does it mean, and why does she doom her husband to take her place?

The Epic of Gilgamesh

This first great world epic makes an immediate appeal to students, with its folkloric story of the hairy man Enkidu raised in the wilderness. Links spring up with Biblical stories like that of Esau and John the Baptist or hairy European figures like Iron John of the Grimms' Fairy Tales. A vaunting hero like Gilgamesh is familiar because of his many descendants, from Achilles, to lords of the <u>Mahābhārata</u> or the <u>Rāmāyana</u>, Siegfried, Beowulf, Knights of the Round Table, James Fenimore Cooper's Deerslayer, or modern heroes like those in Star Wars films. But questions might be raised about how universal such figures really are. Early Chinese and Japanese poems do not feature men who set out to conquer the landscape and even defy sacred beings in order to prove their worth. Setting this epic up against the patriarchs of the Hebrew scriptures reveals interesting differences in concepts of virtue or strength. Also, illuminating contrasts can be drawn with the teachings of Confucius and the values implied in Sima Qian's writing. The disastrous results of the hero's arrogance are of course comparable to those of Achilles' petulance in the Trojan War stories of the Greeks.

Key issues in the epic are the character of the young king and the reasons Enkidu is created to be his companion. The strange upbringing of Enkidu and his poignant loss of natural strength are important to think of in relation to Gilgamesh's behavior in Uruk. Gilgamesh's dream and his symbolic first encounter with Enkidu are revealing, because they indicate what the hairy counterpart of the king represents. Follow the pair of heroes as they set out on their quest for fame, and look closely at their attitudes to the sacred forest and Humbaba. The drama of their meeting with the forest's guardian is a moving one, especially as Humbaba pleads for his life and yet is opposed by Enkidu, who was once a similar wild figure. It is useful to discuss with students what a different kind of figure Ishtar is in this epic from Inanna in the Sumerian poems, for her independence has been lost and her sexuality turned into shame. The arrogant defiance of Ishtar and murder of the Bull of Heaven are sins that bring a terrible punishment, and this tragic set of circumstances rewards close attention. Gilgamesh's journey to find the secret of eternal life is a sort of fairytale appendix to the epic, and it will be easy for students to understand. Overall, the epic offers opportunities for discussion of large human themes such as the yearning for immortality, the relations of humans to the natural world, the definition of heroism, and gendered conflicts.

The most useful study of the Gilgamesh epic is Jeffrey Tigay's The Origins of the Gilgamesh Epic (Philadelphia, 1982), but interesting background can also be found in Thorkild Jacobsen, The Treasures of Darkness: A History of Mesopotamian Religion (New Haven, 1976). Useful interpretive discussions of Gilgamesh occur in early chapters of Max Oelschlaeger's The Idea of Wilderness (New Haven, 1991), Robert Pogue Harrison's Forests: The Shadow of Civilization (Chicago, 1992), and Louise Westling's The Green Breast of the New World (Athens, Georgia, 1996).

Questions for Study and Discussion:

1. Why is Enkidu created, and what does he represent?

2. How would you describe Gilgamesh? What are his values, his energies, his problems?

3. What kind of a relationship grows up between Gilgamesh and Enkidu? What do Gilgamesh's dreams and his fight with the newcomer reveal about it? Why does Gilgamesh grieve as he would for a bride when his friend dies?

4. Why does Gilgamesh want to cut down the forest, and what does this place represent? How do we know?

5. What causes the death of Enkidu?

6. What is the meaning of Gilgamesh's loss of the secret of eternal life?

Poetry of Ancient Egypt

Egyptian lyric poetry is direct, immediate, and remarkably modern in tone when compared to the poetry of ancient Mesopotamia. Students will feel at home at once, in spite of the three- or four-thousand-year difference between themselves and the world of the shipwrecked sailor or the lovers describing their yearnings. "The Tale of the Shipwrecked Sailor" is a marvelous adventure that can be taught with Homer's Odyssey, Virgil's Aeneid, the travels of Ibn Battutah, the Chinese folk epic Monkey, and even Bashō's Narrow Road to the Interior. All these travel narratives utilize the metaphor of life as a journey but also fascinate with the lure of new and strange experiences.

Akhenaton's "Hymn to the Sun" is a beautiful poem of religious devotion that can be read together with the ancient Indian Rig Veda and contrasted with the supernatural attitudes of the ancient Greeks, as well as the monotheistic spiritual traditions of the Bible and the Qur'an. "The Debate between a Man Tired of Life and His Soul" has obvious affinities with the Biblical story of Job, but also with wisdom writings from ancient China and India such as the Rig Veda, the Bhagavad-Gītā, and the Dao de jing. As a dialogic meditation on the purpose of life, it can also be taught with the religious texts we have included from the Bible, the teachings of Buddha, and the Qur'an. "The Song of the Harper" resonates clearly with the teachings in the Biblical book of Ecclesiastes but also contrasts in interesting ways with the Bhagavad-Gītā and the Analects of Confucius and the Dao de jing. In later periods such Japanese writers as Chōmei and Bashō also reflect on the transitory quality of life.

The charming love lyrics from ancient Egypt seem almost to belong to our own world, with their intimacy and fresh evocation of desire. Students will enjoy comparing the situations of the lovers and their attitudes toward each other with the courtship hymns of Inanna and Gilgamesh, poems from the Chinese Book of Songs, the Biblical Song of Songs, and the poetry of love written in medieval Japanese court society as well as the Courtly Love poems of medieval France and Italy.

Because these poems are written in such direct, simple language without ritual tone or heavy metaphorical texture, they do not present serious problems for students. Students can discuss the quality of religious devotion and ways the "Hymn to the Sun," "Debate between a Man Tired of Life and his Soul," and "Song of the Harper" express their metaphysical views in debates or direct address to the deity. Comparison with other religious poetry mentioned above can also be fruitful. Students' attention can be drawn to the settings of the love poems, the attitudes of the lovers towards each other, and the direct ways they express their feelings. Some indication of gender relations in Egyptian society is provided by the relationships defined in the poems.

Background information is available in The Literature of Ancient Egypt: An Anthology of Stories, Instructions and Poetry, edited by William Kelly Simpson (New Haven, 1972), and Echoes of Egyptian Voices: An Anthology of Ancient Egyptian Poetry, translated by John L. Foster (Norman, Oklahoma, 1992).

Questions for Study and Discussion:

1. What kind of deity is addressed in the "Hymn to the Sun"? What qualities are worshiped, and what is the attitude of the pharoah-poet?

2. What kind of creature is the magic serpent in "The Tale of the Shipwrecked Sailor," and what does it teach the sailor?

3. Why is the speaker in "The Debate between Man Tired of Life and His Soul" in such a despairing state? What are the virtues taught by the Soul?

4. Are there significant differences between the male and female speakers in the love poems from Egypt?

5. What are the favorite settings of the love poems, and why?

Genesis

We have included many of the most ancient and culturally formative creation stories from around the globe in The World of Literature. These are the natural works to teach with Genesis: hymns from the Rig Veda, Hesiod's Theogony, the Japanese Kojiki, Book I of Ovid's Metamorphoses, and the Mayan Popul Vuh. Genesis is also important as an influence upon Medieval European literature, and indeed upon all literature from Judaic, Christian, and Arabic cultures because they share this foundational text describing the fall from grace of the original human parents. The Islamic version of the story appears in Sura 20 of the Qur'an. John Milton's Paradise Lost makes the most explicit literary use of the story of Adam and Eve, which is a fascinating modern attempt to explain the narrative in logical, philosophical terms.

Most students will be familiar with the stories in Genesis, especially that of Adam and Eve and the serpent's temptation. In order to make these materials fresh, it is a good idea to contrast the versions of the creation story in Genesis 1 and Genesis 2, and to place the events of the original human pair within the broader context of cosmic formation in Genesis 1. The nature of God is conceived quite differently in the two versions, with the first being a rather formal and distant creator, while the deity who communicates with Adam and Eve is much more personal and interactive. The drama of Eve's willingness to break God's commandment in order to gain knowledge and Adam's desire to accompany her is worth close attention, as is the response of God in cursing not only the human offenders but also the earth. Students can discuss the values implied in the text, as well as concepts of the relation between humans and the rest of creation.

The story of the flood has obvious moral dimensions, with the wickedness of humans causing the kind of divine retribution that appears in many ancient traditions including the Babylonian Epic of Gilgamesh and the Mayan Popul Vuh (though not in the selection in our text). Students can examine the structure of the story for its dramatic pacing, discuss the implied vision of the relation of humans to the natural and supernatural order, and think of its relation to apocalyptic predictions of our own era.

Both the story of Abraham and Isaac and the story of Joseph are concerned with the relation of fathers and sons which are so central to the patriarchal culture of the ancient Hebrews. Students might be asked to think about what kind of social and psychic preoccupations might result in a story such as that requiring Abraham to kill his own son as a sacrifice to his God. Does a tradition of human sacrifice lie behind such a directive, or is this an extreme kind of parable about the way God tests the devotion of believers? The whole question of ancient practices of blood sacrifice is an interesting one to consider in the context of modern values. Joseph represents the opposite kind of problem, with the father's favoritism blighting Joseph's relations with his jealous brothers. Joseph's behavior under the trying circumstances of his imprisonment and later adventures in Egypt can be explored as an example in the ancient world of cross-cultural relations and the complexities of international diplomacy. The almost fairytale qualities of the story can be discussed in allegorical terms, and the drama of Joseph's various trials and triumphs makes for entertaining commentary.

For a general introduction to the earliest books of the Hebrew Bible, and to Genesis in particular, The New Jerusalem Bible (New York, 1985) offers a brief but well-informed and balanced perspective. More detailed commentary is provided in Robert Alter and Frank Kermode's A Literary Guide to the Bible (Cambridge, MA, 1987).

Questions for Study and Discussion:

1. What are the differences between the two versions of the creation story in Genesis 1 and Genesis 2-4? What kind of God seems to be active in each, and what is the relation of humans to the rest of creation?

2. Who is responsible for the "fall" from grace occasioned by the eating of the forbidden fruit? Debate has raged on this question for thousands of years. Look closely at the behavior of all parties, and think about the role of knowledge and innocence implied. Why does God punish the earth as well as the disobedient creatures?

3. What causes the flood, and why is Noah saved? In Chapter 9, why does God endow all creatures with fear and dread of humans, and what does he mean by forbidding humans to "eat flesh with its life" or blood, and what reckoning will be taken for our shedding of animals' blood? What is the function of the story of Noah's drunkenness?

4. Why does God require Abraham to sacrifice his son Isaac? Why is a lamb substituted—that is, killed—to please the deity? What is the function of blood sacrifice, especially in light of the prohibitions to Noah of shedding the blood of other living things?

5. What might Joseph's coat of many colors represent in terms of the whole story of his remarkable life?

6. Is there a meaningful shape to the story of Joseph? What symmetries balance the ending with the beginning? What are the central values of the story? How is the character of Joseph developed?

Exodus

These selections might be taught with other sections of the Hebrew scriptures, or with other foundational texts (including epics), either of an explicitly religious or of a more secular nature; this might include, as examples, some of the dynastic hymns of the Book of Songs (nos. 235, 241, 245) and Virgil's Aeneid. Another natural pairing is with our selection from the New Testament, the Gospel of Mark.

Much of what is at stake here is the very definition of Israel—that is, the meaning of the Jewish experience of the divine. Moses, who has been raised as an Egyptian, is chosen to lead the Israelites out of slavery in Egypt. As both Egyptian and Jew, Moses has a dual identity; recognizing this is crucial for fully understanding the Exodus text.

In coming to grips with Exodus, perhaps the best strategy is to try to allow it to speak to one's own experience—that is, to allow its powerful poetry to function as it has for so many readers who have sought in it liberation from one or another form of oppression.

Students and faculty might usefully consult Eric Voegelin's <u>Israel and Revelation</u> (Baton Rouge, 1957), especially the sections on Moses, as well as the work on the scriptures by Bernard Anderson, <u>Understanding the Old Testament</u> (Englewood Cliffs, NJ, 1975).

<u>Questions for Study and Discussion</u>:

1. What is the significance of the fact that Moses seems to be such an unwilling leader of the newly chosen people?

2. What is the significance of God's calling himself "I AM WHO I AM"?

3. One of the ten commandments is "Thou shalt not kill." How do you square this with God's command in the episode of the golden calf that those who have sinned against him be put to death?

4. Is Moses an epic hero? Compare him with other heroes.

The Book of Ruth

In the Hebrew Bible, the Book of Ruth is placed toward the end, in a collection of materials known as the Megilloth, or "Scrolls." In the Christian arrangement of its Old Testament, the Book of Ruth is located much earlier, as if historically situated, right after the book of Judges. Bernhard. W. Anderson has devised a useful chart which indicates the contents and chronology of biblical materials in the Jewish, Roman Catholic, Orthodox Catholic, and Protestant arrangements (this is found in his <u>Understanding the Old Testament</u>, fourth edition, Englewood Cliffs, NJ, 1986). Students might consider what happens to the Book of Ruth when it occurs in different places within different versions of biblical materials.

One of the issues obvious in this narrative are the lacunae, places where the text does not account for character's actions or motives. It is a feature also found in Kālidāsa's Śakuntalā. These silent spaces invite readers into interpretation. One such is the question of Ruth's motives for leaving Moab and accompanying Naomi back to Bethlehem. Is this an instance, somewhat rare in ancient literature, which dramatizes the love and devotion of one woman for another? Or is Ruth obedient to a patriarchal code of marriage? Note that Orpah returns to her mother's house (1.8) and quickly disappears from the narrative. Ruth, remaining loyal to her husband's family, is inserted into a history of kings. She abandons her own family to align herself with her husband's family. And what of the interwoven subjects of women and land? It appears that the ownership of women is at issue in the text. There is also the question of why Ruth's first child is given to Naomi and why Naomi becomes his nurse. Does the male heir provide Naomi with a replacement for the son she lost? What does this child do for Naomi? Students might ponder why and how the most eloquent words in the narrative which describe Ruth's choice to follow Naomi have been taken and used often within marriage ceremonies.

Because human motives do not seem to be sufficiently explained or, in some cases, explained at all, readers might want to consider whether the text really should be read like a more modern short story or not. Because the characters' motives are submerged or not completely accounted for, other elements of the narrative may emerge as more important. Alexander Globe's discussion of folktale and nationalism in the Book of Ruth offers yet more material useful to teachers. His work is in Approaches to Teaching World Literature, (New York, 1989), edited by Barry N. Olshen and Yael S. Feldman. The book, Reading Ruth: Contemporary Women Reclaim a Sacred Story, edited by Judith A. Kates, Gail T. Reimer (New York, 1994) also offers a collection of essays, some scholarly and some more personal, which could be used fruitfully alongside a study of this text.

Ruth can, of course, be read alongside other biblical materials in the Ancient section of the anthology, and considering the book within that context will likely produce much more rigorous readings of the text. Since female figures are so often erased or represented as secondary to central biblical narratives, considering this text alongside the story of Joseph, for example, sheds a more complete light on both. Like a number of biblical narratives, the socially marginal figures (youngest son, outsider, or, in this case, foreign woman and older woman) are rewarded for their virtue. Because Ruth offers an account of women within sacred narrative it could also be read productively alongside other accounts of women within sacred texts, such as the account of Rābi`ah found in Attar's Memorial of Saints, Christine de Pizan's account of Saint Christine, the more ancient Sumerian materials of Inanna (a text which also includes a sacred courtship), or the sacred Indian writer, Mīrābāī. The women's journeys are worth considering in relation to other sacred journeys but particularly in relation to other journeys found within Hebrew biblical materials.

Question for Study and Discussion:

1. Have students note places where the narrative does not account for motive, or where it leaves out what might seem to be important transitions or explanations. Then have students speculate on the effect and potential meanings created by these lacunae.

2. What appears to be Boaz's motive for marrying Ruth?

3. While this text belongs in both Hebrew and Christian Bibles, God is not an overtly active character in it. What effect does this have? Does it matter? Does this influence what you think the main point of the narrative might be? If so, why? If not, why not?

4. Why is the relationship between Naomi and Ruth so prominent? Why is it that the women say to Naomi, "your daughter-in-law who loves you, who is more to you than seven sons has borne you a male child, a next-of-kin" (4:15)?

5. What do you think is the purpose of the tale? How does it qualify as sacred narrative?

6. Ask students to find out where, in the various versions of the Bible, the Book of Ruth occurs. Ask them then to speculate on how changes in the book's location reflect important differences between these religious traditions. How might the different locations of the text suggest different readings and interpretations?

The Book of Job

Like the rest of the Bible, Job works well in the classroom because it stimulates strong responses and controversy. Many students are so comfortable with the Bible that they can't understand what an English professor might add to their understanding; and many are so angry at it that they can't see any literary value in it. In Job, the literary values are very accessible. As for the "problem of God," the story of the divine wager is mythological enough to compare effectively with the behavior of the gods in <u>Gilgamesh</u>, <u>The Bacchae</u>, or Eastern religious texts like the Bhagavad-Gītā. Students often have an easier time respecting religions that have not shaped their lives, and these comparisons may give them the distance they need to fall in love with <u>Job</u> as literature. The relation of Job to tragedy is a classic literary problem; there is much Job in <u>King Lear</u>. <u>Happy Days</u> is also an interesting text to teach with it. Both of those plays dramatize the problem of human suffering, and like Job they border on the nihilistic.

The two sections of Job included here are so different in style and theme that a class or two could be devoted entirely to describing the differences between them, and calculating the impact they have on each other in juxtaposition. The frame narrative is a folktale portraying the Shakespearian maxim that we are but playthings of the gods; the tale asserts the whimsically absurd nature of the human condition, though at the same time it offers a clear moral response. Job of course has no idea why God is allowing him to suffer. "Why do bad things happen to good people?" is the relevant modern cliche. The prescribed response is an almost Buddhist humility and patience in the face of suffering. How effective could anger at the universe be? (That of course is the Greek tragic hero's response, which may be more heroic, but is certainly less realistic and wise.) Try discussing the frame narrative separately from the intervening poetry: the happy ending (in the last eight verses of the book) will strike many students as inadequate, and there is no reason to dispute this contention. Satan's appearance here is one of only three in the Hebrew Bible. His name means "adversary"; he is not the devil of Christianity, but an argumentative member of God's heavenly court. The text doesn't present a cosmic struggle between Good and Evil, as it may seem to some students.

The poetic chapters offer an entirely different set of problems. In response to Job's outrage over the injustice of his suffering (since he has done nothing to deserve it), God lets loose with a thunderous denunciation of human arrogance, expressed as a long series of sarcastic rhetorical questions. Basically he tells Job to shut up; but the poet is attempting to express the voice of God (or, as I tell my students, the universe itself), and in this bold project he achieves a sublime and vividly detailed vision of the natural world in all its majesty, complexity, weirdness and violence, in which man's ambitions are decentered and reduced to nothing. Many students respond very positively to this speech, since it nicely (and surprisingly) corresponds to a modern post-humanist ecological vision. What kind of religion does it imply? None, some would say. It should be noted that the speech strongly revises the cosmology and moral vision of the rest of the Bible; in fact, nothing in the text even designates Job as Jewish.

Just as importantly, God's speech gives us the chance to discuss Hebrew poetry as poetry. It is constructed entirely of parallelisms, such as "Have you entered the storehouses of the snow, / or have you seen the storehouses of the hail?" Once given this simple insight, students can search enjoyably for the complex structures the poet is able to achieve with this device, which can be deployed in very complex patterns.

When considered together, the two parts of Job are incompatible in important ways. Those who know the rest of the book know that Job is by no means patient in his arguments with his friends. Even in the parts included here, the God of the frame narrative is quite unlike the

God of the speech from the whirlwind, and nothing he says prepares us for the happy ending. In a class small enough for discussion, these insights can be teased out of students' unfolding observations.

Students and teachers who want to read more about Job will find the chapter by Greenberg in Alter and Kermode's Literary Guide to the Bible (Cambridge, MA, 1987) a good start. That book also has a good chapter on Hebrew poetry. Several modern works grapple with the absurdity and the paradoxes of Job: Carl Jung's Answer to Job (Princeton, 1973), Archibald MacLeish's J. B. (Boston, 1958), and Robert Frost's Masque of Reason (New York, 1945). All of these provide excellent paper topics.

Questions for Study and Discussion:

1. How does the text characterize God and Satan? Is God substantially different in the poetic portions than in the prose?

2. How would you account for the repetitions in the prose part, such as 1:7 ff. And 2:2 ff? What effect does the style have on the reader? (Answer: folklore narrative technique.)

3. How many questions does God ask in the poetic speech? Why does he talk in questions?

4. What picture of nature does God present—Eden-like, Sierra Club, or "red in tooth and claw"?

5. What is God's attitude toward the world? How does he portray his creation of it? What is humankind's role in nature?

6. What are Job's replies to God? Is humankind not to search into the mystery of his existence?

7. How natural and coherent does the happy ending seem? How satisfying is it as the conclusion of the story?

The Psalms

The fact that the Hebrew poetic tradition reflected in Psalms appears on the stage of world literature at approximately the same time as the Book of Songs in China and the Vedas in India almost demands some comparison between these traditions. Certainly the Vedas, which are also thoroughly religious in nature, appear to have more in common with Psalms than does the largely secular Book of Songs. However, Book of Songs 241, "God on high in sovereign might" (p. 313), also sings praise to a powerful god and might properly be described as "religious." Students might be asked to compare Psalm 139, the vedic "Hymn of Creation" (p. 177), and Book of Songs 241. Despite the religious nature of all three works, the differences are striking, and students will easily identify some of these—the intensely political nature of the Chinese poem, the highly personal tone of the Hebrew poem, the philosophical nature of the Indian work, etc.

The Psalms reflect a moment in time when monotheism is still a fresh idea and humans are both overwhelmed by the omnipotence and omnipresence of God ("If I ascend up into heaven, thou art there: If I make my bed in hell, behold, thou art there") and troubled that God's people suffer (137). Consequently, students, even those who describe themselves as believers, sometimes find the religious exuberance, the intense expressions of faith, and the outcries of personal unworthiness (as well as the moments of human rancor and vindictiveness) quite distant from their own attitudes.

The great beauty of Psalms comes not from startling imagery nor imaginative language. Scholars have noted that the poetic language of these texts is straightforward and drawn almost entirely from tradition. Indeed, the conservatism of the Psalms is what makes them so difficult to date—pieces written centuries apart can share the same linguistic and literary features. The beauty of so many of these pieces comes from what Robert Alter has described as "a general tendency of biblical poetry toward an intensification or concretization of images and themes both within the line and in the poem as a whole" (see The Literary Guide to the Bible noted below, p. 253). Psalms 23 and 24, both aesthetic masterpieces, might be explored from the perspective of Alter's comment.

A very useful book for discussions of Psalms and other biblical texts is The Literary Guide to the Bible, edited by Robert Alter and Frank Kermode (Cambridge, MA, 1987). Greater detail on Psalms and Hebrew poetry in general can be found in Robert Alter, The Art of Biblical Poetry (New York, 1985). For additional technical detail, see also Hermann Gunkel, The Psalms: A Form-Critical Introduction, translated by Thomas M. Horner (Philadephia, 1967).

Questions for Study and Discussion:

1. Many psalms are presented as cries to God. At the same time, they are not private prayers but are poems that are written down for others to read. Can you discern any tension between the worlds of prayer and of poetry in these pieces?

2. Psalm 8 is simultaneously a hymn praising God and a hymn praising mankind ("For thou has made him a little lower than the angels."). The vedic "Hymn of Man" seems to have the same function. Compare and contrast these two pieces.

3. How do you explain the obsession with enemies that one encounters so often in the Psalms (23, 137, etc.)?

4. One of the features common in the Psalms (and in other early poetic traditions as well) is parallelism, wherein each line of a couplet follows the same grammatical pattern. Trace this feature through one psalm (24 is an excellent example). How do deviations from the pattern heighten the poetic presentation?

5. What attributes do the psalmists ascribe to God? How do they conceive of their relationship to God? How would you answer each of these questions for the Vedas?

Ecclesiastes

Ecclesiastes is attractive as an "alternative" text, one which does not assert the importance of a covenant between man and God. The questions it raises are ones which must be confronted by all people who ask "What is the meaning of life?" In some ways this is the most treacherous of all philosophical questions because it demands an answer that cannot be found. Ecclesiastes addresses this issue.

The scholar C. L. Seow divides this text into four parts. The first, which covers the first four chapters, consists of reflections on the human condition, which is to understand that nothing in this world is reliable, all is in the hands of God. The second section, chapter five, suggests strategies for dealing with uncertainty. Chapters six through eight once again reflect on the human condition, emphasizing that we live in an arbitrary world where none can know God's plan, even if such a plan exists. The final chapters, nine through twelve, deal with the questions of how to cope with risk and death, which are inevitable.

As a guide for dealing with uncertainty in the world, almost any Buddhist text will serve as a good companion piece to Ecclesiastes, but the reader will find particular resonance in Kamo no Chōmei's "An Account of My Hermitage." Horace's Odes express the same carpe diem philosophy. Many other texts, including the Epic of Gilgamesh, deal with the ephemerality of life and human accomplishments.

For further readings and commentaries on this work, see C. L. Seow's Ecclesiastes: A New Translation with Introduction and Commentary (New York, 1997). Students and teachers may also wish to consult J. L. Crenshaw's Ecclesiastes: A Commentary (Philadelphia, 1987).

Questions for Study and Discussion:

1. The narrator of this text from the 3rd century B.C.E. tells us that there is nothing new under the sun. Can we think of anything that is truly new? What would it mean for something to be new?

2. What are we to make of the statement that people who have died are not remembered, nor will people of the future be remembered after their deaths? Is it possible to find satisfaction in the present moment with no thought of immortality?

3. Is it true that all human endeavor is mere "vanity and a chasing after wind"? Is there no human endeavor which is meaningful?

4. Consider the statement, "my heart found pleasure in all my toil, and this was my reward for all my toil . . . . and again all was vanity and a chasing after wind . . . ." Can pleasure—fleeting pleasure—be an adequate reward for our toil?

5. How can we resolve the dilemma the author raises when he asks why we should work if we can only leave the fruit of our toil to others?

6. In addition to these questions, there are a number of provocative aphorisms in this text that can be discussed. These include, among many others:

>"Those who increase knowledge increase sorrow."
>"Vanity, vanity, all is vanity."
>"A living dog is better than a dead lion."
>"The race is not to the swift nor the battle to the strong."
>"There is nothing new under the sun."

The Song of Songs

Works to read with The Song of Songs include the Sumerian Hymns to Inanna as examples of divine eroticism, and Egyptian love lyrics which are secular but share the kind of cultural contiguity that the Mesopotamian material does with the Hebrew Bible. Also the ancient Chinese Book of Songs represents a very old tradition of love poetry with allegorical interpretations. Closer to the modern period is the Bhakti poetry of Ravidas and Mīrābāī from fifteenth century India, with Mīrābāī's lovely eroticism focused on devotion to Rama and Krishna. An interesting contrast is provided by the secular love poetry of the medieval Heian Japanese court tradition, as seen for example in The Tale of Genji. The catalogs of physical beauties offered in The Song of Songs was an important influence upon the development of Renaissance European love poetry as well, particularly in the sonnet tradition whose great exemplar is Francis Petrarch.

The Song of Songs will be familiar to students with strong Judaic or Christian backgrounds, but not necessarily in a literary sense. For most students an initial attention to form will bring the poetry into literary focus and begin to open up its lyricism. Students can be asked to follow the dialogue of the lovers, and to try to characterize the attitudes of each. One question to ask is whether there is any dramatic movement in their relationship during the course of the poetic dialogue. Patterns of imagery can be traced, with emphasis upon the unashamed celebration of the body and the sensuous appeal to precious spices, fragrant herbs, and beautiful animals. Also noteworthy is the strong feminine voice and perspective of much of the poetry, making the dialogue a fully reciprocal and equal love relationship. Many scholars believe that The Song of Songs is the work of a particularly gifted ancient Hebrew poet, who wrote the poems as a celebration of marriage. Knowing that this work has been recited for more than a thousand years at Jewish weddings might help provide an interesting context for discussion of its emphasis on the wholesome joys of love sanctioned by God.

An excellent introduction to The Song of Songs that is based on superb scholarship is found in The New Jerusalem Bible (New York, 1985). Robert Alter and Frank Kermode's The Literary Guide to the Bible (Cambridge, Mass., 1987) includes a chapter on The Song of Songs that offers a fuller discussion.

Questions for Study and Discussion:

1. Who is speaking in these poems, and what seems to be their setting and purpose?

2. How are the poems structured? Is there dramatic or narrative movement from beginning to end? Are particular events described, and if so, what are they?

3. Make a list of major groups of images or metaphors used by the lovers. What do these comparisons tell us about the world of the poems and the aesthetic values of their audience? Are there differences between the way male and female beauty are described?

4. What are the attitudes toward love between man and woman that can be inferred from these poems?

The Rig Veda and the Upanishads

The hymns of the Rig Veda are among the oldest texts in the world. They can be taught along with other ancient collections of poetry, like the Psalms, or the Chinese Book of Songs, to bring out the comparison of religious visions and poetic styles; or with other mythological texts, like Inanna, the Genesis creation story, Hesiod's Theogony and the opening of Ovid's Metamorphoses, the Korean Songs of the Flying Dragons, the Japanese Kojiki, or the Mayan Popul Vuh. A wonderful cross-cultural companion-piece to the Hymn to Dawn especially is the ancient Egyptian Hymn to the Sun. It makes sense to teach the hymns of the Rig Veda with the two short passages from the Upanishads, which were written as a sort of philosophical commentary on them. Many students find these texts to have all the attractive mystery of India in their mix of mythology, religion, philosophy, and meditation.

The Hymn of Creation is especially interesting in relation to other creation myths. It provocatively recounts the emergence out of Chaos of the One, which then seems to divide into two, or perhaps multiplicity. The language is as much mathematical and philosophical as mythical, and its lack of clarity is acknowledged in the final stanza, where we learn that God may or may not know how creation came about. It is possible this is a relatively late hymn, perhaps from the same period as the Upanishads, and sharing their scepticism. The second passage in the Upanishads selection may actually articulate students' questions when confronted with this hymn.

In the Hymn of Man, creation is described in quite another way: the universe seems to be formed of the body parts of a primordial Man (Purusha), who is sacrificed by the gods. This sacrificial act is in some ways itself the act of creation, as its various aspects become the world (space) the seasons (time), society (the castes), and the religious rites that re-enact the first creation and thus sustain the universe. One way of handling this complex imagery in class is to ask what it might mean for man to be the universe. The answer might be explored in terms of macrocosm and microcosm, or the idea that our knowledge of the world is completely internal to consciousness, which suggests the Vedic identity of universe and self, Brahman and Atman. The first passage in the Upanishads selection describes the 101-year learning process before the great god Indra can understand the uttama purusha, the highest Self.

The short Hymn to Dawn describes and worships dawn in the form of a radiant goddess leading a white horse. Here beautiful nature imagery is draped in the fullest possible religious feeling. Most students, of course, have seldom if ever seen a dawn, so they have no idea. Suggest that they watch one, either in their full Copernican mentality, or trying to imagine a prehistoric society's understanding of the sight. Either way, they might begin to see the depth in the hymn's description and feeling. (On the other hand, they might conclude that the ancient poets must have been on drugs—in which case they're probably right, since Vedic rituals involved the hallucinagenic soma.)

The key to appreciating mythology, of course, is in grasping the way its symbols and metaphors fuse various levels of experience, rather than distinguish them analytically: the way the primordial past is made present, and the outside world internalized, ritual order identified with cosmic order; the lighting of a fire with dawn, the opening of the eyes with the world's creation in God's mind. Students must try to grasp that, mythologically, dawn is not like a goddess with a horse, but it is a goddess with a horse; that ritual doesn't just imitate the creation, it enacts it. It will not do for them to object that this is stupid, for it seems human beings naturally think this way unless patiently taught otherwise. Myth ignores logic and causality, but even today it remains the language of dreams.

Questions for Study and Discussion:

1. How many versions of the creation of the world can you find in these hymns? How can there be different versions of the same event?

2. The last stanza of the Hymn of Creation seems to negate the others. Is this scepticism a religious or philosophical attitude? Do you find it in the Upanishads selections?

3. Try to chart the various creations from the sacrifice of Man. What could it mean to say "Man is this universe"? Is this Man the "Supreme Person" of the Upanishads?

4. Try writing a Hymn to the Sunset to compliment the Hymn to Dawn. What symbols and metaphors would be appropriate to the end of day and the arrival of night?

5. Try to paraphrase the Psalm of Vassishtha. What contradictions get in your way?

The Rāmāyana of Vālmikī

The Rāmāyana is an action packed narrative featuring an epic struggle to save a woman from the clutches of an evil fiend. This great battle depicting the exploits of valiant warriors and their animal helpers describes the classic conflict between good and evil, reassuring us that evil cannot triumph in the world. And yet there are problems even in a world where good is triumphant. Despite his success on the battlefield and the restoration of his kingship, the work ends on a subdued and melancholy note as Rama endures the loss of his wife and the death of his mother.

The Rāmāyana includes elements found in similar epics from many parts of the world. Stories of the descent of the wife to an underworld realm abound in literature—from the story of Demeter in the Near East to the story of Izanami in Japan to the story of Sita's disappearance in Kālidāsa's Śakuntalā and the Ring of Recollection. The hero with animal helpers is also a familiar motif—one which is found in the Chinese epic Monkey, in accounts from pre-Islamic cultures of helper horses and camels, and in the Qasidahs.

For background reading, see R. K. Narayan, The Mahabharata: A Shortened Modern Prose Version of the Indian Epic (New York, 1978), which is just what the title says it is and provides a briefer overview of the entire huge text. Veronica Ions's Indian Mythology (London, 1967) gives background and context for the bewildering array of Indian deities.

Questions for Study and Discussion:

1. It is revealing to compare the description of individual combat between Rama and Ravana with that of heroic battle encounters in other cultures. What are the main differences between the

account of combat in the Rāmāyana and in, for example, the Tales of the Heike (or in any other comparable representation of battle)?

2. Consider how the Rāmāyana contrasts two extreme societies in conflict, one which is ultimately good and one which is seen as the ultimate evil. How does this compare to the juxtaposition of different societies we see in the Kojiki, or in the Arthurian legends?

3. Discuss the depiction of Sita as loyal wife of a hero to depictions of Penelope in Homer's Odyssey.

4. As Rama goes into combat with Ravana, he declares: "I swear to thee either Ravana or Rama will cease to exist in the world!" Discuss this classic conflict between good and evil. What other works of literature or cinema express the same idea? Can good or evil ever prevail in the world?

5. Discuss Rama's response to the supposed death of his brother Lakshmana. How does he express his grief? How does he express his feelings about surviving when his brother dies? How does he feel about war when such a price must be paid?

6. In Chapter 117 Rama says he guards his honor jealously. Is this a good thing? Consider what are the implications of this assertion?

7. Draw comparisons between this story, in which the hero is assisted in his quest by animal (bear and monkey) helpers, and other texts with comparable helper-animal motifs (for instance, the Chinese epic Monkey).

8. Consider the implications of Sita's return to the earth. Why does she choose to do this? What does the fact that Rama loses Sita tell us about the limits of his power?

The Mahābhārata

The Bhagavad-Gītā, written in the first century CE is generally regarded as the most important of several religious texts incorporated into the body of the Mahābhārata. The central issue presented here focuses on the conflict between the irreconcilable virtues of duty and compassion. It also reveals a solution to a schism that had developed in Hindu belief at that time. One teaching held that in order to attain Brahman one must follow the dharma, or duty, appropriate to one's caste. Another doctrine held that the way to achieve this union was to withdraw from the world and purge oneself of all material and physical burdens. Krsna's argument is intended to resolve this dilemma.

For further background on this text, consult Eknath Easwaram, The Bhagavad-Gītā (Petaluma, CA, 1985). For more about Krsna [Krishna], see Milton Singer, ed., Krishna: Myths, Rites, and Attitudes (Honolulu, 1966).

Questions for Study and Discussion:

1. Consider how virtues are presented in this text. When Arjuna and Duryodhama visit Krsna to enlist his aid, Krsna is scrupulously fair in his response. Contrast this fairness to Solya, who

agrees to help the Kurus, but also agrees to betray them. Further contrast this with the position of Bhisma, who rejects every form of dishonesty.

2. Ask yourself why the Pandavas have endured nobly the hardship of thirteen years of banishment and only now, reluctantly, have chosen to go to war against the Kurus. What precipitates this confrontation after so long a time?

3. Consider lines 157-60: "When the family is ruined, / the timeless laws of family duty / perish; and when duty is lost, / chaos overwhelms the family." Duty and morality are seen in terms of the family, rather than in terms of the individual. Contrast this to the way Western philosophy tends to focus on the individual. What are the implications of this notion for Arjuna, who is advised to be true to his own <u>dharma</u>, even if it leads to the destruction of his family and the insurance of chaos?

4. In lines 34-35 of the Second Teaching," Arjuna says: "The flaw of pity / blights my very being . . . ." Consider how this passage illuminates the fact that some fundamental virtues are irreconcilable. (For instance, compassion and justice are both admirable, but each excludes the other.)

5. Consider the frightful implications of Krsna's advice in the Second Teaching, lines 150-4. "Look to your own duty; / do not tremble before it; nothing is better for a warrior / than a battle of sacred duty." Wherein lies our duty? Is it to our self? Our family? Our country? Our God?

6. Think about lines 167-8 of the Second Teaching: ". . . you will be despised / by those who held you in esteem." To what extent is our sense of self defined by how others see us?

7. Lines 193-204 of the Second Teaching establish the contradiction between men of deeds and men of words, the man of action and the contemplative man, the warrior and the poet. Can this duality be resolved? Can these positions be balanced without being compromised?

8. Krsna advises us to "be intent on action, / not on the fruits of action," and says that by doing this we can transcend good and evil. Do you believe this assertion?

9. What are we to make of Krsna's statement in the Second Teaching, lines 249-52: "When suffering does not disturb his mind, / when his craving for pleasures has vanished, / when attraction, fear, and anger are gone, / he is called a sage whose thought is sure"? Compare this to Ecclesiastes, which argues that there is a time for suffering and for craving, for attraction, fear, and anger.

10. Consider in Chapter LXVI how Krsna advises lying and deceit as a strategy for defeating one's enemies. Is this consistent with heroic action? How does Yudhisthira justify his lie? How is Yudhisthira's deceit repaid after he goes to heaven?

The Vimalakīrti Sutra

The title alone makes the Vimalakīrti Sutra seem rather daunting and the subtitle, "The Dharma-Door of Nonduality," makes it appear downright esoteric. Nevertheless, this is very approachable as a religious and philosophical text. Also, there are several important issues raised in this text that need to be addressed and whose implications have a significant impact on how Buddhism's influence was felt throughout East Asia. The Vimalakīrti Sutra also challenges the word-oriented foundations of the Western philosophical tradition.

Insofar as we can speak of Eastern and Western philosophical traditions, the Vimalakīrti Sutra ironically stands at that point of distinction. It uses words to argue that words, and therefore logic, cannot articulate the truth. Useful comparisons might be made with the opening section of the Dao de jing and a contrast can be made with the assertion found in the opening lines of the Gospel of John, which associates the word with God. Kamo no Chōmei's An Account of My Hermitage suggests the popularity of this work throughout East Asia.

A good summary and interpretation of this sutra can be found in William R. LaFleur's The Karma of Words: Buddhism and the Literary Arts in Medieval Japan (Berkeley, 1983). Another useful source for seeing the impact this sutra has had on the cultures of East Asia is Richard B. Mather's article, "Vimalakīrti and Gentry Buddhism," in the journal History of Religions vol. 8, no. 1 (August, 1968): 60-72.

Questions for Study and Discussion:

1. Since the Vimalakīrti Sutra denies that words can articulate the truth, in what ways does it succeed and in what ways does it fail in its purpose?

2. Consider what expresses Truth for us. Is it thoughts? Words? Experiences? If it is the latter, to what extent can words ever be an accurate expression of experience?

3. How would you compare Saint Vimalakīrti's silence to Rene Descartes's "cogito ergo sum"?

4. Much of Western philosophy is based on a concept of dualism that sees a distinction between self and other, a distinction between the word and the thing the word signifies. How does the Vimalakīrti Sutra seek to overcome that distinction?

5. Is it possible to write or even think except in dualistic terms?

6. Does language really help us to think clearly, or is it merely misleading, an impediment to grasping Truth?

7. Consider how Saint Vimalakīrti embodies the notion that one can have a religious vocation and still be a part of the secular world. Are these two things necessarily incompatible?

8. Consider how in China this sutra was used to reassure believers that a religious devotee could still be a part of his family and be responsible for his family. On the other hand, in Japan Kamo no Chōmei uses this same sutra to make the argument that devotion to Buddhism means rejection of family.

Asvaghosha

Asvaghosha, about whom we know very little, might have lived at roughly the same time as the author of the life of Jesus found in the gospel of Mark. But the events described by Asvaghosha, unlike those described in Mark, took place several hundred years earlier and have obviously undergone a radical process of "mythologizing." The emphasis in the Buddha-Karita is on the supernatural and the transcendent. The struggle described on its pages assumes a cosmic dimension that is very much at odds with other accounts of the Buddha, particularly in the Theravada tradition, where the human dimension of the Buddha's existence is emphasized. One of the features of Asvaghosa's account is that many episodes are explained or motivated by reference to former incarnations of the Buddha. Stories about these earlier lives of Buddha, who achieved Buddhahood only after a succession of noble existences, are called "jataka tales" and are freely adapted in the Buddha-Karita. Buddha, who began as a Hindu reformer (that is, if scholars have reconstructed his life correctly), has clearly by the time of Asvaghosha been completely drawn into the rich and imaginative religious world of India. Students should be encouraged to read Asvaghosha, Mark, and Muhammed Ibn Ishaq in succession. Each of these works presents the life of the founder of one of the world's great religions, and each is plainly meant to inspire, but these works share little else. Students can be asked how they explain the radically different style of these works and what that difference might tell us about the relationship of the biographer to the figure he describes and about the religious culture of which each author is a part.

It is essential that the teacher spend some time discussing the way the life of the Buddha found in the Buddha-Karita, however supernatural or even fantastic it might first appear, reflects essential Buddhist teachings. Although Buddha appears very far removed from the common believer, his life is a model which all of us can follow. We may not live in a palace, surrounded by luxury and protected from reality, but we all, at least in the Buddhist analysis, live in a false illusion that prevents us from seeing the suffering that surrounds us and will soon be our own (we all age, fall ill, and die). We too must renounce the world of appearance, the Buddhist teaches, including our own families (cf. Mark 3:31-35), if we are ever to find the truth. And the final act of enlightenment, which we all seek to attain, will be almost against the distractions of others and our own weaknesses. In other words, students should be asked to try to find the human-all-too-human stratum of this ostensibly other-worldly narrative.

The style of much Indian literature, and certainly that of Asvaghosha, is elevated and ornate. It tends also to turn its back on the mundane detail in favor of cosmic struggle and lofty religious meaning (a style parodied in Monkey?). So when the Indian text turns, as it sometimes does, to such things as "trickling phlegm and spittle . . . grinding teeth . . . and loathesome nakedness" as this text does (see p. 277), we are plainly meant to pay attention. And the message in this latter example is central to Buddhism: the world of lofty appearance, and indeed the literature that describes that world, is simply one more illusion that a language of reality might occasionally be allowed to challenge and subvert.

Perhaps the most readable complete translation of Asvaghosha is Buddhacarita, or, Acts of the Buddha, 2 volumes in 1, edited and translated by Edward H. Johnston (Calcutta, 1935-36; second ed., New Delhi, 1972). A good introduction to Buddhism is Richard H. Robinson and Willard L. Johnson, The Buddhist Religion (Encino, Calif., 1977). See also Edward Conze, Buddhist Thought in India (Ann Arbor, 1967).

Qustions for Study and Discussion:

1. What features of this "life" are shared with other heroic figures of world literature? (e.g., miraculous birth, the prediction of a prophet or sage, etc. (On this topic, see Lord Raglan, The Hero.)

2. Why is it that the king tries to shield his son from "reality"? In what sense, if at all, is this episode paralleled in the life of all those who would follow the Buddha's path?

3. The fourth of the four passing sights is quite different from the first three. What is its significance and how does it stand in counterpoint to the other three?

4. Consider Mara as an Indian Satan. What is the basis of his onslaught on the Buddha (one can not help but think of the "temptations" of Jesus in Matthew 4)? How does Buddha finally prevail?

5. Nirvana is one of the most difficult concepts of Buddhism. Indeed, it is a state that supposedly transcends human understanding in every respect (a bit like the Tao in this regard at least). Asvaghosha's account of the death of the Buddha is an account of entry into Nirvana. Granted that no ultimately satisfactory answer can be given, what does this state seem to be?

The Book of Songs

The poems from this early Chinese collection can be compared with three other ancient poetic traditions that come from roughly the same period of time: the epic Homeric poetry of early Greece, the Indian Vedas, and the Hebrew Psalms. What such a comparison highlights is the mundane nature of so many of the poems from The Book of Songs. The collection, to be sure, includes religious pieces and pieces that are accounts of legendary figures from the past, but many of its most famous poems describe very common emotions that any student can understand and even identify with (poems 76 and 81 are particularly good examples). This characteristic of the Book of Songs should be emphasized and can be used to make a strong point about the universality and timelessness of certain human situations and feelings.

The Book of Songs obviously emerges from an agricultural society that has an intense involvement with the details of such things as seasonal change and the plant world. Even when the poetry in this collection seems to transcend that world, as in the narrative of Hou Chi, the hero-founder of the Zhou kingly lineage (see no. 245), it returns to mundane, essentially agricultural concerns: after a miraculous conception and birth, and being rescued as an infant from a series of dangers, the hero distinguishes himself by planting "large beans . . . fat and tall" and making "paddy-lines . . . close set."

One of the most striking features of the poetry of The Book of Songs is the use of nature imagery and the way such imagery is juxtaposed with narrative elements. Much study of this text has focused on the relationship between these images, which often begin a poem and are called xing-images ("evocative images"), in Chinese poetics, and the remainder of the poem. Sometimes these relationships are transparent (see poem 20, 23, etc.) while other times they are problematic (see poem 1, 41, etc.). This provides the teacher with an opportunity to talk about imagery in general and how it can be used to create a mood or a texture that can not always be linked to other parts of the poem in a clear and logical fashion.

The poetic line in The Book of Songs, as noted in the introduction, is only four syllables (=four Chinese characters) and thereby stands in stark contrast to the much longer line-length in Homer, the Vedas, and Psalms. This presents a very difficult challenge to translators, as does the fact that these poems typically rhyme. The fact that a poet as great as Ezra Pound has translated The Book of Songs, and has done so in a way that is very free but also makes for great English poetry, presents the teacher with an excellent opportunity to talk about translation and its perils. We should note here in passing that perhaps the fact that this collection has been translated by a sinologist-poet as deft as Arthur Waley and also by an English poet of the genius of Ezra Pound seems almost to have intimidated later would-be translators.

Much of the secondary scholarship on this text is highly technical. Perhaps the best introductions are those of Stephen Owens and Joseph Allen in the newest edition of the Arthur Waley translation: The Book of Songs: The Ancient Chinese Classic of Poetry (New York, 1996), pp. xii-xxv & 336-383. This volume contains an excellent bibliography of other works on this Chinese classic. For those wanting to jump into the more technical poetic qualities of this text, consult Pauline Yu's The Reading of Imagery in the Chinese Poetic Tradition (Princeton, 1987).

Questions for Study and Discussion:

1. Some have argued that the position of women in pre-Confucian China, which this text reflects, is much better than in later times. Do you see any evidence in the poems anthologized here that women occupied a position of some power at this time?

2. The Book of Songs became a Confucian classic. Can you see any difficulties this text might pose to a stern Confucian? (Consideration of this question might need to wait until students have read Analects.)

3. Much has been said in the Peoples Republic of China about The Book of Songs as "the voice of the common people." What is meant by this is not that the common people, who were presumably illiterate, wrote these songs down, but that they ultimately derive from the "folk" and reflect their concerns. Does this seem likely to you?

4. Compare and contrast the use of nature in this collection with nature as it appears (or does not appear) in Psalms, Homer, and the Vedas.

5. If there are any heroes in the poetry of this text they would be King Wen (235 and 241) and Hou Chi (245). How would you compare these heroes to other heroes in The World of Literature?

Confucius
The Analects

Student reaction to Confucius' Analects is often lukewarm, particularly in comparison with their typically strong reactions to Laozi. Confucius can seem so avuncular and commonsensical as to pose very little challenge, and certainly no threat, to the student reader. There are topics in the Analects, however, that run contrary to much current student behavior, and emphasizing such topics can provoke lively classroom discussion. One such topic is li or what is usually translated as "rites" and includes everything from behavior at lofty temple ceremonies to those interpersonal actions we call "etiquette." Confucius seems to have believed that social order is best maintained when we all know our position in the social "pecking order" and follow the completely predictable behavior that the rites assure. One scholar has suggested that Confucius and his disciples might have spent much time together actually rehearsing ritual behavior, thereby turning social intercourse into a "dance" in which each movement, although entirely predictable, is evaluated by how "natural" it has become. Thus, it is possible to present Confucian teaching as going quite contrary to the informality and egalitarianism that typifies so many American settings, the classroom included.

It is worth noting that Confucius does not present arguments but, for the most part, makes assertions. He is a voice of authority. In this respect, Confucius resembles the New Testament Jesus more than the Greek philosopher Socrates. We must keep in mind that what we have in the Analects are memories of a teacher who has already been posthumously elevated in the teachings of his followers to a lofty position—perhaps not a "divine," but surely a "sage" or someone possessing astounding insight and wisdom. Thus, whatever might actually have passed back and forth between Confucius and his disciples is reduced in the recollection of later disciples to short dialogues and pithy sayings. We might think of Confucius' sayings as "wisdom literature" and contrast it to what we typically think of as philosophical discourse. And, of course, we might discuss with the students whether or not their various traditions have similar stocks of wisdom literature.

Some recent scholarship on Confucius, particularly David Hall and Roger Ames' Thinking Through, Confucius (Albany, NY, 1987), presents the Master as more like a contemporary pragmatist than like a philosopher who believes in abstract truths and ultimate realities. While their claims go far (putting Confucius alongside Richard Rorty and Jacques Derrida!), Confucius' teachings, at least as they are preserved in the Analects, seem derived as much from specific situations and questions as from abstract principles. Indeed, some scholars have noted that the Master answers the same question quite differently depending upon the student asking the question, presumably tailoring his answers to the needs and personality of the student. This can touch off a discussion of philosophical systems that proceed from some notion of divine or abstract truth and those that work from "immediate" contexts (and, for that matter, whether Confucius really fits neatly into either of these categories!).

Confucius has become something of an industry. Thus, a teacher can ask, before students begin reading the Analects, what images or stereotypes come to mind when one says "Confucius." These can vary all the way from the "fount of curious wisdom" parodied in the off-color "Confucius say" jokes to the Confucius who is supposedly responsible for the recent growth (now gone somewhat flat) of the Asian economies. Often students come to Confucius expecting the esoteric or arcane and come away from the text, as some of our students have told us, feeling that Confucius is "much less exotic than Plato!"

A recent, provocative study of Confucius that has drawn the Master into the realm of much more serious discussion among Western philosophers is Herbert Fingarette, Confucius: The Secular as Sacred (New York, 1972). A very rich resource on Confucius' thought as well as the entire gamut of early Chinese thought is Benjamin I. Schwartz, The World of Thought in Ancient China (Cambridge, MA and London, England, 1985). For a detailed translation and study of the

Analects that will long be discussed and debated, see E. Bruce Brooks and A. Taeko Brooks, The Original Analects: Sayings of Confucius and his Successors (New York, 1998).

Questions for Study and Discussion:

1. One famous Western scholar describes Confucius as an "agnostic." Are you comfortable with such a description? How would you describe the Master's attitude toward the supernatural?

2. Benevolence or "humaneness" (ren) is mentioned more in the Analects than any other virtue. What seems to be the relationship between this virtue and ritual? One modern Confucian refers to the "creative tension" in the Analects between benevolence and ritual. What could this possibly mean?

3. Confucius is honored in China as the first great teacher. In fact, the birthday of Confucius is celebrated in some parts of China as "teachers' day." How would you describe Confucius as a teacher? How would you compare him to other famous teachers in this volume (Jesus, Socrates, etc.)?

4. Confucius has become a symbol of Chinese conservatism, particularly among many modern Chinese. Others have said that while he may not have been a radical, he certainly was a reformer. What evidence can you find in the Analects for either of these positions?

5. Obviously learning is central to Confucianism (see 1.1, 5.28, etc.). What seems to be the content of the learning Confucius advocates?

6. In your opinion, could the near contemporaries Confucius and Socrates have carried on any meaningful discussion with one another at all (assuming, of course, they could have spoken the same language)? In other words, were the cultural differences so extreme as to make a significant exchange of opinions impossible? Imagine a discussion between the two. Can you find any similarities that could be used to begin to construct a genuine dialogue?

Laozi
Dao de jing

Students often react strongly to Laozi, and it works well to provoke a lively discussion between those who are sympathetic to Dao de jing and those who believe that the text is, as one of our students put it ever so eloquently, "baloney." One can approach the text more or less radically. A radical approach, sure to stir up a significant amount of discussion, might stress Laozi's attack on "knowledge," particularly the type that one acquires through hard effort and study. "Surely no good Daoist," the teacher can say provocatively, "would be in class today." One must ask, as one reads this small text, what would motivate Laozi to take such extreme positions. A possible answer, although not without historical problems, is that Laozi's teaching is a strong reaction against Confucian formalism and the Confucian notion that we must apply ourselves diligently in order to improve.

Scholars continue to disagree strenuously on the precise date of Dao de jing. Part of the problem is that this small book is entirely unlike all other Chinese texts from the early period. For example, in contrast to other early philosophical texts, it has no references to persons, places or historical events. Chinese texts, in general, tend to be very much embedded in a real world—think of Confucius, for example, speaking to named disciples and making frequent reference to figures from the past—but Laozi's text seems to float above the world of specific historical reference. Some scholars, particularly among the Chinese themselves, still place the text as early as the sixth century BCE, while others, particularly Western specialists, date the text as late as the third century. It must be said that recent archaeological discoveries in China of early manuscript versions of Laozi have tended to push the date of the text back to at least the last decades of the fourth century.

Dao de jing has been interpreted in a variety of different ways. While many of us read Laozi as an advocate of non-aggressive action, simplicity, and withdrawal, others have read the text as intensely political. The Chinese historian Sima Qian, for example, saw Laozi as connected to later Chinese philosophies that advocated a ruthless ruler who, in his treatment of the people, "empties their minds but fills their bellies" (3). Others read Dao de jing as a manual of sexual practices, taking some of the feminine symbolism of the text quite literally (see especially 6). The point to emphasize is that this little text is difficult and, at times, so mysterious that it can indeed be read in a variety of ways. It is this very indeterminacy, no doubt, that is partly responsible for the appearance of so many translations, many of them with quite variant interpretations of what it is Laozi is trying to say. An interesting exercise for students is to search out a series of different translations (every library has at least three or four versions, some have fifty or sixty) and compare the interpretations of a single chapter (for example, compare the first chapter in the translations of D.C. Lau, Stephen Mitchell [1988], Alistair Crowley [1995], Ursula K. Le Guin [1997], Arthur Waley [1934], and others, including that of the brilliant but strange sinologist Peter Alexis Boodberg, which begins:

> Lodehead lodehead-brooking : no forewonted lodehead;
> Namecall namecall-brooking : no forewonted namecall.
>   Having-naught namecalling : Heaven-Earth's fetation.
>   Having-aught namecalling : Myriad Mottling's mother.)

Whatever one assumes to have been the line of possible influence between Confucius and Laozi, it works well in the classroom to compare and contrast these two extremely influential thinkers from ancient China. This, for example, can be done quite fruitfully from a feminist perspective. In Analects, women are mentioned only twice and both references are pejorative. In Laozi, however, feminine imagery abounds and is always privileged over the masculine (see, for example, 28 and 61). However, one must note that a part of Laozi's "paradoxical" argument is to contend that those things that we call strong are really weak and those things we call weak are really strong. Thus, he does not call for female emancipation but argues that women, although ostensibly weak, are in reality strong. Students can be engaged in a discussion of whether this constitutes progress or only reinforces female subordination.

Benjamin I. Schwartz, cited earlier, has a good chapter on Laozi, but he is less provocative on this subject than A. C. Graham, Disputers of the Tao: Philosophical Argument in Ancient China (La Salle, IL, 1989), pp. 215-34. Several of the translations, especially that of D.C. Lau used in the anthology, have excellent introductory material on Laozi. A recent useful introduction and commentary on the text is Michael Lafargue, The Tao of the Tao Te Ching (Albany, 1992).

Questions for Study and Discussion:

1. If the Dao cannot be put into words (ch. 1), what is the use of writing a book about it?

2. In what sense does the beautiful produce the ugly (ch. 2)? Does language necessarily ensnare us in a world of contrast and judgment? (This discussion can be enriched after reading Zhuangzi.)

3. One of the most prominent modern specialists on ancient Chinese thought, A. C. Graham, has argued that there is one emotion that unifies all of Dao de jing and that emotion is fear. Do you agree? Is this nothing more than a manual on how to stay out of trouble?

4. Much of the text of Laozi consists of rhythmic, rhymed lines. In other words, it is poetry. Why might poetry be a more appropriate form for Laozi's thought than discursive argument?

5. Chapter 80 of Laozi is one of the first utopian visions from ancient China. What are the characteristics of this utopia? How does it compare to the later utopian vision of Tao Qian (p. 1008)?

6. When Buddhism came into China in the first centuries of the common era, it was often confused with Daoism. Do you see any similarities in the content of this text and a Buddhist text like the Lotus Sutra? Do you think Laozi would have agreed with the first noble truth of Buddhism that "all existence is suffering"?

Zhuangzi
On the Equality of Things

Students are likely to find Zhuangzi enticing but confusing. They will often expect a teacher to reduce this text to a clear and consistent message. To attempt to do so is probably a mistake. Zhuangzi is an anti-rationalist who tries to undermine the arbitrariness, relativity, and instability of all the conceptual structures, especially language, with which we surround ourselves. Thus, he is constantly trying to challenge and upset even our most basic ways of thinking. To use rationality as the primary tool in an attack upon the rational, however, would be precisely to validate rationality. So Zhuangzi typically takes another approach—that of antecdote, of a form of mocking argument that sometimes turns against itself, and of paradox.

Central to Zhuangzi's attack on the rational is the idea that we carve up the world—one could say carve up "the Dao"—through a form of self-centered assertion. That is, as soon as one says "I," the "other" appears; proclaiming a "this" produces a "that"; the simple act of affirmation, in a certain and very arbitrary sense, makes something so; the announcement of any "beginning" implies something before the "beginning"; etc. Such thinking is radical and can reduce one to despair. But this does not happen in the case of Zhuangzi. Instead, he finds joy in the possibility that we can quiet "the pipes of man" and hear the "pipes of earth" and the "pipes of heaven," that we can stop the clamor of words and arguments in order once again to experience the wordless harmony of the Dao.

Zhuangzi lived in a disputatious time. While he obviously enjoyed philosophical argument, especially with his good friend and philosophical rival Hui Shi, Zhuangzi remains a skeptic about the ultimate merit of such dispute ("Suppose that you and I have a dispute. If you beat me and I lose to you, does that mean you're really right and I'm really wrong?"—p. 358). Zhuangzi's writings provide the teacher with a good opportunity to question the notion that reason is the best way to the truth. "But," one might ask further, "what are the dangers in the freedom and spontaneity Zhuangzi seems to advocate?"

There are many sections of Zhuangzi, beyond his chapter "On the Equality of Things," that a teacher might find useful to supplement classroom discussion. Two complete English translations of Zhuangzi can be recommended: <u>Wandering on the Way: Early Taoist Tales and Parables of Chuang Tzu</u>, trans. by Victor Mair (New York, 1994) and Burton Watson, <u>Chuang-tzu</u> (New York, 1968). The latter has a useful introduction. For those wishing to delve more deeply into recent Zhuangzi scholarship, a good collection of essays can be found in Victor Mair, ed., <u>Experimental Essays on Chuang Tzu</u> (Honolulu, 1983).

Questions for Study and Discussion:

1. Zhuangzi argues that right and wrong only exist after "they are established in the mind" (p. 353). But elsewhere he speaks of an "ultimate" that the "ancients attained" (p. 354). Are these two ideas consistent? Discuss.

2. In section 8 (p. 355), Zhuangzi presents a series of paradoxes, some of them probably drawn from other thinkers of his time (beginning with "There is nothing under heaven larger than the tip of a downy hair at the end of autumn." Can you "make sense" of any of these paradoxes? What might be the function of such paradoxes in Zhuangzi?

3. The "Butterfly Dream" is possibly the most famous anecdote in Zhuangzi's writings (p. 359). What is the point of this anecdote?

4. Perhaps the greatest paradox in Zhuangzi is that he is simultaneously a profound critic of language and perhaps the most creative writer of ancient China. Discuss this apparent paradox. Can you imagine philosophical circumstances that might spawn an attack on language such as one finds in Zhuangzi? (Hint: It was precisely at this time that the Confucians were elaborating the notion of "rectification of names," which attempted to fix language in a way that was normative—e.g., "a father who does not act as a father is not a father," etc.).

5. Zhuangzi captured the traditional Chinese imagination more than any other figure of the ancient period (see, for example Zhang Heng, 385). How would you account for this?

6. Some have compared Zhuangzi to Ecclesiastes. How are the two works similar and how are they different?

Mozi
"Shedding Light on Ghosts"

We know very little about Mozi. He must have lived in the 5th century B.C.E. because he attacked Confucius (551-479) and was in turn criticized harshly by the Confucian philosopher Mencius (372?-289). Some scholars have argued that he derives from the artisan class and reflects the austere pragmatism that might have characterized this group. Certainly his philosophy is characterized by a pursuit of "benefit" that shows, at its best, a deep concern for the well-being of all people and, at its worst, a serious neglect of the subtle aspects of human psychology and spirituality. For example, Mozi rejects music because he believes that the performance of music is extravagant and therefore drains economic resources that could be used elsewhere. Music is thus reduced, in his attack, to nothing more than a needless expense.

What is particularly significant in Mozi's writing is that, unlike his predecessor Confucius, he makes arguments. Sometimes these arguments might seem unconvincing or presented rather awkwardly, but he is initiating a new style, one that does not rely simply upon his own authority and is not presented in short dialogues but in protracted essays. In the case of "Shedding Light on Ghosts," the argument is quite simple: we can prove ghosts exist by examining the numerous reports of their existence in the records of the past. In other words, simply look at the textual evidence. Underlying this argument is the claim, made at the outset, that when human beings do not believe in ghosts and spirits they are more likely to behave badly. The latter point returns us to Mozi's insistence upon what he sees as beneficial. That is, human beings should believe in ghosts and spirits, because such a belief will benefit human society.

Traces of a dialogue tradition can be seen in Mozi's rhetoric. Throughout his essay he uses a form of self-interrogation to advance his argument (e.g., "On what grounds shall we base our argument? Mozi said, 'One ascertains whether . . . .'"). He also anticipates possible objections to his argument and tries to counter these. This latter characteristic anticipates philosophical debate and thereby reflects the increasingly lively philosophical atmosphere of the Warring States period in Chinese history.

The fact that Mozi felt the need to argue so strenuously in favor of the existence of ghosts and spirits tells us that he lived in an age of growing skepticism. Such skepticism is particularly characteristic of followers of Confucius. While the Master seems to have exercised caution on this topic (see <u>Analects</u> 11.12), some of his followers proclaimed outright that spirits did not exist and that religious ritual was important for its psychological and sociological effects only. This points to a great divide in the Chinese tradition that continues until the present day. On the one hand, China has a rich tradition of belief in the supernatural—indeed, a world populated and permeated by ghosts, spirits, and other strange forces—and, on the other hand, China has one of the world's oldest and most "hard-nosed" traditions rejecting such "superstitions."

The ultimate fate of the followers of Mozi is one of the mysteries of Chinese history. We know that in the time of Mencius, the followers of Mozi "filled the world," to quote Mencius himself. Certainly Mencius felt that the tradition of Confucius was on the defensive and needed to defend itself very aggressively against the Mohists. A century or two later, Mohism seems to have disappeared entirely. Some have suggested that the followers of Mozi might have suffered greatly in the harsh warfare at the end of the Warring States period. Like their Master, they may have been specialists in military defense who rushed to the aid of small states struggling to survive. And, like the states themselves, these Mohists might have perished in the conflict.

The best translation of the works of Mozi remains that of Y. P. Mei, <u>Mo-tse, the Neglected Rival of Confucius</u> (London, 1934).

Questions for Study and Discussion:

1. Mozi seems to believe that human beings will not behave if they do not believe in the possibility of some form of supernatural retribution. Do you agree?

2. Are you convinced by Mozi's use of historical records to prove the existence of ghosts and spirits? Under what condiditions can such an argument be convincing?

Qu Yuan
"On Encountering Sorrow"

Students often have a difficult time with "On Encountering Sorrow." The difficulties arise at several levels of interpretation. First, this lengthy poem is extremely ornate in language and filled with references and allusions that only the most tireless specialist could begin to track down. Second, the perspective, even the gender, of the narrator seems to shift suddenly from one section of the poem to the other, sometimes leaving the reader quite confused. Third, the poem is filled with emotions of alienation, arrogance, and, especially, self-pity that the student-reader can find tiresome. "On Encountering Sorrow," to be sure, is a complicated work and has spawned quite different readings. Here are three:

a. The poem is basically autobiographical and expresses Qu Yuan's deep distress over the fact that his ruler, the king of the southern Chinese state of Chu, rejected his advice and followed the recommendations of his courtier-rivals, recommendations that eventually brought the destruction of the state. Qu Yuan, in this interpretation, imagines his ruler as a desired lover who rejects him despite his exemplary beauty and uprightness.

b. The poem is fundamentally an artistic expansion of a southern Chinese tradition of shamanic performance. In this poetic rendition, the shaman repeatedly soars into the skies to encounter his or her guiding spirit but fails to establish contact and finally turns back to home and the very world he or she had tried to escape.

c. The poem is an expression of more general human feelings of religious frustration. We are summoned by god or seem to be promised the joys of heaven, here portrayed rather erotically, but our efforts to achieve such a goal always fall short, and we are left trying to understand why, "worthy" as we surely are, we continually fail.

None of these interpretations, alone, is entirely satisfying. "On Encountering Sorrow" therefore presents an excellent opportunity for a teacher to put the initial burden of interpretation into the hands of students. We have taught this poem rather successfully by beginning roughly as follows: "I've never felt that I entirely understood this poem, and I'd very much like to know what you all think it is saying?" What emerges from such a broad question can, in the case of this work at least, be quite interesting . . . and sometimes delightfully surprising.

Of course, the teacher has to try and explain why this poem has had such immense appeal in China. There are several possible answers. First, everything we know about Qu Yuan comes to us through a biography written by Sima Qian, and the latter clearly had an agenda. Qu Yuan, in Sima Qian's presentation, is a frustrated scholar-minister who suffers exile and rejection because he did what every good political advisor is supposed to do: speak frankly and honestly. But since the honest advisor invariably suffers for his frankness, he can only bemoan the fact that he is "born in the wrong time"—that is, in a time when the king does not have the sage discernment to know who is speaking honestly and who is simply telling him what he wants to hear. This theme has had immense appeal in China among scholars who had been taught by the Confucian tradition that they should speak frankly when asked their opinions, but who also quickly learned that frankness almost always brought disaster. Second, Qu Yuan committed suicide as a way of showing his sincerity. The teacher should explain that the status of suicide in China is quite different from that in the Judeo-Christian West. Far from being a sin, it is in certain situations the only way to demonstrate the purity of one's commitment. The power of "On Encountering Sorrow" was enhanced by the poet's suicide and has therefore been seen as emerging from the heart of a man of great purity (it must be admitted, however, that some Chinese scholars, from the beginning, questioned whether or not Qu Yuan's suicide was really necessary, and Mao Tse-tung, much later, attacked the traditional Chinese attitude toward suicide described here, arguing that one should always reject suicide and remain alive to struggle). Third, Chinese poetry, like the poetry of so many other traditions, moves along the continuum from straightforward simplicity to ornateness and even preciousness. Many of the scholar-readers who proclaimed this poem a masterpiece did so in part because they admired its elaborate rhetoric and saw it as presenting an entirely different model of poetry from the shorter, more straightforward works found in the Book of Songs. Many are the worlds of poetry, and the bookends of the Chinese tradition, which can be seen very early: the anonymous Book of Songs and the "Songs of the South" authored by Qu Yuan, the first great Chinese poet we know by name. Fourth, Qu Yuan became a folk hero whose life is still repeatedly honored by the "Dragon Boat Festival," celebrated on the fifth day of the fifth lunar month (the summer solstice).

    David Hawkes remains not only the best translator but also the best interpreter of Qu Yuan's works. His lengthy introduction and textual notes are invaluable to anyone who would teach this text in any detail. See The Songs of the South: An Anthology of Ancient Chinese Poems by Qu Yuan and Other Poets, translated, annotated and introduced by David Hawkes (Hammondsworth, 1985), pp. 15-95. For a study of the complex way in which subsequent Chinese scholars tried to deal with the myth of Qu Yuan, see Laurence A. Schneider, A Madman of Ch'u: The Chinese Myth of Loyalty and Dissent (Berkeley, 1980). Students should be encouraged to consult a good encyclopedia on the topic of the "Dragon Boat Festival," to see how a poet, in China, has become the center of one of the most important holidays of the year.

Questions for Study and Discussion:

1. The first lines of the poem surely encourage an autobiographical reading (1-8). When in the poem do you begin to question such a reading? Or, should this poem force us to expand our notion of what constitutes autobiography? (We should not forget that several recent studies of autobiography have treated such works as Freud's Interpretation of Dreams and T. S. Eliot's "Four Quartets" as essentially autobiographical.)

2. What seems to be the narrator's attitude toward the political world? Are these attitudes specific to the Chinese world or do they possess some more general mixture?

3. On one level, this is a poem about flight—both its attraction and its ultimate impossibility. What does flight represent in this poem?

4. What is it that keeps the narrator from a successful encounter with the god or gods he/she pursues?

5. The narrator bemoans the fact that "no one understands me." What other texts in The World of Literature reflect this same frustration?

Rhyme-Prose (Fu) and Han Dynasty Poetry

The five poems included in this section may seem, at least at first glance, to be so varied as to make any general statement impossible. These pieces can, however, be divided into two categories: poems of social consciousness and poems of personal struggle and consolation . . . perhaps we could say "extroverted" and "introverted" poems. Some traditional Chinese scholars, who were fond of drawing such divisions, might use the term "Confucian" to describe the extroverted poems of social consciousness and "Taoist" to describe the more introverted poems of personal struggle and consolation. However we choose to describe these categories, "On the Wind" and "Fighting South of the Ramparts" would clearly belong to the first type and "The Owl" and "The Bones of Chuang Tzu" would belong to the second type. "Verses Sung to a Tatar Reed Whistle" is not so easily categorized. The teacher should note that unlike the other four poems, the narrative voice in this case is a woman, which may by itself enable the poet to transcend or escape categories which may have derived largely from male experience. At any rate, later Chinese poets were sometimes thought of as basically "social" and "political" in orientation (e.g., Du Fu, p. 1025) or "personal" (e.g., Li Bai, p. 1022). Such categories, however persistent, are over-simplifications—certainly many Chinese poems fit neither category neatly—but they provide an opportunity for a discussion of the various, sometimes contrary, functions of poetry.

All five of the poems in this section are quite accessible and introduce general human issues while simultaneously reflecting important aspects of the Chinese literary and cultural tradition. For example, "On the Wind," raises the general issue of class and how this can radically alter one's perception of even the most basic natural phenomenon. At the same time, the setting for this poem is the court where a minister, in traditional Chinese fashion, presents a subtle (perhaps not too subtle in this case) admonishment to his ruler. In the case of "Verses Sung to a Tatar Reed Whistle," we encounter the pain, initially, of being separated from one's homeland and then, secondarily, the pain of being separated from one's own children, raising the question of precisely what we mean by "homeland." But, within the Chinese cultural tradition, this poem also reflects the profoundly ambivalent relationship that existed between the Chinese and the non-Chinese people to the north (called "Tatar" here). Or, we find in "The Owl" and "The Bones of Chuang Tzu" the eternal issue of how we console ourselves, particularly after all has not worked out as we had hoped and we feel the approach of the end. Within the Chinese cultural tradition, such feelings often get expressed as "Taoist" even though the precise configuration of this "Taoism" might vary considerably from one writer to another—sometimes with an almost joyful tone and other times with a tone that is deeply pessimistic.

The poetry of this period, at least the pieces included in the anthology, tend to be longer than those of the Book of Songs and introduce poetic themes that one does not find in the earlier collection (for example, it would be anachronistic to speak of "Taoist" themes in the Book of Songs). However, one theme that does appear in the Book of Songs (see nos. 185 and 234) and recurs in the Han dynasty poetry represented here is that of the cruelty of warfare. "Fighting

South of the Ramparts" is an anti-war poem that succeeds admirably in portraying the horror of the battlefield without becoming overly sentimental. It has been much read and admired by Chinese readers for almost two millennia—and yet the horror has continued, in China and virtually everywhere else. Students might be asked to consider and discuss the great wealth of anti-war literature that exists in so many literary traditions alongside the fact that human violence continues to escalate. What, if anything, might this indicate?

For general background to these poetic works, and many other pieces in this anthology, two general histories of Chinese literature might be recommended: Ch'en Shou-yi, <u>Chinese Literature: A Historical Introduction</u> (New York, 1961) and Liu Wu-chi, <u>An Introduction to Chinese Literature</u> (Bloomington, IN, 1966). Good introductions to specific poets and, sometimes, specific pieces can be found in William H. Nienhauser, Jr. ed., <u>The Indiana Companion to Traditional Chinese Literature</u> (Bloomington, 1986).

Questions for Study and Discussion:

1. The <u>fu</u>, of which "On the Wind" is a famous example, often merges rich, even florid, language with what is essentially a remonstration. Why might a tradition of speaking to the king in this way (or, at the least, imagining speaking to the king in this way) develop?

2. How does Jia Yi find consolation? Would you describe his vision and the "Nothing" he finally embraces (line 103) as fundamentally optimistic or pessimistic?

3. What images appear in "Fighting South of the Ramparts" to convey the sense of tragedy and forlornness that pervades the poem? How would you differentiate this poem from the famous anti-war poem in the <u>Book of Songs</u>, "Minister of War" (#185, p. 310)?

4. What is it about Tatar life that the Chinese wife detests and what might this tell us about Chinese notions of civilization? But, then, how does the conclusion of the poem complicate notions of homeland and "barbarian" frontier?

5. Notice that Zhang Heng's "The Bones of Chuang Tzu" begins with a journey not unlike and probably inspired by Qu Yuan's "On Encountering Sorrow." But suddenly his journey ends with "a man's bones lying in the squelchy earth." What do you make of this sudden movement from the soaring journey to the most mundane scene imaginable?

6. Why do you think the poem, "The Bones of Chuang Tzu" ends with the narrator saying that his response to all he had heard from the skull was that he "Poured. . . hot tears upon the margin of the road?"

Sima Qian
Records of the Historian

The writings of Sima Qian we have included here almost demand comparison. As a historian, indeed the "father of Chinese history," it is useful to read his work alongside that of the Greek historian Thucydides. The former claims that he, like Confucius, is primarily one who simply sifts and selects from the tradition, honoring his forebears, while the latter is harshly critical of his predecessors and insists that he is doing something entirely new. Despite these quite different stances, Sima Qian surely does innovate at times, and he also is more inclined than the rationalistic Greek to react emotionally both to his lofty duty as a historian and to the difficulties and tragedies of the characters (Xiang Yu one among them) he describes. Sima Qian's letter to Ren An also can be compared to other autobiographical writings. It should be noted, for example, how he repeatedly views himself with regard to a tradition—e.g., life as a eunuch is disgraceful precisely because men of earlier ages, Confucius included, have regarded eunuchs as a disgrace. Sima Qian, surely, is not Rousseau, proclaiming himself unlike anyone who has lived, but is someone who can only see and understand himself through the lineaments of traditions.

Sima Qian's "Letter to Jen An" is a document filled with pain, and students often do not know quite how to react. As a response to Jen An, a friend who was under sentence of death and was eventually executed, the letter seems cold-hearted—that is, Sima Qian is more interested in telling his own story than offering help to a friend. But it seems likely that this letter was never intended to be a private communication. Sima Qian probably seized the opportunity of Jen An's plight to write a public letter explaining why he himself had suffered the horrible punishment of castration. There is a tension in the letter, which students might want to explore, between deep and almost irredeemable humiliation and the hope of eventual vindication. We have also found that some students find Sima Qian, as he presents himself in his letter, "arrogant," while others find him filled with self-hate.

Sima Qian writes his history so that the great people of the past might not be forgotten (see p. 389). That is, he grants immortality and, in the course of this action, assures himself and his father of immortality as well. In fact, Sima Qian draws comfort from imagining a time when he, a great rememberer of the past, would himself be remembered (see p. 394). This can touch off a very fruitful discussion of the whole issue of remembering, which is so central to the Chinese tradition. Confucius himself is supposed to have said that "The gentleman hates not leaving behind a name when he is gone" (15.20). Obviously, being remembered is contemplated with more satisfaction when one sees herself or himself as a part of a larger entity—a family, a culture, etc.—than when one identifies primarily with one's own individual identity.

Sima Qian obviously relishes the drama of extreme situations. Xiang Yu, Nie Zheng, and Meng Tian are all brought to moments of crisis. How a person reacts at such moments, Sima Qian seems to believe, reveals much about character. And Sima Qian seems particularly interested in acts of resolve, even ultimate resolve. This, of course, raises the larger issue of heroism. Students can be led into a discussion of whether or not the startling resolve of Xiang Yu, Meng Tian, and Nie Zheng, all of whom commit suicide, should be regarded as heroic or simply cowardly or foolish. It is wise to note, in the course of such a discussion, that there are values reflected in these stories very far removed from those of most student readers. For example, Nie Zheng acts on behalf of someone who appreciated him. In early China there was a saying that "a man dies for someone who appreciates him as surely as a woman makes herself beautiful for a lover." In other words, if someone recognizes a person's true worth at a time when that person is living in obscurity or through difficult times, the person so recognized owes unflinching loyalty and service to the "recognizer."

Much of Sima Qian's huge history has been ably translated by Burton Watson in Records of the Grand Historian, 3 volumes (1961; revised edition, Hong Kong and New York, 1993). For a study of Sima Qian that attempts to show how his autobiographical writings resonate with his history, see Stephen Durrant, The Cloudy Mirror: Tension and Conflict in the Writings of Sima Qian (Albany, 1995). For a more general introduction to Sima Qian's vast historical project, see Burton Watson, Su-ma Ch'ien, Grand Historian of China (New York, 1958).

Questions for Study and Discussion:
1. Why does Sima Qian undertake this vast historical project and what might his motivations tell us about traditional China?

2. Unlike Thucydides, Sima Qian does not explain to us upon what basis he constructs the speeches and dialogues of his characters. How much latitude can a historian grant himself in this regard before his work becomes "fiction?" Does Sima Qian cross this line?

3. One cannot read the selections included here without feeling that Sima Qian was obsessed by the topic of suicide, a topic which also comes up in his portrayal of Qu Yuan and many other characters. What does he seem to be telling us about this "desperate" act?

4. Discuss the peculiar role played by Nie Zheng's sister, a role Sima Qian has enhanced considerably from earlier versions of this story. Why would a historian like Sima Qian find her particularly commendable?

5. How do you react to Sima Qian's explanation of the origin of much great literature— i.e., that it is often the result of great personal suffering, even physical mutilation (see p. 394)? Do you find any examples elsewhere in this anthology where the production of literature seems quite plainly a compensation for a deep sense of failure or humiliation in the world of action?

Hesiod
Theogony

The Theogony as a creation story stands as a natural contrast to the Biblical Genesis and the Japanese Kojiki, as well as the Mayan Popol Vuh. Each of these major cultural origin narratives is a compilation of earlier oral materials whose rather loose, episodic, and awkward structure indicates its folk origins. The Odyssey and the Aeneid also include some references to the gods or events of the Theogony, as of course does Ovid's Metamorphoses. All these works can be fruitfully taught together.

The opening events of the creation story of Theogony are revealing in the gendered way we move from neuter Chaos to Earth who is parthenogenic at first—able to reproduce without a mate—but then to a male-dominated pantheon that nevertheless includes strangely powerful female beings like Hecate. Bloody father-son rivalries for succession are typical of Indo-European origin stories; the overthrow of Ouranos by Chronos and Chronos by Zeus can be examined closely as tiny dramas revealing paternal fears central to the early Greek mind. Close attention to the function of the mothers in these dynastic wars reveals residual power to affect events. Once Zeus has taken over the divine world, students can evaluate what values are encoded in his fathering of divine children, and their qualities. In particular the story of the birth of Athena is worth questioning, with Zeus's absorption of her mother Metis, out of fear. Tracing the serpent imagery in the narrative can be quite revealing, as can analysis of the strange figure of Hecate. Students will learn how narratives reveal cultural values, if they look closely at the power relations in the Theogony and examine what the various deities personify. Also the question of how the natural world is presented in the poem is an important one.

The Oxford Classical Dictionary is an excellent basic resource for the materials in the Theogony.

Questions for Study and Discussion:

1. What can we learn about the Greek view of nature from the early events of the Theogony? What seems to be the shape of the cosmos, in contrast to that in Genesis?

2. Is the castration of Ouranos symbolic? What is the significance of the place where Chronos hides, and of the weapon he uses?

3. What do we learn about Zeus in the story of his birth? How is he related to snakes?

4. Why does Zeus swallow Metis, and does this really make him the sole parent of Athena?

5. Trace the imagery of serpents through the Theogony. What do they represent?

6. How do you account for the prominence of Hecate?

The Homeric Hymn to Demeter

The alliance between Hades and his brother gods in the arrangement to abduct Demeter's daughter provides an interesting insight into the sexual politics of ancient Greek culture. Yet the poem is focused on the goddess who guarantees—or can withhold—earth's fertility. It is interesting to focus upon her ability to win back her daughter from the underworld. Students can discuss the way Demeter's responses are dramatized and the powers she wields. Primary attention, however, should be paid to the dramatic story of the abduction of Persephone and the mother-daughter relationship it presents. Look also at the way the landscape and the whole natural world are represented in relation to the goddess and her daughter.

This religious story is famous throughout Western culture. It is very ancient, probably reaching back to preliterate and pre-Greek traditions of reverence for the fertile powers of the landscape which were—as in most ancient cultures—associated with women. The Homeric Hymn to Demeter can be taught in conjunction with other stories of descent to the underworld, such as "The Descent of Inanna" and the Sixth Book of the Aeneid. Fascinating contrasts also exist in underworld materials in Homer's Odyssey and the Popol Vuh that we have not had space to include in this anthology. However, the story of the hero twins' birth in Popol Vuh does deal with similar fertility motifs that have sharply different tonal and visual presentation.

As with all mythic and literary materials from ancient Greece, The Oxford Classical Dictionary (Oxford, 1996) is the best starting place for background material on the myth of Demeter and Persephone. Heavily-edited, romanticized, or simplified versions of the myths that have been popular reference books in schools are quite misleading and should be avoided because they do not do justice to the complex and even conflicting sources of these important cultural materials. An interesting treatment of the myth from the perspective of archetypal theory is C. Kerényi's Eleusis: Archetypal Image of Mother and Daughter (New York, 1967). Marija

Gimbutas's <u>Goddesses and Gods of Old Europe</u> (Berkeley,1982) offers intriguing glimpses into the Neolithic heritage from which Demeter and Persephone descend.

Questions for Study and Discussion:

1. How is Demeter's daughter first presented? What does the setting of her frolics tell us about values associated with her?

2. What do you make of the bargain reached between Zeus and Hades regarding the maiden? Why is the name of the underworld god not mentioned?

3. What are Demeter's powers as revealed in her response to her daughter's abduction?

4. Could the story of the "rape" or kidnapping reveal Greek attitudes toward marriage? Or is this story basically a mother's view of marriage?

5. What does the underworld seem to represent, and what is the meaning of Persephone's sojourn there?

Homer
The Odyssey

The books from <u>The Odyssey</u> appearing here can be read in conjunction with any of the other epic works we have included, Western or Eastern. They work particularly well with the selections from Milton's <u>Paradise Lost</u>, as both treat issues of gender and the dangers of an egotistical hubris which either threatens to, or does, lead to an heroic downfall.

It would be helpful, at the outset, to make students aware that the term "epic" comes from the Greek "epos," or "word." Through its noble language, the epic serves as a foundation for its culture, and students are sure to recognize Western attitudes expressed in <u>The Odyssey</u> that are very much with us today. Among those certain to generate discussion is the "double standard" of Odysseus (in Book 5), who shares the bed of a goddess on his way home to a wife who is expected to remain chaste during his twenty-two year absence. The question of a masculine cultural paradigm also takes center stage in Book 23, "The Great Rooted Bed," in which Homer paints a portrait of a Penelope who is very much the equal of her famous husband.

A useful approach to Books 9, 12, 21 and 24 is to explore the nature of the hero as a "speaker of words" and "doer of deeds." When does Odysseus's heroism become or approach <u>hubris</u> (overweening pride)?

For a treatment of <u>The Odyssey</u> in the context of ancient Chinese literature (particularly the <u>Book of Songs</u>), see Shankman and Durrant, <u>The Siren and the Sage: Knowledge and Wisdom in Ancient Greece and China</u>. Scholarly treatments of gender issues can be found in Gregory Crane's <u>Calypso: Background and Conventions of The Odyssey</u> (Frankfurt am Main, 1988), and Lillian Doherty's <u>Siren Songs: Gender, Audiences and Narrators in The Odyssey</u> (Ann Arbor, 1995). For an interesting example of the pervasive influence of the classics on popular culture, see Kevin Thomas, "The Natural: Our <u>Iliad</u> and <u>Odyssey</u>."

Questions for Study and Discussion:

1. When she appears to Telemachus in Book 1 (and throughout The Odyssey), Athena takes the form of a man. Why would the goddess of wisdom assume a male persona when she appears to humans?

2. In Book 5, Odysseus turns down Calypso's promise of immortality for him. Why is this significant?

3. Why should hearing the Sirens' song bring destruction to the listener? What is the song about?

4. In the first half of The Odyssey, Homer has Odysseus endure many tests, thus accentuating his heroism. In the second half of the poem, before he reveals his true identity, Odysseus tests others to see if they pose a threat. Why do you think he tests his old and feeble father, Laertes, who cannot possibly be a threat to him? What does this reveal about Odysseus's character?

5. Reread Odysseus's account of the construction of the Great Rooted Bed. Keeping in mind the nature of an epic as a foundational document, what is the significance of his speech to the work as a whole?

Sappho
Poems

Sappho and her legacy are inextricably bound with the connection between erôs, or sexuality, and spirituality. Works with which she might thus be read include Plato's Symposium, the biblical Song of Songs and the love poems in the ancient Chinese Book of Songs (an especially revealing comparison can be made between Sappho 16, in which the Greek poet flaunts convention, and Book of Songs 76, in which the narrator, in anticipation of adverse criticism from her family and the public sphere, recoils from such self-assertion). Works chosen from later periods might include selections from Petrarch and the letters of Abelard and Heloise, as well as Pope's Eloisa to Abelard. Sappho's poems might of course also be read in the context of the Western classical tradition, especially insofar as their emphasis on intense personal and subjective experience contrasts with the more martial vision of the Western epics.

Students should be made aware of how Sappho transposes—some might say subverts—elements of the classical epic tradition to suit her own purposes. In Homeric epic, it has been said, you are what others think of you. Sappho's lyrics, in contrast, celebrate subjective states of mind for their own sake. In this she is peculiarly contemporary, and students are thus likely to feel at home with her verse from the start. Some might even find it clichéd (as in the descriptions of love-sickness in the last two stanzas of poem 31), until it is pointed out that she, in essence, invented the clichés with which they are familiar. In fact, as Page du Bois states, she might be said to have invented, in Western literature, the fully individuated human consciousness, which sometimes stands in contradistinction to the accepted cultural mores of its time (as in poem 16).

It would also be useful to inform students that poem 1 follows the formal conventions of the "cletic hymn," consisting of three parts: the invocation to the goddess by name using characteristics needed for the appeal to follow, a recounting of the goddess's past exploits to favorably dispose the goddess to the appellant, and the making of the request. In both this poem and in poem 31, the implicit connection of love with divinity should be explored, especially if these poems are read in conjunction with some of the works suggested above.

Students should be made to hear the lilting sound of the Sapphic stanza, which consists of five lines. The first four (of eleven syllables each) correspond metrically, and the fourth (of five syllables) is abbreviated. J. V. Cunningham, in his translation of poems 1 and 31 included here, attempts to simulate this form in English syllabic verse, although the translator substitutes lines of nine syllables for Sappho's lines of eleven syllables. As we discuss in our section on translators of Homer, Greek verse is quantitative; that is, it consists of syllables that are held for longer or shorter periods of time. The first four lines of the Sapphic stanza are scanned as follows:- u - - - uu - u -- ; the final line of each stanza is scanned as follows: - uu - -.

The Modernist poet H. D.'s The Wise Sappho (London, 1988) is a sympathetic, evocative, and highly poetic appraisal of Sappho's verse that is sure to appeal to the interested student. Contemporary critical readings of Sappho can be found in Ellen Greene, Rereading Sappho: Contemporary Approaches (Berkeley, 1996). For Sappho's relation to epic, see Leah Risman, Love as War: Homeric Allusion in the Poetry of Sappho (Königstein, 1983).

Questions for Study and Discussion:

1. How does the "proof" Sappho offers in poem 16 work to illuminate the poem as a whole?

2. How might Sappho's experience in poem 16 be said to be similar to that of Helen? How might it be different?

3. In poem 31, sometimes called "Love's Pathology," what is the significance of portraying the effects of love in terms of physical infirmity almost to the point of death?

4. Give some examples of how Sappho appropriates what might be called traditional masculine themes of her time and turns them to her own use.

5. How do the examples you have given above, in question 4, work in the context of the poems?

6. Describe the different styles and strategies of the two translators of Sappho represented here. What are the stylistic principles of the two translators? Which do you prefer, and why?

Pindar
"Olympian 14" and "Pythian 3"

Pindar can profitably be taught alongside many different lyric poets. Pindar initiated the tradition, in Western literature, of the greater ode, known for its sublimity. It would be worthwhile looking at the poems in our anthology that were inspired by Pindar; namely, Horace's Pindaric imitation and Friedrich Hölderlin's "Patmos." The two Pindaric odes we have included might also be read in conjunction with Sappho, for Pindar and Sappho, respectively, represent the public and private ancient Greek lyric. Because of the public nature of this poem, Pindar's odes inspire comparison with the dynastic hymns of the roughly contemporary Book of Songs. (See particularly songs 235, 241, and 245.)

When we think of occasional poetry today, we often assume that such poetry is not particularly elevated or sublime. If a poet is asked to compose a poem for a particular patron that he or she may not even know very well, if at all, for a particular occasion whose significance may not personally concern the poet, we might assume that such a poem is mere hack work. Pindar was an occasional poet—but he was a sublime one; indeed, he was the greatest of Greek lyric poets. Students should be encouraged to see how both of these poems are deeply occasional, and to try to discover how the poet's words develop out of his assigned task. Students should also be made aware of the centrality of poetry in Greek culture. It is no mere diversion for an ancient Greek.

Elroy Bundy's monographs on Pindar (Berkeley, 1962) decisively created a before and an after in Pindaric scholarship and interpretation, but they are too technical for the layman. The thrust of Bundy's important work is that Pindar's odes must be seen as occasional; that they are poems in praise of the victor who had been successful in the athletic games, and that virtually every word of each poem is intended, directly or indirectly, to praise the victor (and, by implication, the victor's family, who commissioned the poem). Frank J. Nisetich's introduction to his translation of the poems, Pindar's Victory Songs (Baltimore, 1980), discusses the importance of Bundy's work. So does William H. Race's Pindar (Boston, 1986), which is a very readable, helpful introduction designed for the nonspecialist. Also interesting is Donald S. Carne-Ross's Pindar (New Haven, CT, 1985), which is full of suggestive insights; Carne-Ross's love for his subject glows through his lively prose, and his deft sensibility and broad acquaintance with the whole range of European poetry make this book special.

Questions for Study and Discussion:

1. What is an encomium?

2. How does the occasion of each poem determine how it is organized?

3. Why does the poet ask Echo to "go / to the dark walls / of Persephone's house" at the conclusion of "Olympian 14"?

4. What may be some of the artistic reasons that "Olympian 14" is so brief? What might this have to do with the nature of the victor, or his family?

5. In "Pythian 3," Pindar makes connections between the arts of poetry and of healing. Can you find them in the poem? Why does Pindar make these connections?

6. In the final episode of "Pythian 3," Pindar refers to himself (at least in his role as encomiastic poet). How is this self-reference connected to the central theme of the poem? Can you find other instances in the poem where Pindar refers to himself? What is the purpose of such self-references?

Thucydides
The Peloponnesian War

Thucydides can obviously be taught in a segment on the writers of ancient Greece. In that context, he will be seen to be a wonderful exemplar of his own subject, i.e. the Athenian character in the fifth century B.C.E. Students might compare his rationalism with that of Pentheus in the Bacchae. He might also be profitably taught in juxtaposition with Sima Qian, whose reverence toward his predecessors and whose humility stand in stark contrast to Athenian boldness and impatience.

Students need to understand the difference between the Athenian and Spartan characters: restless entrepreneurial brilliance and impatience vs. stolid and somewhat faceless conservatism. Thucydides shows how Athens thrived so long as responsible leaders, such as Pericles, ruled the city. Pericles was himself rather proud (Athens' achievements are so evident for all to see, he tells his audience in his famous funeral oration for those who died in battle in the first year of the war, that he and his fellow Athenians are "far from needing a Homer for our panegyrist"). But after Pericles perished in the plague, power fell into less responsible hands, such as those of Alcibiades. The increasingly icy pride of Athens is in full view in the dialogue between the Athenians and the islanders from Melos who do not wish to take sides in the conflict. They attempt to make the case for their autonomy and free their Athenian oppressors, but they are met only with scorn. The Athenians show neither fear of the gods nor pity for the powerless. Since the ability to feel fear and pity are, for Greek philosophers like Aristotle, essential elements in a morally balanced soul, the Melian dialogue (if dialogue it can truly be called, when one side has not the slightest interest in budging from its position of superior power) shows that Athens has lost its moral authority.

Eric Voegelin discusses Thucydides in historical context in The World of the Polis (Baton Rouge, 1957). Despite the fact that it was written more than forty years ago, it is still incisive and informed by a profound philosophical acumen. See also W. Robert Connor, Thucydides (Princeton, 1984). If you have some French, check out Jaqueline de Romilly, La construction de la vérité chez Thucydide (Paris, 1990). For the tragic elements in Thucydides, see Colin Macleod, "Thucydides and Tragedy" in his Collected Essays (Oxford, 1983). On the pride of Thucydides, see K. J. Dover, Thucydides, Greece & Rome: New Surveys in the Classics, No. 7 (Oxford, 1973). The chapter on Thucydides by Werner Jaeger in his masterful Paideia: The Ideals of Greek Culture (Oxford, 1965) is still worth consulting.

Questions for Study and Discussion:

1. What are the traits of the Athenian character, as the Corinthian envoy describes them? What are the Spartans like?

2. Can you find instances of pride in Pericles' funeral oration?

3. Can you find contemporary parallels with the conflict between Athens and Sparta?

4. In section 46 of the Melian dialogue, after addressing the males in the audience, Pericles finally turns his attention to the women for a few brief words. Does this paucity of attention to his female listeners say anything about Pericles and perhaps, by implication, about Thucydides himself?

5. In the Melian dialogue, does it appear to you that Thucydides himself believed that "might makes right"? Is this the message Thucydides intended for his readers?

Euripides
The Bacchae

This play works well in a course focused on drama in world literature, with its archaic materials compared to Śakuntalā and the Ring of Recollection, Japanese Nō Theatre, and Shakespeare's King Lear. The wider mythic context for Dionysus is presented in very old form in Hesiod's Theogony, though little information about the god himself is included. The only literary materials in our anthology that seem analogous to the Bacchae's focus on the mysterious powers of nature are the ancient Sumerian hymns to Inanna, the figures of Enkidu and Ishtar in The Epic of Gilgamesh, and the bloody ritual games of the Mayan Popol Vuh. All of these works seem to derive from a stage of cultural development in which both the terror and the joyous power of the natural world were intensely important subjects for literary exploration. A modern work which approaches the relation between human arrogance and wild nature is Nguyen Huy Thiep's short story, "Salt of the Jungle." Asking students to read the Vietnamese story in conjunction with Euripides's tragedy should provoke interesting discussion related to present day environmental concerns.

The Bacchae is the most archaic play Euripides wrote, both in language and subject-matter. Greek scholar E. R. Dodds believes that the playwright was reworking very old materials associated with the long tradition of sacred celebrations of the god Dionysus, and that he thus produced a play quite different from his characteristically ironic, secular treatments of mythic themes in other plays. One way to see the uneasy combination of ritualistic, liturgical traditions and secular reasoning that gave such an idea to Dodds is to contrast the events at the heart of the plot, such as the Herdsman's report of Maenad behavior or the chanting of the Maenad Chorus, with Dionysus's addresses to the audience at the beginning and his speeches at the end which seem to explain his actions. Choral passages make clear Dionysus's ecstatic effect on worshipers and his powerful associations with wild animals, plants, and the independent fertility of the earth.

Students will find the world of this play quite alien, but close attention to themes and values established in the opening scenes can help make it understandable. Dionysus explains his purpose to reestablish his mother Semele's reputation in Thebes and punish those who have slandered it. He sets forth the problem of blasphemy and focuses it firmly on his aunt Agave and her son Pentheus, filling in the audience on family history. Asking students to discuss family relationships might be a good idea, especially if they notice the closeness in age and appearance that becomes obvious between the cousins Pentheus and Dionysus. Clearly they mirror each other, yet they are antagonists who see the world in radically different ways. Analyzing their first meeting and then following their clashes up to the point of climactic reversal helps students see the dramatic structure of the play and understand how Pentheus seeks to impose a militaristic masculine will on the androgynous stranger. When Dionysus persuades Pentheus to dress as a woman and spy on the Maenads, something crucial has happened that bears close examination. Nietzsche's argument in The Birth of Tragedy that this play is about the clash between Apollonian reason and Dionysian irrationality or ecstatic life force is a provocative notion to test by close reading of the play. It is odd that Apollo is only mentioned briefly once in the play if Nietzsche is right, but there is no doubt that Pentheus represents an extreme of human arrogance that is disastrous, and that some balance between human control and the independent forces of the natural world is necessary.

E.R. Dodds's Introduction to his edition of The Bacchae (Oxford, 1959) is as rich a treatment of the nature of Dionysiac religion and the traditional elements of the text as one can find. Dodds also places the play within the context of Euripides's whole career in useful ways. Friedrich Nietzsche's The Birth of Tragedy provides a view of the play as a clash between Apollonian and Dionysian visions of life that has influenced all discussion of the text in our century. Nietzsche ignores the dimension of gender that is so important to Pentheus's behavior, and he emphasizes Apollo's symbolic presence when in fact that god is only mentioned once. Nevertheless, it is important to be aware of this influential and provocative analysis. An excellent recent interpretation of the play is Robert Bagg's Introduction to his translation, The Bakkhai (Amherst, Mass., 1978). Charles Segal's essay "Euripides's Bacchae: The Language of the Self and the Language of the Mysteries" in his Interpreting Greek Tragedy (Ithaca, New York, 1986) offers another useful critical angle on the play.

Questions for Study and Discussion:

1. What is it about Dionysus that Pentheus objects to so intensely? What does this reveal about Pentheus's character and motives?

2. How does the Maenad Chorus communicate the nature of the god Dionysus? Look for specific images that define his power. Who are these women, and why did Euripides make them his Chorus? Why are Dionysus's worshipers chiefly female?

3. Who are Cadmus and Teiresias, and what is the meaning of their dispute with Pentheus about whether or not to pay homage to the new god?

4. How does the Herdsman's report of spying on the Maenads satisfy the young king's purpose in calling for his testimony? Why is Pentheus so obsessively interested in the women who are worshiping the god?

5. What happens when Pentheus tries to coerce the stranger with physical force? How is Pentheus responding personally to him?

6. Why does Pentheus change his mind about going to see the Maenads? Look closely at his responses to Dionysus.

7. Are we supposed to approve of the fate of Pentheus and his mother's punishment? What does this grisly conclusion have to do with the major themes of the play, particularly the need for reverence toward Dionysus which lies at the heart of the god's justification for his actions, and indeed at the heart of the genre of Greek tragedy?

Plato (I)
The Apology

For undergraduates, this is perhaps one of the most accessible and provocative of the Platonic dialogues. It complements and/or contrasts well with a number of selections in this anthology. Thucydides's rendition of the speech of the Corinthians on the character of the Athenians, as well as his representation of the Melian Conference, provide a useful portrait of the Athenian mindset of Socrates's time. The biblical book of Ecclesiastes and the Analects of Confucius, as well as "The Second Philosophy and Spiritual Discipline" of the Bhagavad-Gītā all address themes raised by Socrates in his defense.

With the themes of "Question Authority" and "Know Thyself" at its core, this work always elicits enthusiastic responses from students. As discussion proceeds, you will likely find that students are divided into two camps: those sympathetic to Socrates and those who find him too arrogant and believe, along with I. F. Stone, that he "had it coming." A useful classroom strategy is to conduct a mock trial in which students discuss what they consider to be the pros and cons of Socrates's ideas, and then vote for conviction or acquittal—or for any of the other punishments or rewards proposed in the dialogue. Students should be asked to justify their votes and the appropriateness of the suggested punishment or reward. The instructor can play devil's advocate for both sides in the process of coming to judgement.

Students and teachers will find I. F. Stone's The Trial of Socrates (Boston, 1988) informative and controversial. For a more in-depth and scholarly approach, see E. de Strycker's Plato's Apology of Socrates: A Literary and Philosophical Study with a Running Commentary (New York, 1994).

Questions for Study and Discussion:

1. How is Socrates, by his own account, different from other teachers, and what is the significance of this difference?

2. What does Socrates mean when he tells the Athenians that, by putting him to death, they will do more harm to themselves than they will to him? Do you agree? Why or why not?

3. Socrates states: "He who would really fight for justice must do so as a private citizen, not as a political figure, if he is to preserve his life, even for a short time." Do you agree? Why or why not?

4. Discuss the statement: "An unexamined life is not worth living." What are its implications?

Plato (II)
The Republic ["The Allegory of the Cave"]

This selection is among the evocatively symbolic passages of The Republic. With the epiphanic and transfiguring event of "seeing the light" as its theme, it might usefully be read alongside Exodus and the gospel of Mark, or such Asian works as the Analects and the Dao de jing, as well as passages from the Bhagavad-Gītā.

Keeping in mind Socrates's thoughts on the nature of knowledge and the place of the teacher expressed in The Apology and The Symposium, a useful classroom approach might be to focus on why, for most of these authors, enlightenment should bring with it a sense of responsibility for others. Students might also be encouraged to reflect on why so literary a device as "allegory" is found in a "philosophical" work that ostensibly deals with the nature of the perfect state, and to explore the issue of enlightenment versus ideology—that is, truth versus opinion—implicit in this episode.

For this, as for all the Platonic selections included in this anthology, interested students and teachers are encouraged to explore the work of Eric Voegelin for a non-traditional, fresh, and provocative re-reading of Plato.

Questions for Study and Discussion:

1. Why would those still in the cave want to kill the person trying to lead them to freedom?

2. Why do you think Plato has Socrates, at the end of this passage, insert the disclaimer, "Heaven knows whether it is true: but this, at any rate, is how it appears to me"? Does this in any way diminish the authority of what has come before? Why or why not?

Plato (III)
The Symposium

With a subject of near-universal appeal, the nature of erôs (love), this seminal work of Western philosophy works well with a number of other Western texts in this anthology. It combines particularly well with, for instance, the poems of Sappho and the letters of Abelard and Heloise, as well as with Pope's Eloisa to Abelard. Asian works with which it might usefully be read include the Dao de jing of Laozi, especially those sections dealing with passion, desire and the feminine.

Students are invariably drawn to, and often find most appealing, Aristophanes's fanciful and (to most students) "romantic" account of love as finding the one who makes us whole. They will also be surprised to learn that platonic love, a concept with which most of them are familiar, is erôs-driven. In the centerpiece of the work (i.e., Socrates's disclosure of what he was taught by Diotima) students may well be perplexed when they realize that in this clearly male-dominated work where the feminine is banished with the flute girl, the central speech belongs to a woman and is presented in the language of physical love and reproduction. This aspect of the text is fertile ground, as it were, for classroom discussion, since it introduces students to the theme of the nature and limits of human knowledge.

For scholarly treatments of gender issues in The Symposium, the following are useful sources: Page duBois's Sowing the Body: Psychoanalysis and Ancient Representations of Women (Chicago, 1988); David Halperin's "Plato and the Erotics of Narrativity" in Plato and Postmodernism (Glenside, PA, 1994), edited by Steven Shankman; and Steven Shankman's In Search of the Classic: Reconsidering the Greco-Roman Tradition, Homer to Valery and Beyond (University Park, PA, 1994), especially chapters 1 and 14. Denis de Rougemont's perennially fresh and controversial classic, Love in the Western World (Princeton, 1956), is a very accessible treatment of many of the issues raised in this Plato selection.

Questions for Study and Discussion:

1. Give a brief synopsis of each of the speakers' thoughts on the nature of love.

2. What aspects of the others' speeches does Socrates use in his speech?

3. Why do you think Plato makes Socrates's teacher a woman?

4. Having now read The Symposium, how would you characterize the concept of "platonic love"? What does love have to do with knowledge and ideas?

Catullus
Poems

As the great Roman poet of love, Catullus makes an interesting comparison to the Greek poet Sappho who was his model in many ways. Comparing Catullus's poem 51 with Sappho's poem 31 in our text shows how closely Catullus adapted one of her most famous works. Our introduction to Sappho explains the stanzaic form she used, and students can see stylistic similarities in Catullus even in English translation. Other poetry that can be profitably read with Catullus is the love lyrics from ancient Egypt, the Hebrew Song of Songs, lyrics from the ancient Chinese Book of Songs, and Japanese court poetry of the middle period. All of these poetic traditions are characterized by delicacy, irony, and longing. Catullus is distinguished among them by the tough detachment that controls his expression of passion, preventing self-indulgence. Within the Roman tradition, Catullus's relation to Virgil is something like that of the Laozi to Confucius in Chinese culture.

One of Catullus's most famous poems is "Come Lesbia mine, let us but live and love" (Number 5). In the original Latin its meter is the eleven-syllable line (hendecalyllabic). The English translation attempts to approximate it with ten-syllable, iambic lines. This meter, so close to colloquial speech in English, seems the most appropriate way to communicate the fresh directness of Catullus's Latin style. Word choice is also simple and direct, like his Latin.

Poem number 8, "My poor Catullus, play no more the fool," is written in "limping iambics" accepting the poet's humiliation in love at the same time that his feelings are constrained by a crisp matter of fact tone. Here is Catullus's characteristic honesty and refusal to indulge in self-pity. Number 11, "Aurelius and Furius, comrades sworn," uses the bond of warrior friendship as a contrast to the unfaithfulness of his lover. His friends' mission to deliver a defiant message to her is likened to heroic journeys across the globe, and she is thus painted as a dangerous barbarian enemy.

Number 51, "That man is seen by me as God's equal," is written in the Sapphic stanza of the Greek model, as mentioned above. Students should compare Catullus's imitation with Sappho's poem and note the lyric directness of both. Students can consider whether Catullus is able to add anything to the original, or whether his poem is merely a translation.

The famous couplet "I hate and love," or "Odi et Amo" in Latin, number 81, has long exemplified poetic truth to the complexity of emotion by holding two extremes in tension. That love can turn to hate is commonplace knowledge; but the simultaneous experience of the two is here expressed in terms of excruciating physical pain.

The Catullan Revolution (Ann Arbor, 1971) by Kenneth Quinn offers a useful introduction to the historical context of the poetry, as well as sound criticism. Another, broader study of Latin poetry that treats Catullus is Niall Rudd's Lines of Enquiry: Studies in Latin Poetry (New York, 1976). A useful complete text of Catullus's work in Latin, but with English commentary, is The Student's Catullus (Norman, Oklahoma, 1995).

Questions for Study and Discussion:

1. How does the poet seek to compete with cosmic powers in his love for Lesbia in poem number 5? Why would a malicious person wish to count their kisses?

2. Try scanning the meter of poem number 8 to see how it corresponds to the subject of lost love. What is the speaker's purpose, and how does his mood shift?

3. Why does the poet call upon his friends by describing their pledges to follow his call across the world to strange and barbaric places? What connection do those places have to his sweetheart? Is the message described in the poem's second half to be whispered really intended for his sweetheart, or to someone else?

4. How does poem number 51 correspond to Sappho's famous poem 31? Is Catullus's version only a translation, or is it something more? How does the poem's imagery work?

5. Why has the little couplet, "I hate and love" lasted so many centuries? What is its purpose?

Virgil
The Aeneid

While The Aeneid can certainly be read in the company of the other epics we have included, and specifically Paradise Lost, the selections here also allow it to work well with other stories of tragic love. In particular, Ovid's retelling of the Dido and Aeneas story from a feminine perspective in the Heroides, and Pope's Eloisa to Abelard provide a useful counterpoint. Asian works might include Kālidāsa's Śakuntalā and the Ring of Recollection and the Tale of Genji.

Virgil clearly meant his epic to legitimize Rome's claim as not only the political, but the cultural, heir to Greece. As we noted in our introduction, Virgil constantly alludes to Greece's great Homeric epics. One such provocative allusion takes place in Book 12. The instructor may wish to recall, or perhaps even read aloud, the section of Book 24 of The Iliad (not included in this anthology, unfortunately) where Priam begs for pity from a wrathful Achilles in much the same way—indeed, using the same appeals to the father of the person supplicated—as does Turnus from Aeneas. (See also Virgil's reference to this Iliadic scene in Book 2, lines 210-21.) The reactions of the two heroes beg comparison.

The tragic story of Dido and Aeneas in Book 4 is sure to strike a responsive chord with students. It is the pathos of Dido's final encounter with Aeneas—specifically, her passion, his rationalization of political necessity and the almost Abelardian equanimity with which he rejects her claims—that goes to the heart of the ambivalences inherent in Virgil's epic. Students will be interested to learn that, perhaps because of these very ambivalences (we don't really know), Virgil wanted his poem destroyed upon his death.

For further reading, see Steven Farron, Virgil's Aeneid: A Poem of Grief and Love (New York, 1993) and Daniel Garrison, The Language of Virgil: An Introduction to the Poetry of The Aeneid (New York, 1987). Students and teachers interested in making connections with the present are sure to find interesting Dana Burgess's article, "Virgilian Modes in Spike Lee's 'Do the Right Thing.'"

Questions for Study and Discussion:

1. From what land does Aeneas originate? Why is this significant?

2. Why did Dido feel Aeneas should stay with her? What were his reasons for leaving? Who had the more compelling argument and why?

3. Why do you suppose that the final picture we get of Aeneas is one in which he is engaged in a merciless act of vengeance? Is this a heroic portrait?

4. Compare Aeneas's killing of Turnus with the slaying of Priam alluded to in Book 2. Are there significant similarities or differences?

Horace
Odes

Horace can profitably be taught alongside many different lyric poets. His "seize the day" philosophy of our first selection finds parallels in many other poets in other traditions, such as China's Li Bai and Tao Qian. Our second and third selections can be taught alongside other poems that, in a self-reflexive manner, discuss poetry and the writing of poetry. Our last selection is an imitation—that goes its own way—of the Greek poet, Pindar. This would most effectively be read in conjunction with our selections from Pindar, as well as the Pindar-inspired poem by Friedrich Hölderlin that we have included in this anthology. Since the second and fourth selections are composed, in the original Latin, in Sapphics (see below), these poems should be read alongside our selections from Sappho.

Horace is an extremely artful, as well as a very self-consciously literary, poet. Students should be encouraged to appreciate the poems' allusiveness, as well as their directness. Teachers might discuss Horace's treatment of the public and the private, which is intriguing.

The first two selections, in particular, can be taught alongside other poetic translations that attempt to find formal equivalents for effects in other languages. The first poem attempts to imitate, in English, the meter of the Latin. It is called the "Great Asclepiad" and is scanned as follows: - - - u u - // - u u - // - u u - u - (where "-" indicates a long syllable and "u" a short).

Greek and Latin meter is quantitative; that is, syllables are held for longer or shorter periods of time. By contrast, most English verse is accentual, with a certain number of stresses per line. In the first translation, the stresses appear (in English) precisely where, in Latin, there are long syllables.

The second and fourth selections are composed, in the original Latin, in Sapphics, which consist of three lines that are scanned in the following manner: - u - - - u u - u - -. These are then followed by a last line, scanned as - u u - -. The third poem is composed in a meter called the "First Asclepiad" (- - - u u - / / - u u - u -).

Useful general books on Horace are by Steele Commager (written in the 1960s, but still helpful), Matthew Santiroco (Chapel Hill, NC, 1986), and David Armstrong (New Haven, CT, 1989). Particularly recommended is Gregson Davis's book, Polyhymnia (Berkeley, 1991), which shows how Horace draws on the rich tradition of Greco-Roman rhetorical devices to establish meaning in his poems.

Questions for Study and Discussion:

1. What are the qualities of Horace's poetry, as the poet himself implicitly or explicitly describes them?

2. What metrical forms do the translators use, and how are they related to the metrical intentions of the original?

3. Who are Horace's poetic models, and how does he vary from them to establish his own style and meaning?

4. Is Horace a public or a private poet?

5. Can you find instances of Horace's sense of humor? his wit?

Ovid
Metamorphoses and Heroides

Metamorphoses

Ovid's Metamorphoses strives for comprehensiveness. Moving temporally from creation to a recent Roman past, the poem's fifteen books contain a plethora of themes and genres. It features elements from epic (such as hexameter verse, cosmic scope, ecphrasis, catalogues, similes, heroes and gods), tragedy, dramatic monologue, hymns, set speeches, pastoral, epigram, history, myth, and didactic material familiar from oratory and philosophic discourse. However, the selections included in this anthology illustrate only a tiny glimpse into the vastness of the complete text. But if Metamorphoses is comprehensive, it is also somewhat chaotic, leaping from episode to episode without what modern readers (and even ancient readers like Quintilian) consider logical transitions. The presence of some kind of metamorphosis does link all episodes thematically, but it is a loose connection. The omnipresent narrator also continually reminds us that someone is telling the tales, and a close examination of ways the narrator works to shape our responses to the text is a useful exercise. It might prove especially useful in comparison with Homeric and Virgilian narrators. Ovid was, of course, a crucial source for other major authors in the European tradition: Boccaccio, Chaucer, Shakespeare, Milton, Pope, and T. S. Eliot, just to name a few. The <u>Metamorphoses</u> is only one text authors drew from. His other influential texts include the <u>Heroides</u>, the <u>Amores</u>, the <u>Ars Amatoria</u> and <u>Remedia Amoris</u>, his epistles, the <u>Fasti</u> and more.

The Creation story in Ovid begins without ascribing creation to any specific deity: a god, "whichever god it was," separates chaotic sameness into distinct entities. This god, described as "the world's artificer," "the Architect of all, the author of the universe" crafts a better world than had existed before. Such an image resonates, of course, with the implied praise for the human artist and author as well. Notably, the praise for categorization and distinction in creation rests in a tension or balance with the main theme of the text which emphasizes the transgression of category and bodily boundaries as figure after figure transmogrifies into a completely different species of thing or kind of existence. This very tension is worth discussion. Comparisons of the creation account in Ovid with those found in other ancient texts is another obvious strategy for reading and teaching. The figure of Tiresias found in Ovid is usefully compared with his representations in other Greek and Roman texts (e.g., <u>The Bacchae</u>, pp. 517-24), and students may be familiar with his role in Sophocles' <u>Oedipus</u> and Homer's <u>Odyssey</u> (neither episode included in the anthology but often quite familiar to students).

The story of Narcissus and Echo carries many interpretive possibilities. Certainly, the attention it pays to language is one way to explore the tale. The relationship of word and voice to action, punishment, identity, and power form major themes in the short tale. Where the nymph Echo had used words to protect her sisters, these same words offend Juno, who places a curse on Echo: namely taking away her ability to speak only by miming someone else's words. And where Narcissus uses language to protect himself from the advances of lovers, his refusals lead "a youth" to plead with heaven to curse Narcissus: "may Narcissus fall in love; but once a prey, may he, too, be denied the prize he craves" (ll. 129-31). And so, falling in love with his mirror image, loving himself, he cries, "I burn with love for my own self" (219). Dying from catching a glimpse of himself, his death realizes the words of Tiresias (l. 49). But the relationship of word and action is not left unremarked or uncomplicated as Ovid provides two endings to the tale. In one, Narcissus lies in Hades, gazing into the Styx to see his umbra (shadow). In the other, his body dissolves into the soil and is transformed into a flower. The shifting sense of meaning, a sense of linguistic ambiguity and indeterminancy, leaves us far from sure. The two lovers seem to represent extremes of mimesis: one whose voice can only mold to another, can only repeat the other's words; and the other whose desire flows only toward himself, both fated to imbalance in love. The story can, on another level, simply provide an account of how natural phenomena came to be: the echo and the narcissus. The flower was commonly used in Greek funeral rites, and its association with death can also be seen in the <u>Hymn to Demeter</u> (ll. 5-20), where Persephone gathers flowers. When she reaches with both hands for "the Earth's bauble," the narcissus, Hades reaches up from the underworld to abduct her.

<u>Questions for Study and Discussion</u>:

1. What shape does Ovid give to the development of human history at the beginning of <u>Metamorphoses</u>? What elements of Creation are emphasized? Ignored?

2. How does this account of creation compare with that given in Hesiod's Theogony? Genesis? The Egyptian Hymn to the Sun? Texts from the Rig Veda? The creation myths found in the Japanese text, the Kojiki?

3. How is love represented in the tale of Echo and Narcissus? How is "knowledge of self" represented?

4. What is the relationship between the mythic world and the natural world in these selections from Ovid?

5. What representations of the artist are found in Ovid's selections from the Metamorphoses? Examine the narrator's asides and comments on his own story as well as the material found in the Epilogue.

The Heroides

Students need to understand the contours of the mythic story of Dido and Aeneas before jumping in to read this selection, since Ovid's innovations might not be as clear unless students have encountered the more traditional shape given the material. Within epic, of course, like Virgil's Aeneid, Dido represents a temptation for Aeneas. Her world, a softer, gentler world than the warring worlds of Greeks and Trojans, does not allow Aeneas to enact his role as founder of an empire. Typically, Dido is represented as somewhat irrational, even insane once Aeneas leaves her. Her dramatic suicide is often told for horrific effect, or as a way to justify Aeneas's decision to leave her: after all, this hero should not wind up with a mad woman as a wife. Aeneas's loyalty to his people, his duty to found a New Troy, his duty to his father and son rather than to Dido, are represented as indications of his greatness. When students understand this, they can appreciate Ovid's revisions of the tale. Still, Ovid writes the text as a man; and Christine de Pizan thought it needed further revision. A comparison of the shape this narrative takes as it moves from the epic world of Virgil, to the dramatic monologue of Ovid, to the extended argument in defense of women in Christine's City of Ladies, is worth study. The forces of genre, the differences in historical contexts, and apparent authorial intentions are all factors to consider here, as is the way in which stories refuse to hold still. In one sense, Virgil, Ovid, and Christine enact differences we now might understand as "reader-response." Each interprets received narrative just as contemporary readers do when reading even the same text in the same historical moment.

Questions for Study and Discussion:

1. What kind of person is Dido in Ovid's text? What lines are most important in shaping your own response to this voice/persona?

2. How does this Dido understand Aeneas? How does she depict him? Which lines are most important, do you think; in other words, which elements in her description persuade us to view Aeneas in a certain way?

3. Why does Dido make mention of her former husband and brother? How does it help her argument?

4. How are we to understand the act of suicide in the poem? Do you think we need to take historical and cultural differences into account to sufficiently answer this question? What were the attitudes toward suicide in Ovid's Rome? (Students could do some research to help answer this question.)

5. Carefully compare Virgil's account of the Dido and Aeneas story with Ovid's. Then investigate the changes Christine de Pizan made when she borrowed the story to help her defend women in her text, The City of Ladies.

6. How does woman's sorrow in this Latin text compare with other literary accounts of women's grief? Useful comparisons may be found with the ancient Sumerian text, Hymns to Inanna, Qu Yuan's "Li Sao" ("Encountering Sorrow"), The Homeric Hymn to Demeter, Penelope in Homer's Odyssey? Or al-Khansā's laments from early Arabic poetry?

7. How does this text contrast with other texts featuring male figures suffering loss and grief in Ancient and Middle period literature? Gilgamesh? The Bhagavad-Gītā? Job? The Shāh-nāmah?

The Gospel of Mark

For those who are already familiar with the Gospels, reading Mark in a literature class has the beneficial effect of defamiliarizing it, making it fresh. For those who have never read it, reading it can produce the surprising sense, "It's not what I expected." It can be taught in the context of other biblical materials, or in the context of Roman literature of the period, or in the context of other biographies, especially of religious leaders like Buddha (Asvaghosha's Buddha-Karita) or Mohammad (Muhammad Ibn Ishaq's Life of the Prophet), or in the context of other sacred literature, like the Qur'an and the Bhagavad-Gītā. Though approaching it from a literary angle may produce strong reactions in some students, it is not hard to avoid "mistreating" it, and Christian students can be shown that its literary interest only enhances our respect for the text. My personal recommendation is that teachers respect faith-driven interpretations that may emerge in class, since the text itself begs for such interpretations—which are therefore of real critical interest. One can be respectful and still offer challenging approaches that take students far beyond their automatic responses.

Mark is the earliest of the four gospels. It was written about forty years after Jesus's death, and after the Roman destruction of the Temple in Jerusalem. Mark inherited a generation or two of oral testimonies about Jesus, and gave them their first literary form. For this reason, it is of interest as being on the borderline between an oral (folkloric) tradition, and a literary one. Matthew and Luke are in one sense literary elaborations or commentaries on Mark. The price one pays for Mark's ground-breaking originality is his relative lack of literary sophistication, which Matthew and Luke have in abundance.

Some simple structures and attitudes in the book can be brought out right away. First of all, the whole narrative is very lean, with no wasted detail; it leaps right to Jesus's baptism and moves swiftly to the crucifixion. There are three endings; the first, probably original, is quite shocking in its suddenness, and the others patch on more conventional endings. Second, all figures of authority are wrong or evil, and the weak and powerless are favored consistently. It is like those teen movies in which all adults are bad or stupid, and kids save the world. The weak and powerless play a big role in the book, as it focuses on the lower classes. In this it differs importantly from Greek and Roman literature. Third, the apostles are portrayed as amazingly slow-witted, failing to grasp all of Jesus's clues as to who he is, unable to interpret even the simplest parables. This allows the story to proceed (a bit clumsily) like a mystery, in which the revelation is delayed till the very end—though the reader is enlightened in the very first sentence. Fourth, there are a number of surprising rough edges and inexplicable details, like Jesus's statement that he speaks in parables so that people will not understand him, or the appearance of a naked man running away from the scene of Jesus's arrest. And fifth, it should be pointed out that the book is written in demotic, as opposed to literary, Greek, and in a humble style that surprised the late classical world (much as Wordsworth startled the neoclassical poets of his day, or Hemingway startled the novelists of his). The book has virtually no rhetorical polish or ambition, and convinces its audience by its directness and simplicity of speech.

I find the parables a valuable focus in the classroom. They are little stories-within-the-story, and illustrate the narrative style of the whole. There are a few themes that run through the parables, such as the harvest, which indicate metaphorically the themes of the whole book—in this case the "harvesting" of converts, or the apocalyptic "harvesting" of fulfilled history (a strong theme in the book, perhaps reflecting the feeling that destruction of the Temple was a clear sign of the approaching end of the world). Many of the parables are metaphorically about preaching, which is the aim of the whole work—e.g., Jesus sows the seeds of truth or salvation for a later harvest. Ask the class to read the parables as a sequence and see what images and themes emerge. Also, the parable is a distinct literary genre, and one can try to define its features—it is short, concerns common people doing ordinary things, and nearly always has a brain-teasing counter-intuitive twist ("to those who have more will be given"). Once a definition has been arrived at, the task it to identify each occurrence. Some of the later ones in the book are quite short (the fig tree, the doorkeeper). Scholars seem to agree that the parable was originally an oral preaching technique rendered progressively more literary by successive gospel writers. A current thread in parable scholarship suggests that they are likely to be the closest parts of the gospels to Jesus's actual preaching.

If you take an interest in parables as a genre, then there are several other texts in the anthology that might or might not contain parables. Asvaghosah's life of the Buddha contains an interesting analogue of the parable of the prodigal son from Luke's gospel; Zhuangzi's little narratives are often called parables; Augustine's story of the pear tree, and his story of the gladiatorial games might both be thought of as parables; Bede's parable of the sparrow seems to be in the genre; and from Arabia, Farīd al-Dīn Atar's Conference of Birds contains them. Interesting paper topics, to compare Mark's parables with these.

Teachers and students who want to do more reading should see Frank Kermode's little book, The Genesis of Secrecy (Cambridge, MA, 1979), the second chapter of which is an excellent literary treatment of the parables. In addition, the chapters on Mark and Luke (the latter discusses parables in particular) in Alter and Kermode's Literary Guide to the Bible (Cambridge, MA, 1987) are quite useful.

Questions for Study and Discussion:

1. Is the gospel of Mark a "biography"? What are its primary emphases in the life of Jesus? How important to this gospel are Jesus's miracles, his teachings, the details of his life history?

2. How does Mark characterize the Jewish and Roman authorities? What is your impression of the apostles from his narrative?

3. What do you make of the "certain young man" in 14:51? Can you find other details in the narrative that are similarly disconnected?

4. What are the features of the parable as a genre? How many parables does Jesus tell in Mark? Are there marginal cases, which may or may not be parables? Can parables be acted out, as well as told?

5. Consider the differences between the three different endings of Mark. Which of the three do you prefer?

Three Qasīdahs

The three qasīdahs are undeniably challenging for students. Having students locate the distinct sections of the qasīdah (the nasīb, the takhallus, and the gharad) and then review each section's conventional purpose (discussed briefly in the introduction to the texts) provides a useful beginning. Students can usually quite easily locate the main images and emotions in each section, and then work toward an understanding of how these associatively connect into a poetic whole. Working through one poem in class will likely prepare them to tackle one or both of the other qasīdahs on their own, but most students will find even this difficult.

It might be useful for students to read these poems with an eye to locating exactly what makes them difficult to read and understand. This can lead to a discussion of readers' expectations, and how our training as readers can make any unfamiliar texts seem, at first, confusing. Because these texts do not meet Euro-American readerly expectations, we might find them pulling our expectations one way and then another. Noting such responses can help students explore the "horizons of expectations" that each of us brings to reading. This also can reassure students that their initial responses are not "wrong," but rather are situated historically and culturally. The unfamiliar aesthetic strategies and techniques, as well as the cultural difference of texts like the qasīdahs, may help students understand the efforts readers must sometimes make to read across centuries, landscapes, and cultures. The qasīdahs not only disrupt attempts to read logically (rewarding, instead, the reader who reads more associatively), they also disrupt any attempt to identify a single theme or meaning. However, a central relationship exists in all three: namely the relationship between civilization and nature. One can, consequently, read them thematically in relation to the more ancient Middle Eastern literatures or alongside the Chinese Song of Songs. Like The Song of Songs, the qasīdahs derive from oral materials, from a people who lived in close relationship with land and weather. And like many early written poetic traditions, the qasīdahs frequently praise ancestors and tribes, the bedouin equivalent of "nation." Quite unlike the Chinese collection, though, the qasīdahs represent the culmination of a pre-Islamic oral tradition on the cusp of an Islamic transformation; and unlike the ancient Chinese materials, these poems are longer, have a complex three-part structure, and often celebrate a heroic, more nomadic, code of manliness rather than the agrarian culture of a Zhou dynastic world. They are probably best read, then, in relation to later Arabic and Persian materials within the same section or, if paired with materials outside cultural proximity, done so with an eye to important differences.

The qasīdahs might be taught as a group to investigate the genre or studied separately in thematic connections with other texts in the volume. As a genre, they could be compared with any other work that places the persona or main object of the poem in an associative relation to key images drawn from their respective cultures and landscapes. A nostalgic tone is common to all three, although the Arabic qasīdah clearly revels in passion and lacks the elusive and understated quality of, say, medieval Japanese court poetry. Like the early poetry of most cultural traditions, the qasīdahs grow out of an untraceable history of songs and out of a rich but unwritten oral tradition and culture. Romantic and erotic love relationships are common in the qasīdahs, themes obviously present in the poetry of most cultures and eras.

Al-Shanfarā's Lāmiyyat picks up on themes found in Gilgamesh, where the liminal figure of Enkidu may be read productively next to that of the outlaw-poet, for contrast as well as for similarity. Labīd's Mu`allaqah, with a gharad which glorifies the poet's tribe, shares that theme with other literature throughout the collection that praises tribe and nation, such as Virgil's Aeneid, the dynastic odes found in the Chinese Book of Songs, the Persian Sohráb and Rostám, and other epic material from any period. Imru' Al-Qays belongs with the best of the nostalgic love poets. His work can be placed next to Ibn Zaidūn's Nūniyya for Wallāda to see some of the changes in love poetry within a Middle Eastern context from the sixth to the eleventh centuries, or next to the love poetry of the Indian Vidyakara or the Roman poet Catullus to examine important differences in representations and definitions of erotic love.

A good resource for working with the three poems is the translator's book, The Mute Immortals Speak.

Questions for Study and Discussion:

1. Make a list of all the images/objects that seem to have prominence in the poem. Do these images suggest a mood? Meanings? Why?

2. Make a list of all the verbs that seem to have prominence in the poem. Do these suggest a mood? Meanings? Why?

3. Why does the poet in Labīd's qasīdah leave his lover? How does he console himself? And what seems to be the reasons for Al-Qays and Al-Shanfarā's separations from their lovers?

4. What seem to be desirable qualities and actions for men in these poems? For women?

5. How does the world of these pre-Islamic texts compare with the world established by later Islamic materials, like the Qur'ān, the Life of the Prophet, or the other early Arabic poems found on pages 899-902?

6. How does the "heroic" in the qasīdahs compare with the "heroic" established in Ferdowsi's Sohráb and Rostám? In Dede Korkut's tale of Goggle-eye?

7. Compare the portraits of the beloved in these poems with the representations of the beloved in later poetry of the Middle East, such as the works of Bashshār Ibn Burd, Ibn Hazm, or the famous Nūnniyya for Wallāda by Ibn Zaidūn.

The Qur'ān

As the headnotes emphasize, this is a text many Muslims have in the past and present, committed to memory. It is, above all, a living book to be recited; consequently, one way to help your students appreciate the book is to obtain a recording and let them hear the original language. Recordings abound, most recently, the Islamic Book Service in Indianapolis has produced The Holy Qur'ān on twenty-one cassettes (1998). A three-cassette selection of verses is available from A.E.S. in Los Angeles, and another lengthy cassette collection, The Holy Qur'ān & English Translation of Its Meaning is available from The Audiovisual Center/NAIT; distributed by Islamic Book Service (Indianapolis,1991). Since Sūrah 12 is included in our text, the early '90s compact disc recording, A Recital from the Holy Qur'ān Surat Yusuf (Brooklyn, N.Y.) is one recording to note. And if the Qur'ān is read as a sacred text, alongside other sacred texts like the Hebrew Bible, the Christian New Testament, the Vedas, etc., another five-cassette collection produced in the 1990s, Music & Chant from the Great Religions (London & Guilford, CT: Sussex Tapes, Audio Forum) could prove useful.

The Qur'ān is an extremely difficult text to teach well to Western students who frequently know little about Islam. Not only do students find the text very difficult to understand, they also often react negatively to some of its content. Teachers should prepare themselves to provide thorough introductions to this text, if it is incorporated into literature courses. Like many (but not all) great sacred texts, the Qur'ān presents itself as the correct answer to spiritual questions; like many, it responds to other belief systems it considers misguided or decadent. And like many, it ushered in social transformations that altered the way groups and individuals lived their everyday lives. Teachers would do well to acquaint themselves with pre-Islamic social systems and codes to see the innovations Muhammad introduced and to understand just why he was revolutionary and threatening to the dominant powers of the seventh-century Arabian peninsula. Fazlur Rahman's book, Major Themes of the Qur'ān (1980) offers a clear and thoughtful review of Islamic faith in the sacred text. Bell's Introduction to the Qur'ān, which was updated by Montgomery Watt (1977), is still a reliable, somewhat more general, introduction. For an understanding of historical context which may provide crucial frameworks for classroom discussions and lectures, see M. G. S. Hodgson, The Venture of Islam in three volumes (1974) and W. Montgomery Watt's Muhammad's Mecca: History in the Qur'ān (Edinburgh, 1988) . Since interpretations of the Qur'ān have, like biblical interpretations, developed over time, Approaches to the History of the Interpretation of the Qur'ān, edited by Andrew Rippin (Oxford, 1988) provides articles on Qur'ānic commentary. Another book-length study of major Qur'ānic commentaries is Interpretation of the Meanings of the Noble Qur'ān in the English language, 4th edition, by Muhammad Taqi-ud-Din Al-Hilali and Muhammad Mushin Khan. (Riyadh, Saudi Arabia, 1994). Helmut Gatje's book, The Qur'ān and its Exegesis: Selected Texts with Classical and Modern Muslim Interpretations, translated and edited by Alford T. Welch. (Berkeley, 1976), offers teachers and students a range of Qur'ānic interpretations—an important understanding to counter monolithic interpretations. While Western readers understand that various biblical interpretations led to various Jewish and Christian religious sects or denominations, they may need help understanding some of those same dynamics within Islam.

Qur'ānic references to Jewish, Christian, non-Islamic Arab spirituality, to Haggaditic and apocryphal sources, to legends and to two excerpts from the well-known Alexander Romance suggests that this major sacred text arises in a complex cross-cultural and intertextual moment. For believers, the presence of other cultural materials and spiritually and politically powerful figures establishes the Qur'ān as a universal message from Allah to humanity. And it also helps establish a link between what it considers to be the past misinterpreted human history and the present correct revelation. Any comparison of the Qur'ān with biblical material, while fascinating and useful, must recognize that the Qur'ān's rendition of the Joseph story or of the Flood is not intended to be a translation or naive distortion. In fact, biblical materials are often simply mentioned without much detail, as though Muhammad could reasonably assume his audience knew the stories and the ancients to which he referred. His concern was not to translate from one language to another; his purpose was to reveal the divine Book as it was dictated to him. Interestingly, in other writings by Muhammad and his contemporary followers, Christianity is condemned for its belief in the trinity; and rather than understanding the Holy Spirit as part of the trinity, Muhammad thought Mary formed the third aspect or realization of God in Christian trinitarian belief. The Qur'ān holds a place in Islam that Christ does for Christians: it is the ultimate "word" of God that exists as a copy of a same sacred, eternal, heavenly text that has always existed. It is, in other words, co-eternal with God. As a representation of divine word or speech, the text is a text of voicings far more than it is a text of narrative.

As a sacred text, the Qur'ān belongs to the genre of prophetic or visionary literature and, in that regard, shares more with texts like the apocryphal book of 2 Esdras or the Letter of Jeremiah, or with Hebrew prophetic books like Jeremiah, Ezekiel, Isaiah, Hosea, Joel, Obadiah, Amos, Zephaniah, Malachi, and so on, than it does with the narrative selections from the Hebrew Bible found in the anthology. Students could, however, easily examine one of the short prophetic books from the Hebrew Bible themselves to see the way prophecy and revelation occurs within Jewish contexts and then compare that with the revelations of the Qur'ān. In both, the prophet exists as a "messenger" of God, warning, instructing, reminding, glorifying God, but differences are notable and worth discussion as well.

Reading in translation is, of course, problematic. Literary qualities are hard to hear without knowledge of Arabic. Vocabulary from life lived on the Arabian peninsula begins to resonate with spiritual meanings in the way that, say, "the Word" does in the Gospel of John or the way "covenant" can in the Hebrew Bible. The Arabic words "dalla" (lose one's way) or "hada" (travel on the right path), for example, are words found in the Qur'ān that migrate out of the nomadic Jahiliyyah world into Islamic spiritual meaning.

Questions for Study and Discussion:

1. Why do you think the longest chapters, or sūrahs, of the Qur'ān are placed first and the shortest last? (Students may ponder this question and then teachers should tell them that we simply do not know. We do know that the longest sūrahs are ones Muhammad recorded latest in his life. They are placed first. The shortest sūrahs are, generally, the ones Muhammad recorded earliest in his prophetic life and they are placed last. The order and the elimination of interesting variants only occurred in 651 (nineteen years after Muhammad's death). Some have speculated that because of conflicts that emerged in the community, the "textus receptus" of the Qur'ān suppressed material which made references to `Ali and the prophet's family members. This view has been argued by Shi`is. Others suggest that Muslims who prepared the standardized Qur'ān of 651 did not know for sure what the order of the sūrahs was supposed to be and so, lacking a sure chronological order, they settled on a neutral order based on length. The acceptance of the 651 version of the Qur'ān belongs with the Sunni Muslims.)

2. What seems to be the attitude toward non-believers in the Qur'ān? Is there a single view or do different sections seem to contain different attitudes toward non-believers? How do these compare with attitudes toward outsiders in biblical materials? In other sacred texts from other spiritual traditions?

3. Unlike biblical texts, the Qur'ān produces no chronology of a nation or of a life. It is, in fact, rarely narrative. What might this suggest?

4. The Joseph story (Yusef) is usefully compared with the Joseph story in the Hebrew Bible. What is accomplished by each different rendition? Does the Qur'ān have any of the same aims in telling this story? It is the longest continuous narrative in the Qur'ān; what does it accomplish?

5. Compare Yaweh, the God of Israel found in the Hebrew Bible, with Allah, God of the prophet in the Qur'ān. Does this suggest important differences in the cultural frameworks of the ancient Jewish and Arab communities? What role does Jesus seem to play in the Qur'ān? Examine closely the story of Haggar and Ishmael in the Qur'ān and in the Hebrew Bible. How does the Qur'ānic revelation understand these figures?

Muhammad Ibn Ishāq
The Life of the Prophet

Two distinct paths present themselves for studying this document: one can begin by focusing on the small elements, the documentary nature of the biography and its care with attribution; or one can begin by reading through the whole text, noting the larger contours of biographical narrative that are present here and common in other sacred biography.

Within the larger contours of biographical narrative, some episodes share a purpose with parallel episodes in other sacred biography or hagiography (saints' lives). The miraculous birth of the prophet includes a visitation to the mother by "a voice" that carries information similar to annunciation scenes in Christian accounts of Jesus's birth. Muhammad's mother, Āmina d. Wahb, is told that her son will be "the lord of his people," and she is told what name to give him: "Muhammad." And like the star of Bethlehem familiar from Christian accounts of Christ's birth, a tremendous light appears to Āmina d. Wahb the night her son is born (p. 763). Having students consider the accounts of miracles Muhammad was said to have performed when a child and the accounts of events that set him apart from other young boys, helps them see the similarities in sacred biography from one religious tradition to another: the ability to feed the starving and hungry (pp.764-65); the experience of dismembering (pp. 764-65; folklore scholarship has established the importance of dismembering among shaman of many different cultural traditions); precociousness (i.e., the ability to lift his head the night he was born [765]); and the recognition by foreigners/unbelievers that he is special (i.e., the Abyssinian Christians who wanted to take him to their king, or the Jew who, the night of Muhammad's birth, announced: "Tonight has risen a star under which Ahmad is to be born. [pp. 765-66; 763]).

The relationship between Muhammad and Kadīja is worth reading carefully, partly because of the striking difference between this husband-wife relationship and the celibacy or sacred marriages found in other spiritual biographies. Kadīja is Muhammad's employer, "a merchant woman of dignity and wealth," who proposes marriage to Muhammad (pp. 766-67). Having students explore ways Ibn Ish'āq's biography depicts women, especially the figures of Kadīja and later `Ā'isha may challenge the simplistic way Western readers imagine women functioning within Islamic culture, religion, and literature. A comparison of women represented in this selection from Ibn Ish'āq with images of women in the Gospel of Mark or within Hebrew biblical literature can lead to some fruitful discussions, including a discussion of why contemporary Western depictions of Arabic and Persian culture so often focus on women and/or polygamy. Edward Said's work on Orientalism may prove useful background for teachers wanting to pursue such a line of questioning.

Arabic culture, not having a tradition of prophets, first made sense of Muhammad's visions and his teachings by calling him a kahin, (madman), a poet, a demon, or a sorcerer. As an adult, Muhammad is, according to the biography, called by God (Allah) through a series of visions to introduce monotheism to his people and to "perfect" the religion of the prophets descending through Hebrew and Christian writings. Tempted to kill himself rather than bear the shame of being a madman or poet (both despised by the elite Quraysh tribe Muhammad belonged to), the prophet is comforted by both the angel Gabriel who intercepts him on his suicidal mission, and by his wife, Kadīja. Many people despised, doubted, and jeered Muhammad, just as the prophets within Judeo-Christian tradition were jeered. But Muhammad also takes on the role of political leader as his followers battle with non-Muslims who set out to disrupt or destroy the early Muslim community. The importance of vision cannot be underestimated because, of course, through it Muhammad provides his community of believers with the text of the Qur'ān. But Muhammad's night journey, his ascent into heaven, and his vision of hell are also important episodes in the biography, particularly in relation to the other Islamic materials in the anthology like Attar's Conference of Birds, the poetry of Al-Ma'arrī and of Rūmī, and the twentieth-century short story, "Zaabalawi" by Naguib Mahfouz. The episode provides a useful comparison with the spiritual journeys of divine and human figures found in other periods and literatures, as well.

Resources for working on Ibn Ish'āq's Life of the Prophet include the following: Gordon D. Newby, The Making of the Last Prophet: A Reconstruction of the Earliest Biography of Muhammad (Columbia, SC, 1989); Walter Ong, Orality and Literacy (New York, 1982); A. Guillaume's introduction to his translation of The Life of Muhammad (1955), which appears in this anthology; and, for social and historical background, W. M. Watt's biography of Muhammad: Prophet and Statesman (1961).

Questions for Study and Discussion:

1. Identify ways this biography of Muhammad argues for the divine appointment of Muhammad as God's messenger. What events and what kinds of features in the narrative help establish this text as sacred biography?

2. What is accomplished by so carefully attributing the various accounts of events to particular speakers rather than conflating the many traditional stories of the prophet into one continuous or nearly continuous narrative as, say, the apostle Mark does in his account of the life of Christ?

3. What relationship exists between the oral and the written in Ibn Ish'āq's biography of Muhammad? What specific features of the written text show the traces of oral composition and of oral communication from one generation to another or from one witness to a listener and finally to a writer?

4. How are women depicted in this text? How are believers depicted? Unbelievers? So what?

5. Compare this sacred biography of Muhammad with Mark's representation of Christ in the Christian bible. What similarities and differences do you observe? What do these things perhaps tell readers about cultural or historical differences? About religious or spiritual differences?

6. Compare the night journey and ascent into heaven to the spiritual journeys found in other material within the anthology. How does this compare with Inanna's spiritual journey? Gilgamesh's? Aeneas's? The birds in Attar's Conference of Birds? Dante's?

7. Read the biography alongside the selections from the Qur'ān. Does the biography assist you as you tackle the difficult text of the Qur'ān? How so? If not, why not?

Abol-Qasem Ferdowsi
The Tragedy of Sohráb and Rostám (from The Shāh-nāmah)

Ferdowsi explains, within the narrative, that he draws his tale of Sohráb and Rostám from the dehqáns' accounts (l. 29), and he frames the narrative by having us imagine it is being recited by the mobád (l. 31). (Dehqáns were provincial, aristocratic landowners and the mobáds were Zoroastrian priests). These two groups, along with a written source, a Pahlavi prose text called The Book of Kings—supposedly given to the poet by a mehrbán (sometimes understood as a friend, sometimes as a concubine)—are claimed by Ferdowsi as the sources of his Shāh-nāmah. Although source study fails to identify precisely texts Ferdowsi may have consulted, students may notice, here, that a concern for establishing the "authority"of a narrative is a common feature in Ancient and Middle period literatures. What is also interesting is that many accounts in the long Shāh-nāmah are represented as tales sung by mobád, dehqán or recited or read by a mehrbán. So this epic is established as a series of tales told by various storytellers, sharing then, some of the structural elements of several other Middle Period texts like the Conference of Birds, the Thousand and One Nights, or Chaucer's Canterbury Tales.

Students should know that many other Persian epics and an extensive written and oral literature extending back to ancient civilizations exist in Iran's literary repertoire. This epic is not the first, by any means, but it has become the most influential. Like any "history" or "epic," the Shāh-nāmah presents an image of a nation and how its dominant culture wants to perceive its past and its own crucial values. According to Olga Davidson, Sohráb and Rostám "explores the very limits" of Rostám's heroic duty "to protect the king, and by extension, society itself" (Poet and Hero in the Persian Book of Kings, 1994; p. 128). Rostám is allied with farr, a Persian word resonating with multiple meanings but meaning literally "luminous glory." As part of this "glory," Rostám is allied with the concept of divine kingship and above all to the divine forces of fate which compel him to function as their agent. Sohráb, on the other hand, imagines placing Rostám (whom he does not know except by reputation) on the throne of Iran, conceiving of establishing kingship based on merit. Such a notion is contrary to the spiritual and philosophical framework informing the epic, where Yazdán (also Izád), or God, presides over an on-going cosmic struggle between Ahura Mazda (the good) and Ahrimán (the evil), and in which humans function more or less as pawns. Kingship is assumed to be divinely-appointed, as seen in the fact that Yazdán favors Kay Kavús despite his ignobility and foolishness. Sohráb's rebellion threatens farr and, consequently, Rostám kills his own son. The fact that he does not know him, however, adds the dramatic touch that has made this portion of the Shāh-nāmah so well known throughout world literature. Students may want to locate Matthew Arnold's 1853 version of the narrative, The Story of Sohráb and Rustum to see one such influence.

The death of Sohráb preserves the advantage of the ignoble Kay Kavús as well as Shah Afrasiyáb, king of Turán (Turkey). The point here is that the glorious Iranian kingdom exists because of the will of the divine; it does not thrive or fall depending upon human agency. And just as Sohráb's presumption is a sin against God and his divinely-appointed king, so, too, Rostám's rebellious criticism of Shah Kavús is a betrayal of the king. Perhaps for these reasons, both father and son are punished by their mutually-tragic encounter. Of course, Tahminé hides the truth, as do other actors in the fated drama. When Sohráb orders the defeated Hojír to identify the warriors in the Iranian camp, Hojír does not reveal Rostám's identity. Ferdowsi writes:

> One sought his father's camp. One hid the truth,
> And would not speak the words he longed to hear.
> What can one do? This world's already made.
> There is no task that He [God] has left undone.
> The writ of fate was otherwise, alas.
> What it commands will finish as it must. . . . (ll. 622-627)

This view of a fated and predestined world may challenge students' notions; and, in this light, Sohráb and Rostám may be usefully compared with Utnapishtim's discussion of fate in Gilgamesh, the gods' involvements in human affairs in Homer's Odyssey or Virgil's Aeneid, or with the punishment of human hubris in Greek tragic drama like The Bacchae. The narrative, so grounded in the father-son relationship, also bears resemblance, in this respect, to other epic and sacred materials in the volume. Its view of the divine and human aspect is usefully compared with the Indian Mahābhārata.

Because the vocabulary in Sohráb and Rostám preserves a number of the Persian originals, teachers may want to examine Jerome Clinton's full translation of the poem. It has notes which can help with the unfamiliar vocabulary. Students will be interested to learn, for example, that the epithet, "Tahmatán," which frequently describes Rostám, means "huge-bodied." And from Clinton's notes, students learn that "div" means demon, that "Gordafaríd," means "created a warrior," and that "pahlaván" means "hero" and shares linguistic roots with the European term, "paladin." Other useful resources for teachers include Olga Davidson's book (cited above); Dick Davis, Epic and Sedition: The Case of Ferdowsi's Shāhnāmeh (Fayetteville, AR, 1992); M. S. Southgate, "Fate in Firdawsi's 'Rustam va Suhrab,'" in Studies in Art and Literature of the Near East, edited by Peter J. Chelkowshi (Salt Lake City, UT, 1974); Ehsan Yarshater, "Iranian National History,"in Cambridge History of Iran, 7 volumes (Cambridge, 1983). See especially volume 3, pages 359-477; and Persian Literature, edited by Ehsan Yarshater (Albany, 1988).

Questions for Study and Discussion:

1. How do the opening lines of Sohráb and Rostám have bearing on the full text printed in the anthology?

2. What features appear to constitute the "hero" in Sohráb and Rostám?

3. Whereas numerous narratives are built around a son displacing a father, in this narrative that "natural order" is overturned and a father survives his son. What is suggested by this disruption? What keeps Sohráb and Rostám from recognizing one another until the brutal end?

4. How are enemies depicted in this narrative? Kings? Animals? Heroes? And what things are elevated by descriptive passages to places of prominence? Are these the same kinds of things elevated to prominence in Greek and Roman epic materials?

5. What does the figure of Gordafaríd add to the narrative?

6. Why does God (Yazdán) sustain Kay Kavús when he seems so weak and incompetent?

7. What kind of world is depicted in this section of the Shāh-nāmah?

Farid al-Dīn Attar
The Conference of Birds and "The Life and Teachings of Rābi`ah al-`Adawiyya" (from The Memorial of Saints)

One of the striking features of The Conference of Birds is the tension between the images in it (so clearly drawn from nature) and the spiritual arguments these very material images are asked to convey. The image of the shadow, often representing human souls, is key to the story of the birds' creation (see lines 236ff.). The Simorgh "cast unnumbered shadows on the earth" and then gave birth to each of his shadows by gazing steadily at them. Quickened by divine sight (or acknowledgment) the birds (or human souls) are created out of elements of the divine. This seems to suggest that shards of divinity construct the natural world. On the other hand, the nightingale's excuse (lines 113ff.) and the Peacock's (lines 156 ff.) are rebuffed by the Hoopoe who criticizes their attachment to nature. Of course language itself struggles to express spiritual ecstasy and wisdom, but constructing spiritual meanings using images laden with materiality and borrowed so heavily from the natural world is interesting, especially when the spiritual message advocates a transcendence of the natural world. The Hoopoe, for example, criticizes the Peacock, saying: "You think your monarch's palace of more worth / Than Him who fashioned it and all the earth." But the desire to escape or transcend the world is constantly pulled back into it within the imagery of the text. Truth, for example, in line 180 "is like a shoreless sea," and faith and ecstatic union with divinity like "seeing" the Simorgh.

Since a key tenet of Sufism is the idea that only God truly exists, then the world can only be understood as shadows or pieces of the One God that truly exists. A desire for union with the divine sparks the journey of the soul through the appearances of multiplicity to a knowledge of unity. Truth exists, for the Sufi, beyond any particular religion, although Islam is considered the most direct way to God and Truth. As the tale about the murderer who went to heaven suggests (beginning with line 445), the force of unity in the universe is so great that the human understanding of good and evil is also ephemeral in a divine or infinite sense of things. Union with God involves an inward quest to spiritual ecstasy and the annihilation of self and of separateness. But using language, a human (and therefore inadequate) system to communicate these ideas is difficult, especially since language depends upon differences in sounds and words and grammatical functions to produce meaning. So, language which relies on differences for meaning is pressed sometimes to a breaking point when attempting to express spiritual beliefs in

Oneness and the annihilation of differences. Paradoxes and metaphors both carry the concepts but simultaneously bespeak difference. The challenge of using language to carry non-linguistic ideas can be seen in other sacred literatures like the Chinese Dao de jing, the Psalms, or Ecclesiastes. The strain placed on language and meaning can also be found within Christ's parables, like those recorded in the Gospel of Mark (see, for example, Mark 4:1-34 or Mark 11: 33-50), as well as in God's speech from within the whirlwind found in the Book of Job. The view of the world as a wax toy or life as a moth drawn to the divine, figured as a flame, are especially useful episodes in The Conference of Birds which students might study to help them begin to grasp Sufi mysticism.

The journey of the soul toward God has, of course, significant parallel within Islam to the visions Muhammad had, not only receiving the book of the Qur'ān, but also his ascent into heaven, a vision/ascension recorded in Ibn Ishāq's Life of the Prophet. But the journey of the soul is also central to the ancient Sumerian texts celebrating the Goddess Inanna, the heroic journey of Gilgamesh into the otherworld, the journeys of the Hebrew people throughout Biblical literature, particularly the exilic literature recording the journey out of Egypt and the return to Israel. Dante's Divine Comedy (the Commedia), especially its last book, the Paradiso (a section from Dante's work not included in the anthology) may be the European literary text from the Middle Period closest to Attar's Conference of Birds. In Attar's use of dialogue, frame narrative, and embedded tales, we can see structural techniques which are also found in the Thousand and One Nights, Chaucer's Canterbury Tales, Christine de Pizan's City of Ladies, and Homer's Odyssey.

Significant secondary sources include that by Dick Davis (who worked on the translation included in this anthology): "The Journey as Paradigm: Literal and Metaphorical Travel in Attar's Mantiq al-Tayr," Edebiyat new series 4 (1993). This article helps explain aspects of Attar's frame narrative. An interesting source which examines Islamic mystical texts, as well as a number of other crucial texts in Islamic culture, including the Qur'an, is a tape recorded conference on "The Book in the Islamic World" held in 1990 and sponsored by the Center for the Book and the Near East Section of the Library of Congress. Ehsan Yarshater, et. al., have compiled an immense work of over 500 pages on Persian Literature (Albany, NY, 1988), and entries on Attar in the Encylopedia Iranica are also useful. The large 1996 collection done by the Paulist Press, entitled Early Islamic Mysticism: Sufi, Quran, Miraj, Poetic and Theological Writings, includes selections from other Sufi texts which might offer teachers a more thorough context within which to tackle The Conference of Birds, and A. J. Arberry's Classical Persian Literature (1958; reprinted 1994) and History and Literature in Iran: Persian and Islamic Studies in Honour of P. W. Avery (London, 1998) may also supply teachers with important background.

These same resources may also supply crucial background for the selection included in the anthology from Attar's Memorial of the Saints. This short selection which Attar composed on Rabe'a, an early Islamic woman saint, can be read as hagiography, an early form of biography. It is, as the headnote indicates, usefully read alongside the writings of the Indian poet, Mīrābāī, but perhaps most usefully compared to other Middle period writings that we might recognize as biographical, like Christine de Pizan's account of The Life of Saint Christine (an especially useful parallel between two women saints, one Christian, one Islamic) or Ibn Ishaq's Life of the Prophet, which established one model of sacred biography within the Islamic literary tradition.

Questions for Study and Discussion:

1. What kind of language (i.e., metaphors and similes) and what sorts of images help Attar describe the spiritual quest of the soul for Truth?

2. What difficulties do the birds face as they journey toward the Simorgh?

3. What is gained by creating an allegorical journey to communicate spiritual meaning? In other words, why describe the soul's journey toward God in allegorical terms?

4. How does the spiritual journey in The Conference of Birds compare with other spiritual journeys found in the literatures of other religions?

5. In what sense can we understand the account of Rabi'a to be biography?

6. How does this account compare with the life of Saint Christine recorded in Christine de Pizan's City of Ladies?

7. What do the sayings of Rabi'a mean? What purposes do they seem to have?

Usāmah Ibn Munqidh
The Book of Reflections

Students might find it interesting to know that the word "Usāmah" means "lion," particularly since Usāmah's childhood run-in with a ravenous lion is included in the anthologized selections from the over two-hundred-page memoir. The literal title of the text, Kitāb al-I'tibār, means "the book of instruction by example" and suggests that the purpose of the "reflections" or "memoirs" was more didactic than what Western readers usually expect from autobiography. Since the book was written when Usāmah was about ninety, issues of memory and autobiography are, however, useful ways of approaching the text. A recollection contains, of course, more distortions and perhaps a different agenda than a day-to-day diary might. It is a project of self-reconstruction in recollection and so inquiry into ways Usāmah "writes a self" proves fruitful for discussions. One feature, quite noticeable in the way in which Usāmah writes himself and writes his world is the presence of antithesis. If killing a lion was a young man's triumphant victory, it also feeds the jealously of his uncle, a dangerous potential in a powerful and wealthy family (see page 843); and if Usāmah's father was severely wounded in his forearm by an enemy's lance, if strength drained for a time out of his arm and hand because of the wound, that same arm and hand made forty-three copies of the Qur'ān. Usāmah comments, "My father wrote a magnificent hand, which that lance thrust did not affect" (842). Having students watch for the presence of antithesis is useful as they begin to grasp a sense of what Usāmah the writer is attempting to accomplish and how this writer read the world around him.

On the other hand, explanations of events are often laid at God's feet; divine foreknowledge and planning is Usāmah's way of explaining or analyzing events. The section from his book describing the brutish Franks begins, for example, with the words: "Mysterious are the works of the Creator, the author of all things!" Usāmah is amazed at how animal-like, how ignorant, and how rude these European crusaders are, but he also tells us that he befriended one of them and "between us were mutual bonds of amity and friendship" (844). It is, however, clear that the friendship is maintained because Usāmah exercises courtesy and polite restraint, as he does when praying in a mosque that had been taken over by the knights templar (844-46). Because Western students are more accustomed to reading about the crusades from a European point of view, Usāmah's comments on the Frankish character and his amazement at what he reads as their dishonorable marriage practices, are telling moments which defamiliarize the European.

Not surprisingly, Usāmah's book of reflections describes, for readers, a Syrian and Middle Eastern warrior society. Emphasis is on courage, strength, warring ability and who did what to whom rather than a meditation upon ideas. At many points in the full text, Usāmah points to the inability of humans to control events or plan ahead effectively. His father comments that "My boy, war runs itself." But the contrast between Usāmah's careful and exact details which construct a sense of a real, material world experienced by a real person and Ibn Battutah's detached, oftentimes extremely general descriptions of his travels is worthy of discussion, since both Usāmah and Battutah write "non-fictional" accounts of lived experience.

As background to a class discussion or lecture, Philip K. Hitti's introduction and notes which accompany his translation, An Arab-Syrian Gentleman and Warrior in the Period of the Crusades, Memoirs of Usāmah Ibn-Munqidh (Princeton, 1929; rpt. 1987) is invaluable. Additional resources include: D. W. Morray's monograph, The Genius of Usāmah ibn Munqidh: Aspects of Kitāb al-I'tibār (University of Durham Centre for Middle Eastern and Islamic Studies, no. 34 [1987]), and Robert Irwin's article, "Usāmah ibn Munqidh : an Arab-Syrian Gentleman at the time of the Crusades Reconsidered," in The Crusades and Their Sources: Essays Presented to Bernard Hamilton, edited by John France and William G. Zajac (Aldershot, Hampshire, Great Britain, 1998) is useful.

Questions for Study and Discussion:

1. What kind of picture of himself does Usāmah seem to be constructing in his memoirs?

2. What characteristics of human personality and behavior does Usāmah valorize?

3. What kinds of people in his world are cast as "Other"?

4. What role does God (Allah) play in human affairs according to Usāmah?

5. Why does Usāmah mourn old age?

6. How would you describe the compositional or rhetorical techniques Usāmah uses to shape the episodes in his text? What seems to be his purpose in writing?

Abu 'Abdallah Ibn Battutah
The Travels

One of the striking things about this selection included in the anthology is the dated sound of Gibb's early twentieth-century translation. The very first paragraph of the translation is one obvious example, and students might think about how the same sentences could be rendered in contemporary English. An important feature to examine in almost any travel narrative involves the selection of details to be communicated. Students might look at the sections from The Travels included in the anthology to discover what they think the purpose might be for Ibn Battutah's accounts. What is not said also remains tantalizing. At the beginning of the text, for example, he indicates that leaving home was a great sorrow: "it weighed grievously upon me to part from [my parents] and both they and I were afflicted with sorrow" (850), but he also indicates an inner longing drove him to adventure: he was, he writes, "Swayed by an overmastering impulse within me, and a long-cherished desire to visit . . . glorious sanctuaries" (850). Given these two initial emotions, readers might look to see if they recur as Battutah travels throughout the Middle East and India, as well as South and Far Eastern Asia. (It will be noticed that such recurrences are rare.) Battutah seems most taken by the character of individuals and societies he visits, rather than the "glorious sanctuaries," and his recollections of his own emotions are also rather scarce, with the episode of the "Narrow Escape" an important exception.

Like the accounts of other ancient and middle period travelers, Battutah registers some concerns that his literary audience (apparently in Tangiers) might doubt him. Beginning to describe a king in India, Battutah writes that some of the stories he will tell "are marvelous beyond anything ever heard before." To shore up audience confidence in his account, he appeals to God—"I call God and his Angels and His Prophets to witness that all that I tell . . . is absolute truth" (853)—and tries to disarm readers' doubt by acknowledging the strangeness of what he witnesses: "I know that some of [what] I shall relate will be unacceptable to the minds of many, and that they will regard them as quite impossible, but in a matter which I have seen with my own eyes and of which I know . . . I cannot do otherwise than speak the truth" (853). Describing the Indian Sultan for us, Battutah provides details about court ritual, a noticeable attention to specifics which is sometimes curiously lacking in other episodes. When the Sultan of Tunis celebrates a religious festival of Breaking the Fast, a paragraph seems sufficient for Battutah's record, but the Indian Sultan's court fascinates Battutah for many pages in the original (several pages in our selection). Much of Battutah's travels seem rather dry, but the episode entitled in our selection "A Narrow Escape" shows attention to the shaping of plot and event. Battutah builds suspense into the account and attributes the good outcome to God's will and to his own faith.

One of the most fascinating elements of The Travels involves Battutah's method of relating customs he finds both fascinating and either repulsive or superstitious. For the most part, however, it is difficult to tell what his appraisal of an event is because his style and tone aim for a journalistic, detached accounting of events rather than a more emotional, poetic, or judgmental response. And in some cases, he seems to adopt the customs and conceptual frameworks of the cultures he visits. Where we might assume Battutah would resist the magical and superstitious beliefs that lead people to believe in devil possession, we are wrong. When people in the town of Gályúr bring Battutah a woman (called a kaftár) accused of magically eating out the heart of a child by simply gazing on him, he orders them "to take her to the sultan's lieutenant, who commanded that she be put to the test" (859). The test resembles some accounts of witch hunts found in Early Modern European sources. Battutah writes that these women (and sometimes men) were tied to huge jars of water that acted as weights and then thrown into the river. He concludes with the comment, "As she did not sink, she was known to be a kaftár; had she not floated she would not have been one." What exactly he thought of this practice is somewhat unclear, since he points to the impossible dilemma facing the accused but doesn't comment further. He finishes his report of this episode by telling us that the woman floated, that she was consequently burned as a kaftár and that her ashes were collected and smeared all over the townsfolk, "for they believe that anyone who fumigates himself with them is safe against a kaftár's enchantments during that year" (859). Readers leave this account, like so many in the lengthy collection of his travels, wondering what Battutah really thought of what he witnessed.

The most obvious connections to other material in the anthology are with Marco Polo's travel narratives. Sources for teachers preparing The Travels include Ross E. Dunn's book, The Adventures of Ibn Battuta, a Muslim Traveler of the 14th Century (Berkeley,1986); Marina A. Tolmacheva, "Ibn Battuta on Women's Travel in the Dar al-Islam," in Women and the Journey: The Female Travel Experience, edited by Bonnie Frederick, Susan McLeod, et. al. (Pullman, WA, 1993); Adel Allouche, "A Study of Ibn Battutah's Account of His Journey through Syria and Arabia," Journal of Semitic Studies (JSS) 35.2 (Autumn, 1990): 283-99. Abderrahmane El Moudden's article, "The Ambivalence of Rihla: Community Integration and Self-Definition in Moroccan Travel Accounts, 1300-1800," in Muslim Travellers: Pilgrimage, Migration, and the Religious Imagination, edited by Dale F. Eickelman and James Piscatori (Berkeley, 1990), may also prove insightful, though the focus of the collection is not on Battutah. General studies of travel literature and travel narrative, particularly examinations of descriptions and of characterizations of foreignness and "otherness" could obviously enhance a reading of The Travels, as well.

Questions for Study and Discussion:

1. After reading the entire selection, consider the ethos the narrator constructs for himself. What kind of speaker emerges from the passages included here? What kind of person does this world traveler and observer seem to be? How do you know?

2. What attitudes does Battutah adopt toward people he meets and the worlds he encounters? Point to specific passages that seem to carry evidence of these attitudes.

3. What kinds of activities or events seem to captivate Battutah's attention? And what things seem to be missing that you might expect in travel literature?

4. How is China depicted in this account? What attitude does Battutah seem to have toward the great empires and cultures he visits like China or India?

5. Why does Battutah fear the Arabs in North Africa? How do we know he is afraid of them? (For this question, students might be encouraged to uncover a brief history of late medieval Northern Africa so that they understand the dynastic and tribal conflicts that divide the late medieval Islamic world.)

6. How does Battutah represent the "Other" in his travel narratives? What seems to be his purpose in writing?

The Thousand and One Nights

Studies on The Thousand and One Nights are rather plentiful in English in comparison with some of the other Middle Eastern literature of the Middle period. And Western readers are more likely to have read some of this text than probably any other Arabic, Persian, or Turkish text in the anthology. The Arabian Nights in English Literature: Studies in the Reception of the The Thousand and One Nights into British Culture, edited by Peter L. Caracciolo (New York, 1988) provides some thought-provoking background on the reception of this immense text into European (and consequently, American, culture). Often, European and American scholars translating or studying The Thousand and One Nights (hereafter TON) used European aesthetic standards or classical Arabic standards for judging the qualities of this tremendously influential text. And consequently, the text has often been judged as bawdy (which of course it is, as are Chaucer and Shakespeare) or as folkloric (which it is to some degree, also like Chaucer and Shakespeare, except that the TON has also been ordered into a serial text pre-dating Boccaccio's Decameron or Chaucer's Canterbury Tales). It has a majesty often overlooked by Western scholars until just recently, despite the enjoyment the text has provided for Western readers. And it has had to survive the derision of Arabic rhetors and scholars who compared it with the classical Arabic of the Qur'ān and the Qasīdahs and have found it lacking.

The frame narrative is a key to its grandeur and affects how we read all the embedded narratives. This frame retells a narrative familiar, in some ways, to Western readers. A world is turned upside down by sexual sin or trespass and a subsequent curse. Then, through the word, through the power of human art or a civilizing agent, another order is gradually re-established. Narrative holds the promise of redemption, and in these large mythic contours of the frame narrative, the TON also places the promise of redemption in the voice of a woman, Shahrazad. The binary of order and disorder or of thesis and antithesis is not resolved in synthesis; instead, the power of the tripartite narrative or philosophic order is defeated by proliferation of narrative, by an elongation of time, by digression and parentheses rather than by a more focused and united narrative line. As Ferial Ghazoul has noted, "In the Odyssey, Penelope's struggle to gain time is based on a simple device of doing and undoing; she unravels at night what she weaves in the daytime. Penelope marks time in order to delay temporal events, but Shahrazad's art lies in annulling the very limits of time. Penelope's struggle is against given time, while Shahrazad's is against the notion of time itself" (Ghazoul, p.18). She reads TON as a text that is, among other things, concerned with one of the most tantalizing of philosophical concepts, namely time. And it works its labyrinthine representations of time through parallel plots, characters, embedded and mirroring narratives and sub-narratives and sub-sub-narratives, and so on. Time is life, quite literally in the case of Shahrazad and her listeners (and readers), and story is life quite literally but also figuratively for any reader encountering TON. And where time eats away at life, Shahrayar "devours" women. While Shahrazad cannot stop "devouring time" (represented in the figure of Shahrayar), she can turn his hunger into a hunger for stories so that the only women sacrificed to his hunger are literary ones. They are figurative rather than literal sacrifices that feed the lord or sultan Shahrayar (in the fiction of the tale). This is just one of the redemptive moves narrative accomplishes in the larger conceptual frameworks informing TON.

If a sexual trespass launches the disorder in the kingdom of TON, Shahrayar's murder of his wife and her lover seems to cause a wound that must be healed, a blindness that leads to much greater injustice and trespass. Compensating for his own wound (a loss of his own innocence, perhaps and/or his reign of violent, enraged terror), Shahrayar murders virgin after virgin, enacting his own death in an outrageous attack on innocents.

Aside from the literary issues involved in the massive serial text, having students study several of the many English translations of just the opening frame narrative is quite useful and revealing. Students can see the way various translators from different historical periods made sense of the horror of the frame narrative. Richard F. Burton's translation is, perhaps, the most influential one, but the tales have been remade into children's books in the West and a study of these might make a fascinating term project for a student or for a collaborative endeavor.

Some of the most useful texts for teachers preparing the TON include the full translations done by Haddawy in two volumes (the most recent translation); Ferial J. Ghazoul's Nocturnal Poetics: The Arabian Nights in Comparative Context (Cairo, 1996); David Pinault, Story-Telling Techniques in the Arabian Nights (Leiden, NY, 1992); and Muhsin Mahdi, "Remarks on the 1001 Nights," Interpretation 3.2/3 (Winter, 1973): 157-68; A. Hamori, On the Art of Medieval Arabic Literature (Princeton, 1974) and articles he has also written; M. Gerhardt, The Art of Story-Telling: A Literary Study of the Thousand and One Nights (Leiden, 1963); and Nadia Abbott, "a Ninth-Century Fragment of the Thousand Nights," In Journal of Near Eastern Studies (July 1949): 129-64.

Questions for Study and Discussion:

1. How does the frame narrative shape our responses or readings of the embedded narratives?

2. What other texts from the ancient and middle period in the anthology begin their narrative plots with a crime or trespass and a consequent curse?

3. What is the effect of having Shahrazad's name so close in spelling and sound to Shahrayar's?

4. Why does Shahrazad's father tell her the story of the Ox and the Donkey? What meaning does the story have for the frame narrative?

5. What purpose does Dinarzad have? What effect is created by having her in the king's bedroom?

6. Although we have just a small sampling of the great variety of narratives present in the longer versions of the TON, what kind of world and what kind of issues seem important in the selections that appear in the anthology?

7. Any multiple and serial narrative, created out of many separate stories, calls attention to storytelling or "telling" as an issue in and of itself. If the selections present in the anthology make a statement about story telling, what might that be?

The Book of Dede Korkut

As might be expected from a mythic tale with folkloric qualities, names in this text carry meaning. The name "Basat," for example, means "attack-horse," which is exactly what Basat does at the beginning of the tale because he has been raised by a lioness. Tales that feature humans raised by animals are familiar in other mythic material as well, including the Romulus and Remus account of the founding of Rome or the figure of Enkidu found in the epic of Gilgamesh, a text included in the ancient section of our anthology. A striking feature of this narrative is that demarcations of separate beings—animals, humans (the Oghuz people), and the peris (fairy-like figures)—are violated. First, the baby son of Uruz Koja is adopted and nursed by a lioness after he is accidentally left behind when enemies fall on the Oghuz encampment.

Second, a shepherd of the Oghuz people captures and rapes a peri maiden. This violation results in a curse: "you have brought ruination on the Oghuz" (889). The curse is the monstrous, amorphous body (again a chaotic sign of the unnatural) that grows and grows the more the Oghuz stone it, hit it, or kick it. Finally, Uruz Koja splits the fast-growing mass down the middle with his spur and the monstrous shape gives birth to Goggle-eye, a one-eyed child with the body of a man. In the notes to their edition of the Dede Korkut, Faruk Sümer, Ahmet Uysal, and Warren Walker indicate that the name for Goggle-eye, "Tepegöz" originates from "tepe," which means "hill" or "top" or "head," and "göz," which means "eye" (The Book of Dede Korkut: A Turkish Epic [Austin, 1972], p. 199). Because he "delivered" the one-eyed child, Uruz takes him in and raises him with his own son, Basat.

Goggle-eye immediately and ferociously nurses and sucks his wet-nurse to death (a similar motif occurs in the Middle English fourteenth century romance of Sir Gowther, not in the anthology). Again, a violation of taboos and boundaries occurs as Goggle-eye begins to cannibalize his peers. The Oghuz finally drive him out of their community. Given a magic totem (the ring) by his peri mother, Goggle-eye becomes what we might now call a serial killer. But no one can stop Goggle-eye's cannibalism and he feeds regularly on human flesh, killing his "brother," Kiyan Seljuk (Basat's sibling). Holding the Oghuz hostage, he exacts a horrible price, feeding on men and hundreds of the tribe's sheep. Basat, having escaped the carnage by virtue of being away from the community, returns and insists on exacting vengeance for his brother's death. In a scene very similar to Homer's account of Odysseus's strategic blinding of Polyphemous, Basat gets the male hostages to help him put out the monster's eye. But other mythic motifs emerge in this telling of the encounter with the horrific one-eyed monster, including the cave filled with riches, the two swords, one of which has the power to cut off Goggle-eye's head (reminiscent of the moment when Beowulf sees the magic sword in Grendel's mother's cave), and the magical incantations that split open vault doors and free Basat. Some elements of the story remain unanswered: the most obvious, why Goggle-eye would give Basat his magic ring and why the ring didn't protect Goggle-eye from the hot spike the men drive into his eye. Some folklorists have conjectured that the tale has been distorted somewhat in its generations of oral transmission and that the episodes are transposed, that originally Basat may have stolen the ring off of the giant's hand and then blinded him. The traces of that oral arrangement with a more plausible plot line have, possibly, been interpolated into unexplained episode sequences within the written text.

Having students investigate the oral qualities of this text and having them consider both the role of the poet, Dede Korkut, and the bare threads of an Islamic faith woven loosely into a pre-Islamic tale will likely produce fruitful discussion. Comparative study of this text with other mythic material found in the anthology, especially with the Gilgamesh/Enkidu relationship and with Homer's Polyphemous narrative, also prove useful. Some students may also want to think about how and why bodily deformity in the ancient and middle period (and even in contemporary literature as well) often was viewed as monstrous or a sign of evil or immorality. Such a legacy has important exceptions of course, such as the blind Tiresius, a figure who holds great wisdom, but the legacy also frequently casts the deformed human body as an "other" to be destroyed.

Resources for work on the Dede Korkut in English are somewhat scant. Both Geoffrey Lewis's translation (used in the anthology) and the translation done by Sümer, Uysal and Walker include useful introductions and notes to the text. Michael Meeker's article, "The Dede Korkut Ethic," International Journal of Middle East Studies 24.3 (1992) is extremely useful for studying the tale of Basat and Goggle-eye. Seyfi Karabas has written an article on "Social Function of the Dede Korkut Narratives," in Plenary Papers: The Eighth Congress for the International Society for Folk Narrative Research, volume two, edited by R. Kvideland and T. Selberg (Bergen, Norway, 1984-85). C. S. Mundy also has a dated but still useful article exploring the connections between this tale and Homer: "Polyphemus and Tepegöz," Journal of the British Society for Oriental and African Studies 18 (1956): 279-302.

Questions for Study and Discussion:

1. Since the Dede Korkut originated in oral narratives told from one generation to another (only written down much later than its misty and communal beginnings), can you identify some of the oral features still present in this narrative? (Features such as apostrophe, prayer, repetitions, and formulaic phrases are good indicators.)

2. What cultural, moral, religious, and social elements seem to be in conflict within this tale?

3. Why is Basat raised by a lionness? What purpose does this seem to serve as the narrative unfolds?

4. Why doesn't the tale force the rapist-shepherd to raise the son who results from his crime? Does this suggest to us something about the genre we are reading? The literary conventions that surround the tale? Does it say something about Uruz that he agrees to raise the strange, deformed child?

5. How does the contrast between the two boys raised in the same home but hailing from different biological origins help further the meanings in the tale?

6. Compare this text with Homer's account of Odysseus and Polyphemous. Compare the depictions of Basat and Goggle-eye with the depictions of Gilgamesh and Enkidu in the epic of Gilgamesh. How does this relationship between two "brothers" compare with other ancient tales of amity and enmity between brothers found in ancient and middle period literature?

Arabic and Persian Poetry

Poetry chosen for this section of the anthology should, along with the qasīdahs and longer Arabic and Persian poems, provide students with a sense of the range of Middle Eastern poetry from this era. It must be stressed, however, that the range of Arabic and Persian poetry cannot be adequately represented in so few pages. The best strategies for teaching these materials may take one of two paths. Students could read the entire section of Arabic and Persian poetry to uncover the range and diversity of forms and themes which are then discussed much as one discusses any poetic texts and placed in a conversation about Middle Period poetry from China, India, Japan, and Europe. Considerable time could be spent getting a handle on the differences and commonalities found in the various Middle Period poetic traditions. Another route would be to focus on just a few poems or on the poems of just one writer: Ibn Hazm's verses are part of a treatise on love and could warrant significant focused study; Rūmī is often considered the founder of Sufism, and his poetry attempts to express spiritual rapture and so may be useful to study along with Western or Far Eastern spiritual verse, and Ibn Zaidun's "Nuniyya for Wallada" is a longer poem and so also fruitful for study (its theme is profane love).

To give students a sense of the developments, historical contours of the poetic tradition in Arabic and Persian, and a sense, then, of where the poets included in the anthology fit into a literary history, teachers could consult the following: the Cambridge History of Arabic Literature, an invaluable resource which consists of three volumes, two of which are applicable to studying Middle Period literature: Arabic Literature to the End of the Umayyad Period (1983), and 'Abbasid Belles-Lettres (1990). Other more general resources include the Cambridge History of Iran, the Cambridge History of Islam, Persian Literature (New York, 1988), edited by Ehsan Yarshater, and Andras Hamori, On the Art of Medieval Arabic Literature (Princeton, 1974).

More specific studies of regions or genres include: Julie S. Meisami, Medieval Persian Court Poetry (Princeton, 1987), Suzanne P. Stetkevych, Reorientations: Arabic and Persian Poetry (Bloomington, IN, 1994), Annemarie Schimmel, A Two-Colored Brocade: the Imagery of Persian Poetry (Chapel Hill, NC, 1992), L. E. Goodman's study "The Sacred and the Secular: Rival Themes in Arabic Literature" in the Literary Heritage of Classical Islam, edited by Mustansir Mir (Princeton, 1993), and the introductions and notes found in A. J. Arberry's translations of works included in the anthology (see copyright information for his various texts. In addition, bibliographic searches under Arberry's name will uncover his many translations and editions of Arabic poetry.) James T. Monroe's translations, Hispano-Arabic poetry: A Student Anthology (Berkeley, 1974), are particularly useful for additional texts and notes on Hispano-Arabic poetry.

Other valuable assets to teachers are books that discuss Arabic literary criticism. Such work helps teachers investigate the reading expectations or standards of the Middle East of the Middle Period; resources include: G. J. H. van Gelder's book, Beyond the Line: Classical Arabic Literary Critics on the Coherence and Unity of the Poem (Leiden, 1982), and Wen-chin Ouyang, Literary Criticism in Medieval Arabic-Islamic Culture: The Making of a Tradition (Edinburgh, 1997). For a sense of cross-cultural influences, Maria Rosa Menocal's book, The Arabic Role in Medieval Literary History: A Forgotten Heritage (Philadelphia, 1987) is a good place to begin to explore Arabic influences on medieval European literatures. Her work is enhanced by D. A. Agius and R. Hitchcock, editors, The Arab Influence in Medieval Europe (Reading, UK, 1994; 1996) and D. A. Agius and I. R. Netton's collected papers from the International Medieval Congress held at the University of Leeds in 1996, entitled, Across the Mediterranean Frontiers: Trade, Politics and Religion, 650-1450 (Turnhout, Belgium, 1997).

To assist with reading particular Arabic texts dating from the ninth to the eleventh centuries, Stefan Sperl's book, Mannerism in Arabic Poetry: A Structural Analysis of Selected Texts (New York, 1989), is helpful. Suzanne P. Stetkevych's translations of the qasīdahs contain invaluable discussions which can illuminate the readings from other early Arabic poetry found in this area of the anthology: The Mute Immortals Speak: Pre-Islamic Poetry and the Poetics of Ritual (Ithaca, NY, 1993); in addition, Michael Zwettler's 1978 study, The Oral Tradition of Classical Arabic Poetry: Its Character and Implications (Columbus, OH), can help readers understand the oral qualities of the original early Arabic texts. Work on Rūmī benefits from Fatemeh Keshavarz's study: Reading Mystical Lyric: The Case of Jalal al-Din Rūmī (Columbia, SC, 1998), as well as from A. J. Arberry's edition of translated poems. The poetry of Hafiz translated by Arberry (Cambridge, 1947) is a useful resource for work on that poet, and Qasim al-Samarrai's article, "New Remarks on the Text of Ibn Hazm's Tawq al-hamma," in Arabica vol. 30, no. 1 (1983): 57-72, as well as the 1994 publication of "The Ring of the Dove" (London), another translation of Hazm's text on love, are both helpful for teachers preparing to teach Ibn Hazm's poetry from the Tawq al-Namamah.

Questions for Study and Discussion:

1. As with any study of poetry, having students locate main images, themes, and apparent communicative purposes is one obvious place to start working on these texts. Have students consider whether or not they have encountered these images in other Arabic and Persian materials found in this area of the anthology or whether some of these images are familiar to Euro-American culture, as well. Entertain the question of whether an image, familiar to twenty-first century Western readers, really means the same thing when it appears in a fifth century or twelfth century Middle Eastern poem.

2. What range of themes, genres, and purposes seem to characterize the poetry found in the section on Arabic and Persian poetry? How is our understanding of those things enhanced by considering the other selections in the Middle Eastern Middle Period section as a whole? Are there connections between the shorter poems in this part of the anthology and some of the longer pieces of Arabic and Persian literature? If so, what are they? What ideas seem present here that do not seem to occur in the longer works found in the anthology of Arabic and Persian middle period materials?

3. What sense of love is expressed in the selections?

4. What sense of the divine is represented in these poems?

5. What sense of humanity is indicated in these poems?

Kālidāsa
Śakuntalā and the Ring of Recollection

I have had great success with Kālidāsa's play Śakuntalā in class. Students find it beautiful but strangely exotic. They don't know what to make of it until they get some basic guidance in class discussion, and then feel as if they're being let in on a mystery. Kālidāsa is India's Shakespeare, and the play can very effectively be taught with King Lear and other dramas in the book, like The Bacchae, the Japanese No drama, and Beckett's Happy Days; but there are many other equally strong syllabus links. It could be taught with other Indian texts, of course (Kālidāsa is the author of many of the poems collected by Vidyakara, so that is a natural), or with other texts from the same period, or from the international literature of love, or late classical mythology. Ovid, or Book IV of The Aeneid would be compelling companion pieces on most of these grounds; Gan Bao's In Search of the Supernatural and the Kojiki are near-contemporary mythological texts from China and Japan, and Augustine's Confessions, also contemporary, offers a shocking contrast. All of these are startlingly different from each other, though they represent, in a rough way, the late classical stage in cultural development. Turning outside the anthology, it should be noted that the play is most famous in the West as a strong influence on Goethe's Faust; comparing the prologues (or the whole plays) is a productive paper topic.

There are three approaches to the play that have worked for me: first, the Indian theory of the rasas can be explained in several ways. The play is not realistic, and does not try to present the sort of dramatic tensions found in Western narratives; rather, the author concentrates on creating certain moods, and certain combinations of moods, like a painter mixing colors, or an

Indian cook combining spices, or a symphonic composer mixing instrumental tonalities. The play opens with a light, comical prelude, which contrasts in the strongest possible way with the first scene, which strives for speed and violence in the king's hunt; that, in turn, is followed by the sweetest imaginable idyll, when the king witnesses the nymph-like heroine and her attendants in their peaceful glade. It is like hearing the orchestra warming up, then a theme in blaring horns and kettle-drums, followed by soft and melodious violins. Once you become attuned to this aspect of the play, it is not hard to see the many effects that can be achieved by juxtaposition, layering, and combination. A little Indian music will bring the point home nicely: the rasa is something of a tone poem, in which the artist and the listener become attuned to the finest nuances of each note of the scale, or key, before entering into complex effects. Ask students to seek out on their own the purest examples they can find of the various rasas in the play, then focus on the poems or stanzas they have chosen to discover their subtle delicacies.

My body turns to go,	or,	I see fresh footprints
My heart pulls me back,		On white sand in the clearing,
Like a silk banner		Deeply pressed at the heel
Buffeted by the wind.		By the sway of full hips.

It is good for this generation of students to concentrate on such subtle expressions of the erotic rasa, extremely sensuous but never pornographic.

The second approach confronts the play's dramatic structure directly. If students don't notice it immediately, they recognize when it is pointed out to them that all the key turning-points in the plot are curiously absent from the play. In the opening act, the king woos Śakuntalā in disguise, fearful of revealing who he is. Tension mounts as we anticipate the revelation, but amazingly the action is interrupted before it comes; and when the love affair resumes after the comical interlude of act two, Śakuntalā has already learned who the king is. Again their wooing is interrupted, and when act four opens we discover that not only have the lovers been married in the meantime, and consummated their love, but the king has left for the city! The ascetic's visit, and the curse he places on the heroine, is oddly carried out completely off-stage. Throughout the play, moments when the tension is highest are elided. Ask the students to itemize the missing scenes that a Western dramatist would have emphasized and explored.

The third approach has to do with the representation of the heroine and her destiny. Students will be shocked by the combination of misogyny and idealization, horrified by the treatment she endures from her husband, and by her undying love for him even after she has been swallowed by the earth. As the king says,

> She bears with perfect virtue
> the trial of long separation
> my cruelty forced on her.

We may be unable to justify these attitudes to our students, nor perhaps should we want to, but we can try to provoke understanding. Sketching the ideas of dharma and karma for them may help—though I will admit that I focus less on these ideas than I do on the literary inventiveness of the play's dramatic structures (prologue, interruptions and ellipses, the final shift of scene to heaven), the beauty of its poetic tonalities (the rasas), and its strange "otherness" to those of us raised on Greek and Shakespearian tragedies.

For more background and analysis, see Barbara Stoler Miller's extremely useful introduction to her translation of Kālidāsa's plays, Theatre of Memory (New York, 1984).

Questions for Study and Discussion:

1. What are the most evident differences between Śakuntalā and Western dramas, like the Greek tragedies and Shakespeare? Can the play be called a tragedy?

2. A number of key dramatic moments in the plot are not presented in the play. List the scenes you are surprised do not appear. What effect is achieved by their absence?

3. The play examines the relation of the heroic and erotic rasas, but contains comic elements as well. Try analyzing a scene in these terms, finding pure expressions of these moods, and interesting combinations, juxtapositions, layerings, etc. Choose a few favorite poems or stanzas for close reading.

4. Many Western readers at first find the imagery conventional and repetitive (think of all those mango blossoms!). Can you think of a justification for this technique?

5. Is the king cruel, and the heroine passive? Is the play misogynistic? Could this possibly be a happy ending? Find the clearest expressions you can in the final act of the play's ethical vision. What deep truths about human life does the play try to illustrate? How would you apply the concepts of dharma and karma?

Vidyakara
Treasury of Well-Turned Verse

Vidyakara's Treasury may be formal and challenging in the Sanskrit, but in English it appears the simplest and most transparent poetry imaginable. Students find these poems as immediately attractive as the Chinese Book of Songs, or the Tang poets—especially Wang Wei's Wang River Sequence—or Japanese poetry, and for some of the same reasons. They are all excellent choices for introducing poetry to students who tend to assume that, to be poetry, it must be complicated and obscure. The Treasury is also a natural companion to Kālidāsa's drama, since they both display the Indian aesthetic of the rasas. It is hard to suggest Western texts that might work well with it, however, since Europe never produced poetry of this sort—simple pictures of everyday village life among the poor, of children and peasants and farm animals and the jungle, and the jewelry, cosmetics, and smoky rituals of erotic love in the Indian Middle Ages.

The introduction in the book suggests a number of approaches. The crucial perception to aim for is that the poems, while they may be simple snapshots or bits of narrative, all convey moods. They are not as "objective" as they look, then, since they are intended to provoke subtle emotional responses in the reader. They are, in a word, evocative. We can't fully trust our responses, however, since the culture they portray really is quite "other." Thus there is a strong sense of the familiar and unfamiliar at the same time. Most students will recognize the joys of summer, a millenium away and in another world, in poem 226:

> the children, sticks in hand and smeared with mud,
> run after the rising fish,
> yelling "chubhroo, chubhroo!"

or the laziness of the water buffalo, though they've never seen one, in poem 202.

If one reads all thirty-three poems (which take up only seven pages) straight through, one will notice some of the conventions running through them, and be better able to imagine their world—a world of mangoes and lotuses, water buffalo and monsoons. One will discover, for example, that the monsoon is the season of love, since people must stay indoors. Or, if one happens to be away from home, it is the season of heartbreak, as in poem 220:

> one sees the horizon suddenly in a flash of lightning . . . .
> How can the lonely lover spend these nights?

In Satyajit Ray's film <u>Pather Panchali</u>, there is a beautiful scene of the arrival of the monsoon season, in which the imagery of the <u>Treasury</u> poems is still very much alive. I have found it very effective to show a clip from this film in class.

The combination of vivid realism and strong conventionality can make for an interesting discussion. What does originality mean in such a genre? How are stock images used so effectively? Each image—each mango, lotus, or other common object—becomes a symbol which accumulates meanings as we read more poems. What is the relation of tradition to individual talent? Of realism to symbolism?

The cultural otherness of the poems becomes most problematical when it comes to sex and gender. At first we may be startled by the casual references to plump breasts and sexual positions, and be unsure of our responses. Are the poems written from an insistently male point of view, objectivising women? A few poems seem to indicate not; but one cannot forget that India is a strongly patriarchal society where women are oppressed beyond most Americans' imaginings. Only in the final few poems do we get powerful statements from the female perspective, and they are devastatingly disillusioning.

The greatest difficulty of teaching poems like these may be due to their very simplicity. What is one to <u>say</u> about them? Two simple and effective techniques are, first, to have students select their favorites and read them to the class, followed by an explanation of their choices; or, second, to have them try writing a poem or two in the same style. In the latter exercise, one hopes they will discover how economical these poems are, capturing complex scenes vividly with just one or two verbal strokes. As students prepare for such an exercise, teachers might want to point out, as an example, the extraordinary image of the umbrella—"the crystal cage"—in poem 242.

Daniel Ingalls's book, <u>Sanskrit Poetry from Vidyakara's "Treasury"</u> (Cambridge, 1968), from which these excerpts have been taken, would be very helpful for anyone wanting to know more about the poems in the <u>Treasury</u>.

Questions for Study and Discussion:

1. Choose two or three favorites from the thirty-three poems in the selection. Explain your choices. What features of the poems most attract you—their compact imagery? universal themes? cultural otherness? emotional charge?

2. The most striking social themes in the poem are childhood, farm life, love, and the status of women in society. Does the collection display consistent attitudes toward these themes?

3. Look closely at the images offered in the poems—the umbrella, the water buffalo, the winter sun, the wagtail, the crocodile. Are these simple snapshots of everyday life? Or are they, rather, objectifications of human emotions? Or are they symbols with complex meanings?

4. Try writing a few poems of this sort. Describe the techniques you discover, and the points you are trying to achieve in the imitation exercise.

Two Bhakti Poets: Ravidas and Mīrābāī

These poets were first brought to my attention by students who had discovered them for themselves. They have an immediate attraction to students because of the social issues they raise. American students find untouchability shocking beyond words, since it seems the most exaggerated possible case of racism, and Indian gender politics presents an exaggerated form of anti-feminism; yet these two poets, one the voice of untouchables and one the voice of women, respond to their oppression in wholly unexpected—that is, in wholly un-American—ways. The Mīrābāī poems can effectively be taught in conjunction with the biblical Song of Songs, the life of the Arabic female mystic Rābiʿah, and the life of St. Christine, in Christine de Pizan's The Book of the City of Ladies. The first fuses the language of religion and sexual passion; the second shows a quite different religious response to female oppression, Muslim rather than Hindu; and the third is typically Christian in its stress on renunciation. Mīrābāī's life also brings to mind the situation of Shahrazad in the Arabic The Thousand and One Nights.

It is hard for an American to imagine what untouchability means, and an excellent way of approaching Ravidas would be to have students (or one student) read up on the subject and present it to the class. Even in the twentieth century, it was a common practice among the upper castes to avoid being touched even by the shadow of an untouchable—the resulting pollution would require an immediate bath. In a shop, an untouchable would put his coins in a special dish, and water would be poured over them before they were picked up by the shopkeeper.

It may not be possible to understand these practices overnight, but they will provide interesting background for Ravidas's poems. All of his poems are concerned with the poet's social status, but, oddly, they do not express outrage. Rather, they find a spiritual solution to the problem, in everyone's true equality in the eyes of the Lord. Several poems gently lampoon the upper castes's ritual practices: the holy books are written on palm leaves, though the palm tree is ritually impure; a Brahmin girl is so obsessed with purity rituals that she finds worship impossible; and from the cobbler's point of view, the human body (as opposed to the soul) is portrayed as so much impure meat. For all his religious idealism, Ravidas is a worldly realist.

The long "peddlar" poem portrays the four stages of life, from childish illusion to the shivering and quaking of old age.

Most of the poems address a quite general, formless god, though Krishna (Hari, Murari, Govind) appears now and again as an especially friendly god, and Ram (the Rama of the Ramayana) is often invoked as a name for god. The poem on the name of god uses a common trope in Indian scriptures, the totality of god indicated by this sort of contradiction:

> Your name: the little lamp, the cruse [a small vessel],
> your name the wick.
> Your name is the oil that I pour into the ritual lamp.

In the Bhagavad-Gītā we read,

I am the rite, the sacrifice,
the libation for the dead, the healing herb,
the sacred hymn, the clarified butter,
the fire, the oblation. (Book 9)

Or, in the Rig Veda,

When, with Man as their offering,
The gods performed their sacrifice,
Spring was the oil of sacrifice,
Summer its fuel, Autumn its gift.

Ravidas's poems provide a wonderful opportunity to examine elaborate metaphors. For example, the body is figured in successive poems as a cage, a tree, a puppet, a house, a bullock, and a store.

Mīrābāī's poems display a sort of mysticism, as she portrays herself consistently as a lover (in quite literal terms) of her god Krishna. This is the same Krishna we found in the Bhagavad-Gītā, but in later centuries he was developed in the direction of a whimsical, musical, childish, handsome, winsome, flirtatious, seductive, blue-skinned god, always pursuing and being pursued by country girls. The Bhagavad-Gītā's Krishna is the exact opposite in some ways: he demands absolute obedience to dharma, which is composed mostly of caste regulations. Mīrābāī's life is a well-known, oft-told legend of domestic oppression common in India. Married to a prince who died shortly afterwards, she developed a strong spirituality and sought out Ravidas as a spiritual master. Her family, outraged at her flouting of caste laws and her refusal to remain sequestered as a woman, attempted to poison her, but Krishna saved her. Her religious devotion and her songs made her immensely popular, adding to her family's outrage. She left home and became a wandering saint, and when her family tried to drag her home again, she entered a temple and disappeared. In a country where today widows have no status and often become wandering paupers and pilgrims, and where "bride-burning" is still a social scandal, the story and the songs of Mīrābāī have an immense popularity.

Her poems are, first of all, ecstatic. Though they are likely to appeal to students because of their passion and because the legend implies a sort of feminist power, they are likely to shock American sensibilities as well. Like Ravidas, she responds to her oppression in a surprising, Indian way. Her relation to Krishna is extremely subservient, and may seem to embody all the patriarchal, anti-feminist values that her life story would seem to oppose. He is the ideal bridegroom, the ideal husband, and she is "a virginal harvest for you to reap."

Though both poets are attractive, exciting and interesting in class, Ravidas and Mīrābāī test students' willingness to tolerate the otherness of a very different culture.

Questions for Study and Discussion:

1. How would you describe Ravidas's response to his own untouchability? Anger, revolt, attack, sarcasm, moral superiority, irony, comedy, concession, humility, servility: which of these best characterizes to that crucial question? What does his religious devotion have to do with his lowly caste position?

2. In "Oh well born of Benares, I too am born well known" and "Mother, she asks, with what can I worship?" how does Ravidas address the upper castes?

3. Pay attention to the metaphors Ravidas uses for the human body, and for human life. What are the four watches of the night?

4. Mīrābāī is often called an Indian feminist. How do you assess that claim?

5. Mīrābāī's relation to Krishna is certainly ecstatic and passionate, but does it qualify as mystical? What is the relation of sexual passion and religious devotion in these poems?

Gan Bao
In Search of the Supernatural

Students typically enjoy these brief stories of the supernatural. Still, Gan Bao is not easy to teach precisely because his stories are more entertaining curiosities than profound literary works. Moreover, a reader of modern narrative will find that these stories read a bit like outlines, with virtually no space given to character development and with plots that leap very quickly from one event to another. Some background explanation therefore becomes essential. Gan Bao was a historian—indeed one of the most prominent historians of his time. In the preface to his anthology of over five hundred stories, of which we have selected only five, he makes it clear that he has collected these stories, some of them perhaps more properly called "anecdotes," as a supplement to the historical record. That is, Gan Bao plainly believes in the supernatural and, while not quite vouching for the reliability of each of his stories, feels that they should become a part of the public record. Thus, the stories in Gan Bao's In Search of the Supernatural are not highly adorned nor elaborately developed but are presented in a straightforward, matter-of-fact manner. That being said, Gan Bao is a great writer who writes classical Chinese in a direct, strong fashion than has won him the admiration many subsequent stylists.

The story of the supernatural becomes a staple of Chinese literature and Gan Bao is one of the forerunners of this form. Why, we might ask, do stories of this type proliferate and gain such a large audience? This is, of course, a worldwide phenomenon that students might be asked to discuss (many of them will have read Stephen King or regularly will enjoy films that contain supernatural elements). But perhaps such stories especially flourished in China in part because they provided some escape for an educated readership that was steeped in this-worldly Confucian classics and serious historical texts. Moreover, for those in traditional China who believed in ghosts and spirits, and many clearly did, the supernatural world was believed to interweave with the world of the living—it was not at all the "totally other" of certain Western traditions. As Lu Xun, the great modern writer and scholar put it, "In China no clear division can be drawn between the world of men and the world of ghosts."

Despite their brevity, these stories present themes that have considerable appeal and recur in later Chinese literature as well as finding correspondences elsewhere in world literature. "Han Ping and His Wife," for example, is a story of a tragic double suicide provoked by a greedy prince. As is common in such supernatural stories (though surely not in "The Old Man and the Devils"), there is some redemption—the dead lovers are joined together by the interlaced catalpa trees that grow from their graves. "Married to a Ghost," by far the longest of the five stories included here, deals with a sexual relationship between a human being and a ghost, a very common theme in Chinese literature. In this story, though not in some later Chinese stories of this type, the relationship blesses both the living and the dead.

A full translation of Gan Boa's stories can be found in the excellent In Search of the Supernatural: The Written Record, trans. by Kenneth J. DeWoskin and J. I. Crump, Jr. (Stanford, 1996). For those who read French, Remi Mathieu's Gan Bao: A la recherche des esprits (Paris, 1992) is highly recommended. The discussion in Nienhauser, Op. cit., p. 716-18 (under Sou-shen chi) is very useful.

Questions for Study and Discussion:

1. Some scholars have said that fiction in China grows out of historical writing and that Gan Boa's stories, in particular, tend to be presented as history. Can you see any elements in at least some of these stories that one might identify more with historical than fictional writing (a boundary difficult to draw, of course, both in China and in the West!)?

2. "Horse into Silkworm" is, on one level, a bizarre explanation of the word for mulberry, sang. But it is also a moral tale dealing with an old and widespread theme: the all-too-hasty promise to marry whoever grants a wish or fulfills some request. In your opinion, does the story end unhappily or does the earlier return of the father offset what subsequently happened to his daughter?

3. In the story "Married to a Ghost," when do you think Lu begins to realize that he is involved with ghosts? Who motivates the action in this story, Lu or his supernatural counterparts? Can you think of any strong cultural reason why the ghosts are so eager for Lu to marry their daughter?

4. What do you make of the story "Dead Drunk?" Is it only a witty piece of entertainment or can you imagine some message here? (There might indeed be a bit of satire in this story aimed at Taoist stories that were becoming common in Gan Bao's age concerning Taoist practitioners who had supposedly disappeared from their graves or who had been dug up and found alive in their coffins.)

Tao Qian
Poems

Tao Qian is one of the most accessible as well as one of the most beloved of all Chinese poets. He rejected the ornate style of his contemporaries and wrote in a manner that is relatively easily read. Students, however, are sometimes baffled by his "lack of ambition," as one of our students once put it. Certainly Tao Qian longs for home, for wine, for nature, for poetry, and for desultory reading. One must understand such longings within the context of what was expected of an educated man in traditional China. Basically, the educated had memorized classical texts throughout the duration of their youth so as eventually to serve the state, often as magistrates who presided over counties and had complete responsibility for everything from taxation and military conscription to adjudicating court cases. The pressure of such service was enormous, the dangers considerable (Tao Qian himself probably averted disaster by resigning from one post just before his patron fell afoul of the law and was decapitated). Counterbalancing what we might describe as "Confucian state service" was a tradition of a higher way, usually identified with Taoism, especially Zhuangzi. This latter tradition insisted that the purest man turned his back on government service and the reputation and wealth it so often brought. Tao Qian chose this "higher way" and has been respected among later literati in part, perhaps, because he did what so many of them wished they had the courage to do. He is the poet of all of us who have been tempted to throw up our hands and walk away, even if that walk is toward poverty.

Virtually every educated Chinese knows well Tao Qian's "Peach Blossom Spring." One might ask why this particular utopian vision, as simple as it is, has had such enormous appeal throughout Chinese history. First of all, the piece is daringly subversive: the best society, it seems to claim, is hidden from meddling government officials (officials who would destroy the utopia if they could). Second, it is a simple, agricultural society (much like the utopia of Laozi, chapter 80) and the Chinese have usually identified the happy life with the rural village rather than the city (Chinese utopian fantasies virtually never center upon real wilderness!). Third, the approach to the cave (and the rebirth it represents?) has a beautiful dream-like quality. And it is the fisherman's journey through the peach blossom spring that gives the piece its name. Students who read this piece tend to notice the irony of the conclusion and the message it carries—i.e., that should we actually find a happy society we would quite automatically take steps to destroy it. However, this particular message, although surely implicit in the story, has not been as important to Chinese readers as the dream-like journey of the fisherman toward the rural utopia and the nature of its happy and hospitable residents.

The Seas and Mountain Classic, which is the topic of one of the poems included here, has a fantastic geography that described amazing creatures who supposedly lived around the edges of China. At an early time, this book was accompanied by pictures of these unusual and entirely imaginary creatures. To be sure, this book (and the equally imaginative Story of King Mu, which dealt with a fantastic journey of an early Zhou king to the far west of China) is the exact opposite of the serious, historically grounded Confucian classics, which all serious scholars supposedly made their lifelong companions. Thus, Tao Qian opts for imagination—indeed, fiction—and this is a conscious reactions against the constraints of history and Confucian discipline.

Tao Qian is acutely aware of the flight of time and wishes to spend his "one single life" in a quiet "resting place." Because he speaks so much of drinking, students will sometimes try to turn him into a raucous frat boy. This, assuredly, he is not. Wine for him clearly serves an almost metaphysical function, enabling him to establish contact with some greater "profundity."

Excellent translations of Tao Qian's works can be found in James Robert Hightower, The Poetry of T'ao Ch'ien (Oxford, 1970). A recent study by Stephen Owen, one of the West's best scholars and writers on the topic of Chinese poetry is "The Self's Perfect Mirror: Poetry as Autobiography," in Shuen-fu Lin and Stephen Owen, ed., The Vitality of the Lyric Voice (Princeton, 1986), pp. 71-102.

Questions for study and discussion:

1. Returning, refuge, and finding oneself are recurrent themes in Tao Qian. To what extend are these themes shaped by the Chinese experience—especially that of official service—and to what extent are they universal longings that you can find expressed in other works throughout this anthology?

2. What view of our world emerges from Tao Qian's poems "After Drinking Wine," and in what way is wine an antidote to our situation in this world?

3. The society of "The Peach Blossom Spring" has escaped from government. How is this potentially subversive message softened somewhat by the final events of this piece?

4. Chinese poetry, as Tao Qian's works illustrate so well, tends to be presented as fundamentally autobiographical. This encourages us to read these poems as literal expressions of particular moments in the poet's own life. That is, the author and the persona implicit in the poems are easily treated as the same. Do you see any problems with such an approach?

The Lotus Sutra

It is important to remind students that Buddhism began in India (see pp. 265-288) and only spread to China in the first centuries of the current era. Moreover, it was Mahayana Buddhism that became popular in China and Japan, as opposed to the Hinayana (or, more properly, "Theravada") that penetrated most of Southeast Asia. Mahayana Buddhism, at least as it appears in the Lotus Sutra, teaches the doctrine that the Buddha is eternal and that all living beings share in the Buddha's nature and can gain salvation through faith and devotion. This "supreme enlightenment," which all Mahayana believers seek, is known in Sanskrit as anuttara-samyak-sambodhi, an unwieldy term that appears in this story from the Lotus Sutra. The teachings of Mahayana Buddhism, unlike the more austere and lonely path pursued by adherents of the Theravada doctrine, promises eventual salvation to all—salvation that will come through the guidance and love of the Buddha and the numerous Bodhisattvas who serve him.

The problem that informs the Lotus Sutra, and can be seen to some degree in the first paragraphs of the section included in the anthology is this: how can it be that the human being who became Buddha through his arduous personal striving and who then taught his disciples to follow his example could now proclaim himself a Buddha from the beginning of time and urge his disciples to put aside their earlier beliefs to follow a yet higher way? Put somewhat differently, how does a Mahayanist negotiate the fact that Theravada Buddhism seems to have been the earlier doctrine of the Buddha? The answer to these questions begins with the distinction between a lesser and a higher truth. The Mahayana teachings are described as a higher truth supplanting the earlier teachings. Buddha himself, the Mahayanist argues, did not reveal this truth until late in his own life and then only a few of his disciples "got it." Chapter four of the Lotus Sutra begins with the aged disciples, who had until this time adhered to the lesser way, finally understanding that they have now heard a higher Law and have thereby "gained great goodness and benefit." In other words, they have just converted from a Theravada to a Mahayana perspective. And the story they tell reflects their own story to the Mahayanist view.

The father in the story from the Lotus Sutra represents Buddha, just as the father in the biblical story of the prodigal son represents Jesus. But notice that in the Buddhist story it is the father who initially goes in search of the son and then proceeds to bring his son to recognize the truth slowly and carefully. The father does not reveal himself all at once because he knows that this would be too much for his son, just as it would be too much for us if the Buddha did not first lead us with lesser doctrines and thereby prepare us for supreme enlightenment. A part of the Buddha's nature, exemplified here by the kindly father, is to strive tirelessly to bring all beings to the recognition that "we are all like the Buddha's sons."

The "Translator's Introduction" to Burton Watson's highly readable translation of The Lotus Sutra (New York, 1993) is recommended. Kenneth Ch'en's Buddhism in China: A Historical Survey (Princeton, 1964) provides excellent information on Mahayana Buddhism and its appeal in China. On the Lotus Sutra, see Ch'en, pp. 378-382. Many excellent books on Mahayana Buddhism are available. Edward Conze's books are particularly readable (see, especially, Buddhist Thought in India: Three Phases of Buddhist Philosophy (Ann Arbor, 1970).

Questions for Study and Discussion:

1. What is the significance of the son's first vision of his father? How does the father proceed to narrow the enormous distance between himself and his son who feels so completely unworthy?

2. How would you explain the extremes that are a part of this story—i.e., the father is unbelievably rich, the son (and then the father) work clearing away excrement, etc.?

3. Why do you think that the parable is such an important part of religious literature both in the East and the West? Put somewhat differently, why do religious teachers invariably resort to story-telling rather than pure doctrinal exposition?

Four Tang Poets: Wang Wei, Li Bai, Du Fu, Bai Juyi

The poetry presented in this section, drawn from the work of four of the greatest Tang poets, is highly diverse. There is always a tendency to flatten and stereotype the vast richness of Chinese verse. Because of this tendency, we have purposely tried to select pieces that reflect a range of topics and a variety of forms (from the short quatrains of Wang Wei to Bai Juyi's rather lengthy narrative poem, "A Song of Unending Sorrow"). If there is anything that unifies the diversity one encounters in the poets of the Tang, it is their very enthusiasm for poetry itself and their practice of incorporating verse into so many aspects of their lives, both private and public. Few occasions, at least among the educated elite, were complete unless adorned in some fashion by verse. Thus, one might begin a discussion of Tang poetry with the last poem in this section, Bai Juyi's "Madly Singing in the Mountain" (p. 1033), a poem that expresses, perhaps better than any other, the sheer joy of writing poetry. Next, one can turn to Wang Wei's "Lazy about Writing Poems," which seems to be a renunciation of poetry but is itself a poem and hence a reaffirmation of what it would seem at first glance to deny.

Reading Chinese poetry reproduced without footnotes can be a daunting task precisely because Chinese poems are firmly rooted in a real world of place names and historical references. One can, of course, scurry to scholarly editions that explain every proper noun and all the numerous allusions that fill almost every Chinese poem. While such research obviously enriches Tang poetry, our experience is that students themselves usually derive only marginal "added value" from such a process. Most of the poems included here communicate well without knowing all the references (with Du Fu's "Autumn Meditations" as the most problematic). What is ultimately more important for beginning students than the proper nouns that dot these poems is an awareness of the four seasons and the features of each. Tang poetry is often fixed in a specific season and the mood of the poem grows from the time of year it portrays. "Autumn Meditations" will not be cheery, and chrysanthemums, however beautiful in and of themselves, are "sad" flowers because they are the final beauty that precedes the end (winter=death). Students should be encouraged to attend to the nature images that are scattered through so many of these poems and to try to understand how these images resonate with human feelings. (Keep in mind that Chinese poems, though often containing image after image drawn from nature, are almost invariably "about" human situations and the feelings they provoke).

As Stephen Owen has noted so aptly in his discussion of Tang poetry, "The autonomous literariy of the Western tradition is alien here: though he longed for the honor of posterity, Tu Fu (=Du Fu) did not sit down to write 'the great Chinese lyric' as Milton and Keats sat down to write the 'English epic'" (see below, Owen, p. 6). What he means, as noted above, is that Tang poetry was usually occasioned by some event—it was what an educated person did in certain situations. Owen goes on to note that exile was the one event, however, that often provoked a more private voice. There is an older antecedent for this in the anthology: Qu Yuan, whose poetry also supposedly resulted in large measure from exile. Of the poems included here, Du Fu's "Moonlight Night" is a poem of exile, written while he was separated from his home by war, and his "The Man with No Family to Take Leave Of" can be read as a return from exile and the estrangement it brings. And, of course, Bai Juyi's "A Song of Unending Sorrow" is in part a song about exile, albeit not his own. The larger issue, we believe, that motivates such poems and that is reflected in one way or another in many poems not dealing with exile per se, is the intense Chinese attachment to home and family: "A living man, but with no family to take leave of— / how can I be called a human being?" ("The Man with No Family to Take Leave Of," lines 31 & 32).

When reading Li Bai's poems entitled "Drinking Alone by Moonlight," one must of course recall Tao Qian. Tang poets revered Tao Qian more than any other poet of the Chinese past, and his eremitism (<u>and</u> his bibulousness!) profoundly influenced their own verse. Without doubt, Li Bai is writing his verses about wine with Tao Qian as his model. It is fascinating to follow this theme of wine-drinking to Japan (see pages 1074-75) where it appears, at least as exemplified in this anthology, with considerable wit (see especially nos. 341 & 343) and brevity!

The best single book on the subject of Tang poetry is Stephen Owen, <u>The Great Age of Chinese Poetry: The High T'ang</u> (New Haven, 1981). Owen has several other books about Chinese poetry, and all are fascinating reading. See especially his <u>Traditional Chinese Poetry and Poetics</u> (Madison, 1985). All of the poets included here, along with many other Tang poets, have been translated extensively. The books cited in the "Acknowledgments" (pages 2234-35) are a good place to find sources for additional study. Many additional translations are also noted under the entries of individual poets in Nienhauser.

Questions for Study and Discussion:

1. Wang Wei's quatrains are perhaps the high point of this particular poetic form. How are nature images used in these pieces?

2. As mentioned above, Li Bai's poems of drinking are written with Tao Qian as background. Can you see any other Tang poems included here that appear to echo Tao Qian? (See "To My Cousin Qiu, Military Supply Official").

3. There are poems in this collection of strong social protest. Li Bo's "Fighting South of the Ramparts" is a powerful anti-war poem that obviously is a rewrite of its anonymous forerunner of the same title (see pages 382-83). But what is the focus of protest in Wang Wei's "A Wealthy Woman of Luoyang" and what earlier Chinese poem does it appear to echo?

4. The very fact that some have considered Du Fu's "Autumn Meditations" the greatest of all Chinese poetry says much about the Chinese poetic aesthetic. Discuss the art of these poems and consider why they might have had such appeal to Chinese literati-readers.

5. Chinese poems tend to be rather muted in the expression of romantic feeling. Bai Juyi's "A Song of Unending Sorrow" is often cited as an exception to this tendency. Discuss the theme of romance as it appears in this piece and compare the issue as it arises in "The Story of Ying-ying."

Yuan Zhen
The Story of Ying-ying

This story works extremely well in the classroom precisely because so many students will find Chang's ultimate abandonment of Ying-ying as either inexplicable or inexcusable. But, if we take the narrator's comment at the end of the story at face value, and there is little evidence here that it is meant to be ironic, then Chang has finally taken the proper action: "His contemporaries for the most part conceded that Chang had done right to rectify his mistake" (p. 1041). The interpretative problem arises, at least to some extent, from the fact that many students have been shaped by a strong Western tradition, though surely not without its own counter currents, that valorizes the romantic sentiments of the individual—e.g., "love conquers all!" We should bear in mind that marriage in traditional China was essentially a family affair—that is, an alliance of two families—and had very little to do with romantic attachment. In fact, the romantic feeling was often seen as posing a dangerous challenge to "family values." Consider, for example, Bao-yu's attachment to Dai-yu in Dream of the Red Chamber, which must ultimately be relinquished because of his family's preference for the more stable Bao-chai (pp. 1639-76). Thus, Chang's final action in this story becomes quite understandable, even admirable, within such a cultural context. If the teacher of this story is lucky enough to have a culturally diverse classroom, she might find students, as we often have in our classroom, who will defend Chang's behavior and thereby stimulate a lively discussion. (Cultural note: Do not allow students to argue that the relationship between Chang and Ts'ui Ying-ying is inappropriate because they are cousins. Cross-cousin marriage was allowed if those concerned did not share the same surname, which these cousins, who were related only on the maternal side, did not.)

Of course none of the debate about Chang can diminish the fact that the story is largely about Ying-ying, and seen from her perspective, the story is a tragedy. One might criticize her for her sexual aggressiveness, but she is for the most part portrayed as a beautiful, sensitive, and extremely cultured young lady. One can argue that the story is the fantasy of a male who wants to have everything—the pleasure of a sexual encounter with a woman who is portrayed as desirable in every "high-class" way and, at the same time, the moral superiority of ultimately rejecting her. Such a reading, though surely not without merit, makes it difficult to explain the extremely broad appeal of this story, which was ultimately transformed into one of traditional China's most famous plays, Wang Shifu's thirteenth-century masterpiece The West Chamber Story (Xixiang ji) Perhaps, then, the appeal of the story exists to a large degree in the very complexity of Ying-ying's character. While little can be said about Chang beyond his initial attraction to Ying-ying and his eventual capitulation to what we might call "Confucian expectations," Ying-ying continues to fascinate readers and resists reduction to any stereotype.

As noted in the introduction to this text in the anthology, Chang's forsaking Ying-ying can be compared with Aeneas' departure from Dido in The Aeneid. However, the differences in these texts are highly revealing and touch upon several general but important issues in East-West comparison. First and most obviously, The Aeneid is presented in the highly elevated language that typifies the classical Western epic, whereas the Tang chuanqi (which literally means "Passing Along the Curious"), represented here by "The Story of Ying-ying," is presented almost as a piece of historical gossip. Second, very much in accord with this striking stylistic difference, the story of Aeneas and Dido, certainly an extraordinarily powerful tale in its own right, presents a world of extreme emotion and heightened drama—the main characters are no mere mortals! However, Chang and Ying-ying, whatever else we might think of them, act very much on a constrained and quiet stage. For example, in The Aeneid Dido burns herself to death as Aeneas sails away, while Ying-ying quietly weeps as she writes her good-bye to her former love. This contrast is, of course, easily drawn, but such a contrast points to an important characteristic of Chinese literature: it tends to be very much embedded in this world and to retain the tone of a historical record even when it is obviously fictional (there are, of course, exceptions, Monkey being a noteworthy one).

For a collection of chuanqi tales with a useful preface, see Karl S. Kao, Classical Chinese Tales of the Supernatural and Fantastic—Selections from the Third to the Tenth Century (Bloomington, IN 1986). For an excellent translation of the great play that evolved from this story, see Wilt L. Idema and Stephen H. West, The Moon and the Zither: The Story of the West Wing by Wang Shifu (Berkeley, 1991). The brief entry in Nienhauser is also helpful for background on the chuanqi tale and provides additional bibliography.

Questions for Study and Discussion:

1. The author (Yuan Zhen) appears as a character in this story (spelled within the story as "Yuan Chen") once as a poet who writes a poem about the whole affair and once as someone who "was especially close [to Chang] . . . and so in a position to ask him for an explanation." What impact does this have on the way we readers regard the tale and its presentation?

2. What is the image of the "cultured woman" that emerges from this tale? (See especially p. 1037.)

3. How do you explain Ying-ying's strong initial repudiation of Chang ("you substitute seduction for rape") followed so quickly by her capitulation?

4. Confucian readers in China were always concerned about whether a work sustained their conservative values or threatened them. From what you know, is this story fundamentally supportive or undermining of Confucian morality?

Two Song Poets: Su Dongpo and Li Qingzhao

The selections of Chinese poetry included in The World of Literature conclude with the writings of two remarkable Song dynasty poets, Su Dongpo and Li Qingzhao. The tradition was to continue and has even flourished up to the present time. But Su Dongpo and Li Qingzhao are good representatives with which to end our consideration of this great poetic tradition precisely because they reflect with such clarity and power so many of the tradition's major characteristics and themes. It is admittedly difficult to teach these two poets, despite their directness and relative lack of the kinds of allusions that complicate Tang poetry. The problem is that both Su and Li are exceedingly mature poets—both are struggling with loss and disappointment and are finding comfort in simple things (see Su's "White Crane Hill" and Li's "The Beauty of White Chrysanthemums"). Young students sometimes have difficulty with the tone of quiet sorrow that pervades so many of these verses. It is well to remind them of several circumstances beyond the understandable sorrow that each poet feels at the loss of a beloved mate (Su's "Ten years—dead and living dim and draw apart" and Li's "Thoughts from the Women's Quarters"). First, there existed no strong belief in an afterlife in elite Chinese thought—at least not in the sense of a Christian or an Islamic heaven. One treasured life and the human memory which kept the past and the people one loved alive and watched these slowly slip away with some pain and nostalgia (rarely with rage, though, since one always knew this would happen!). Second, the "official" philosophy, which was imbibed in youth in the form of the Classics, was essentially optimistic. That is, it held out the possibility for constant self-cultivation and growth and taught, moreover, that a good man (invariably a man in this case) could and should serve the state and serve in a way that would benefit both the emperor and the people. But one's actual experience of such service so frequently brought disillusionment for it was filled always with stress and often with danger and made one long for the security of home. Moreover, the government servant was sometimes required to compromise his values, a problem presented poignantly in Su's "New Year's Eve II." Thus it is, also, that Su bemoans "Not staying a herdsman all my life" and elsewhere says that he may look like an official "but inside I'm not."

There are important moments in these poems when Su and Li reflect on poetry itself. Su notes that poetry, like painting, should reflect "[c]lean freshness and effortless skill." The two arts of painting and poetry were considered in Tang and Song China to be intimately intertwined, and many great poets, Su included, were also known as great painters. Since so many of China's greatest landscape paintings come from the Song period, it works well for the teacher to show a slide or two of famous Song paintings and ask the students to reflect on any aesthetic or thematic resemblances they discern in these two ostensibly quite separate art forms. Li's comment on poetry is the realization of the poet's power as she memorializes a chrysanthemum that "will fade but be remembered in this poem" (and in this sense will join with the orchids of Qu Yuan and the chrysanthemums of Tao Qian). The words of the poet, she understands, freeze time and thereby preserve whatever they memorialize—a fact the great French poet Ronsard (1524-1585) also knew well, although his most famous expression of this concerned a woman and not a flower:

> When you are very old, at eve, by candlelight,
> Sitting by the fire to unwind your skein and spin,
> You'll sing my verses, and in wonderment will say:
> 'Ronsard so honored me when I was young and fair.'
>
> Then every servant girl of yours, on hearing this,
> Thenceforth, though she be half asleep at humdrum toil,
> Will rouse herself to listen when she hears my name
> And lines that bless your name with everlasting praise.
> (The Muse Spoke French, Santa Maria CA, 1994; p. 31)

A fascinating question is the degree to which one can or cannot discern a specifically female voice in Li Qingzhao's work. Surely she had thoroughly mastered the conventions of a poetic tradition largely shaped by men and was widely admired by male readers or it is doubtful her work would have been preserved. Surely, also, the narrative voice in her poems is female, but male poets in China often appropriated the female voice (Qu Yuan is a noteworthy example). And surely her poems are unusual, with an emotional intensity rarely matched elsewhere in the Chinese tradition. But the question remains open as to whether one can identify something distinctively female about her poetry.

For more of Su Dongpo's poetry, see Burton Watson's translation: Su Tung-p'o: Selections from a Sung Dynasty Poet (New York, 1965). Lin Yutang's famous study, The Gay Genius (New York, 1947), though somewhat popularized, is a good read. Kenneth Rexroth and Ling Chung have translated all of Li's poems in Li Qingzho: Complete Poems (New York, 1979). On the issue raised in question five below, see Timothy Wixted, "The Poetry of Li Ch'ing-chao: A Woman Author and Women's Authorship," in Pauline Yu, Voices of the Song Lyric in China (Berkeley, 1993).

Questions for Study and Discussion:

1. What is the function of dreams in these poems and what associations does dreaming seem to have here and elsewhere in the Chinese tradition?

2. There is an immense amount of longing for the countryside throughout the Chinese tradition going back at least to Tao Qian and expressed here by Su's "Long Ago I lived in the Country." How do you explain this emotion, and how would you compare Chinese longing for the countryside with what one so often encounters in the Western tradition?

3. As so often throughout the earlier Tang period, Tao Qian appears as an ideal in Su's poetry. Why would the image of Tao Qian be a particularly important but painful one for Su Dongpo?

4. Li Qingzhao's poem "A Morning Dream" is not only intensely personal but can also be read as intensely political. Discuss the intertwining of the personal and the political in this dream of encountering the immortals An Ch'i-sheng and O Lü-hua.

5. Why would a poet like Li Qingzhao claim that she has "No fine poetic thoughts" in the midst of what is obviously a very fine poem ("On Plum Blossoms")?

Wu Cheng'en
Monkey

Journey to the West (or in Waley's translation "Monkey") is often categorized as one of the six great novels of Ming/Qing China (fourteenth through nineteenth centuries). The other one these six represented in the anthology is Dream of the Red Chamber (the remaining four being Romance of the Three Kingdoms, Chin Ping Mei or Golden Lotus, Water Margin, and The Scholars). The rise of the novel in China roughly corresponds temporally with the rise of the novel in the West and might have been stimulated by some of the same factors, urbanization one of the most important of these. It is noteworthy that Wu Cheng'en (1506-1582), the author of

Journey to the West, was a slightly older contemporary of the great Spanish novelist Miguel De Cervantes (1547-1616) and their masterpieces have certain similarities. First of all, Don Quixote and Monkey might both be labeled "picaresque novels," although in some ways Journey to the West satisfies the stricter definition of this term better than Don Quixote, and each abounds with humor. Second, both of the central characters in these two novels, Don Quixote and Tripitika, are regularly upstaged by their memorable companions, Sancho Panza and Monkey, two of the most unforgettable creations of world literature. Third, as C. T. Hsia has noted, both are works of "satiric fantasy grounded in realistic observation and philosophical wisdom" (see Hsia reference noted below, p. 116). However, there are striking differences too. Journey to the West, although deriving ultimately from a historical event, takes place on a cosmic scale and ultimately deals, often on an allegorical level, with the search for salvation within a Buddhist doctrinal framework. Don Quixote is concerned with quite different issues—the relationship between illusion and reality (not absent from Journey to the West but not the major theme), and the genre of romance writing itself, etc. Still, these two works can be read and discussed side by side as important landmarks in the rise of the novel, a genre that will eventually dominate the literary world in both the East and the West.

The marks of an oral story-telling tradition are obvious in Journey to the West and in the other early Chinese novels. Certain historical events, in this case the amazing journey in the seventh century to India of the Buddhist monk Xuan Zang (called "Tripitika" in Waley's translation), caught the popular imagination and became the basis for stories, typically told in a public market, which were then strung together into story cycles. Since the earliest Chinese novels develop from this process, they often appear as a series of episodes bound together almost entirely by the presence of the same characters and little else. In this case, however, the numerous episodes (let us not forget that the full English translation runs to four volumes) are emplotted by the fact that the travelers have as their goal India, the land of the Buddha, the home of the scriptures, and, in a very important sense, the source of salvation.

The character Monkey upstages Tripitika in the novel. In fact, the pious monk, who is based upon a historical figure of enormous perseverance and courage, is turned into a rather passive and at times cowardly figure who only succeeds on his journey largely because of his animal helpers, Monkey the most important of these. The ultimate origin of the character Monkey is something of a mystery, although some have suggested the idea for such a figure may derive ultimately from Hanuman, the monkey hero of the Ramayana, another work with which Journey to the West might be compared. Monkey represents impetuosity, rebelliousness, an abundance of life that is not always properly contained. He is almost always lovable; and also almost always out of control. He is also very funny, and it is probably the humor of the novel as much as anything else that has attracted so many Chinese readers. In fact, one useful approach to the two brief chapters of this novel included in the anthology is to focus on the character of Monkey and consider precisely what there might be in Monkey that has made him a figure of the popular imagination known to young and old alike in China for almost five centuries.

A useful introduction to the Chinese novel, with a provocative chapter on Journey to the West, is C. T. Hsia, The Classic Chinese Novel: A Critical Introduction (New York, 1968). A more scholarly, updated study is that of Anthony Plaks in Four Masterworks of the Ming Novel: Ssu ta ch'i-shu (Princeton, 1987). Anthony Yu's complete translation of this novel is a masterpiece, and his introduction is particularly useful: Journey to the West, 4 volumes (Chicago, 1977-1983).

Questions for Study and Discussion:

1. Discuss the element of social satire in these chapters, particularly as they pertain to the family and the problem of the son-in-law.

2. Pigsy represents lust and gluttony, just as Monkey represents impetuosity and rebelliousness. However, Wu Cheng'en also makes Pigsy, as well as Monkey, a humorous and very endearing character. Discuss humor in the story and how that softens the allegorical, religious intent that serious readers have so often found in the novel.

3. A striking feature of this novel, and one that makes it rather unusual within the Chinese tradition, is the way it mixes the most fantastic elements (the fights, for example, which invariably become contests of magical power) with the most mundane (e.g., an obsession with bodily functions). How do the fantastic and the realistic intertwine in this chapter and what affect does this have on the reader?

4. What might Mr. Kao and his daughter represent? (They are, after all, witless players—perhaps we should say victims—in a cosmic drama.)

The Kojiki

The creation myths of Japan make a striking contrast to the Biblical stories of creation. Instead of a single, omnipotent, and transcendent God, the Japanese version of creation shows us something much more human: a male and female couple who create the world through acts of procreation. They proceed in a rather hit and miss experimental fashion until they get it right. Probably the most effective way to engage these myths is to pick out the story line of each segment. While the stories may seem cluttered with unfamiliar images and symbols, students should be reminded that in mythology everything means something, even if we do not know what that meaning is. We are challenged to interpret these images in significant ways, rather than simply writing them off as "alien," hence unintelligible. Once the story lines have been identified, students can go back and discuss the details of imagery to see how these enhance the story.

For comparable stories of creation, see Genesis in the bible, the "Hymn of Creation" from the Indian Rig Veda, Hesiod's Theogony, and the Mayan Popul Vuh. For comparable stories of the descent to the underworld see The Descent of Inanna and the Mayan account of "[The Hero Twins in the Underworld]." Although not included in this volume, the familiar story of Orpheus and Euridice also provides a useful comparison, and is represented in Ezra Pound's Canto I. (Pound's Canto, it will be recalled, is a translation of Book XI of the Odyssey.)

There are very few secondary sources or commentaries on the Kojiki in Western languages, even in specialized academic journals. The translation here might be read in conjunction with Donald Phillipi's translation (Princeton, 1969) to note important differences in expression. Otherwise, by making comparisons and contrasts with creation myths from other cultures, and by consulting more general works on creation mythology, one can find these stories quite accessible. As an aid toward this end, see Joseph Campbell's The Masks of God: Creative Mythology (New York, 1976).

Questions for Study and Discussion:

1. In the stories presented here we see two distinct cycles. In the account of Izanagi and Izanami the female figure is clearly given a subordinate role, whereas in the story of Amaterasu and Susanoo, the female deity is given the predominant role. How might we account for this reversal?

2. When Izanami gives birth to the fire deity, she is burned and dies. When Izanagi tries to bring her back from the land of the dead, what parallels are visible with the Greek story of Orpheus and Euridice or the myth of Demeter and Persephone? Are there similar myths in other parts of the world?

3. When Izanami pursues Izanagi back to the land of the living we are seeing a struggle between the forces of life and death. What images or actions suggest life force? How are the forces of death represented?

4. When Izanagi returns to the land of the living he bathes to purify himself from the pollution of death. Specifically, he washes, in turn, his left eye which has seen the corruption of death, and this produces the sun goddess, Amaterasu; his right eye, which produces the moon god; and his nose, which has smelled the corruption of death, and produces the storm god, Susanoo. Consider the symbolism of these newly created deities.

5. Early Japan was characterized by a communal farming society. When we look at Susanoo's transgressions, how do these reflect crimes that would be considered intolerable to an agricultural community?

6. After Susanoo is banished to the earth for his crimes, he ceases to be a trouble making renegade and becomes a heroic figure who saves the farmer's treasure. How can we account for this transformation?

7. When the farmer's daughter is threatened by the eight-headed, eight-tailed serpent, what does the serpent represent? Why is Susanoo, the god of storm and rain, the appropriate deity to subdue the serpent?

8. The story of Amaterasu hiding in the rock cave reflects a prehistoric solstice ritual. What parallels might we see between this and the Western Christmas or Hanukkah celebrations which also coincide with the solstice?

The Manyōshū

The poetry of the Manyōshū (the title means "a collection of ten thousand leaves") is remarkable within Japan's literary tradition for the variety of form, content, and language it displays. After the Manyōshū, and until modern times, virtually all Japanese poetry was either thirty-one syllable tanka or the even shorter seventeen syllable haiku. The Manyōshū is the only place where we find choka, the longer poetic form. After the Manyōshū, poetry content was dominated by a demand for elegance in imagery and vocabulary and by a high degree of subjectivity. Poetry was used exclusively to express the poet's feelings. Only in the Manyōshū do we find occasional poetry celebrating public events at court, poetry which provides social criticism, or poetry of the common people. All traditional Japanese poetry falls into an alternating five and seven syllable meter, but Manyōshū poetry has a range and freshness of vocabulary and image not found in later poetry.

The poetry in this collection can be usefully compared to other collections of Japanese poetry, such as the court poetry and haiku. These poems can also be compared to the great verse of Tang China, in which one can identify examples of poetic borrowing. And, of course, Japanese poetry can be contrasted to the poetry of India, Arabic, and Persian poetry, as well as to more familiar European poetry.

For further examples of Manyōshū poetry, see the anthology, Manyōshū (Princeton, 1981), published by Princeton University. For a detailed discussion of many of the poems presented here, see Robert Brower and Earl Miner, Japanese Court Poetry (London, 1961). A slightly more recent volume is Edwin A. Cranston's The Courtly Tradition in Japanese Art and Literature (Cambridge, 1973). For a study of the life of Hitomaro, see, Ian H. Levy, Hitomaro and the Birth of Japanese Lyricism (Princeton, 1984).

Questions for Study and Discussion:

1. In Hitomaro's poem "Imperial Procession," identify the many examples of parallelism and show how they work to reinforce the celebratory message of the poem.

2. Consider the envoy(s) attached to the long poems and the way they serve to draw attention to and crystalize certain meanings in the poem.

3. In Hitomaro's "Lament on Leaving His Wife," identify three stages of separation as the poet makes his departure from his beloved.

4. In "Lament on Leaving His Wife," notice how the poet raises his grief to cosmic proportions, eventually speaking in terms of the movements of the sun and the moon, then abruptly brings the reader back to his immediate and intensely felt grief.

5. Consider Tabito's poems in praise of wine and see if you can identify a Daoist worldview borrowed from China.

6. In Okura's "Dialog of the Destitute," identify the speeches of the two speakers and compare their relative levels of destitution. Notice how one man finds some modest comforts even in poverty, whereas the other finds causes for intense chagrin, what are they? What are the one man's comforts and the other's regrets?

7. Although the "Songs from the East Country" were written long ago in a country far away, how distant are the sentiments they express or the images they use from your own experience?

Japanese Court Poetry

Japanese court poetry reflects a thousand year tradition of literary production in Japan and, indeed, these poems are still being written today. This poetry is exclusively in the 31 syllable form of the tanka and the poems themselves are dominated by what one critic has called "the tyranny of elegance." What was considered elegant in terms of image, sentiment, or vocabulary was strictly banned from this body of literature. While nature imagery is the norm for these poems, it is important to realize that nature serves only as a vehicle to reflect the feelings of the poet; no attempt is made to give an objective description of nature. As we move from the poems of the Kokinshu (905 CE) to the poems of the Shin Kokinshu (1210 CE) we see a pervasive and increasing tone of melancholy in the works. One of the characteristics of these poems is that they were written with the expectation that they would be interpreted in a variety of ways, and therefore they often have a resonance which lends itself to multiple interpretations.

There are several ways to begin working with the poetry in this selection. In the poem cycle formed by the last thirteen poems in this entry, one could, for example, try to identify the images and meanings of the poems that illuminate the process of association and progression that link one poem to the next. The common theme shared by these poems is the first stirring of love. In this case, it is an uncertain and one-sided affair, but gradually we see the lover acknowledging his feelings toward his beloved, even though she may not be aware of his feelings. Although literary historians today have not clearly or fully identified the principles of association and progression that link these poems, we know from ancient commentaries that such principles governed the arrangement of poems in contemporary anthologies. Students can be challenged to follow a line of progression and association in the poems presented here. The clearest example of progression can be seen in the last four poems of the sequence, which follow the seasonal development: from winter snow to the cherry blossoms of spring, to the willow shoots of later spring, to the rainy season of early summer. This is emblematic of passion, as it grows from cold indifference to mild feelings of love, then toward the summer heat of full passion. In most cases, however, the poems are linked in pairs, as we can see by comparing Fujiwara Teika's poem "Yesterday, today" with Emperor Komyo's poem "How strange it is." The line "Yesterday, today" in the first poem corresponds to the phrase "These days" in the second. Both poems speak of a "vacant reverie." And although it is not apparent from the translations, both poems employ the verb omou, meaning to feel love. This is continued in the next poem in the sequence by Lady Reizei, which also uses the reverie, the feelings, and the words that show time as "days spent." Thus, there is a common theme of beginning love running though the whole sequence, a progression of images that is seen intermittently, and an association formed by shared vocabulary linking adjacent poems. These principles are often hard to see in Japanese and may be impossible when filtered through translation, but it is important to know that the poems are not placed randomly.

Within the Japanese tradition these poems can be contrasted to the earlier poetry of the Manyōshū and the later haiku poetry. Comparisons and contrasts might also be made with the longer, more socially engaged poetry of China, the poetry of Korea, the poetry of India, and to the poetic traditions of Europe.

For a detailed discussion of the conventions of this poetry, including aesthetics and possible interpretations, see Robert Brower and Earl Miner, Japanese Court Poetry (London, 1961) and Arthur Waley, Japanese Poetry: the Uta (Oxford, 1919). For a discussion of the way these short poems can be linked in sequence, see Robert Brower, Fujiwara Teika's Hundred-Poem Sequence of the Shoji Era (Tokyo, 1978). For further examples of this poetry, see Helen

McCullough's Kokin Wakashu (Stanford, 1985) and Laurel Rasplica Rodd's Kokinshu (Princeton, 1984).

Questions for Study and Discussion:

1. A 31-syllable poem is miniscule by the standards of most of the world's poetry. In what way can such short poems be meaningful? Can these even be regarded as poetry, or should they rather be considered as epigrams?

2. What are the images used in Japanese court poetry and how do they compare with those used in the earlier collection, The Manyōshū, and in the poetry of other nations? Court poetry was strictly controlled by what some have called the "tyranny of elegance." In contrast to The Manyōshū, with its often powerful images, we should keep in mind in addressing this and other questions that the court poetry is unrelievedly elegant as a result of a restriction of themes and even vocabulary considered suitable for poetry.

3. How is a complex theme such as religion dealt with in such brief poetry? For one thing, the poems show a primacy of feeling over thought as a way of viewing the world—a highly subjective stance. The brief flashes of insight found in these poems might be likened to the Zen experience of satori. (The poem "What now is real?" seems especially to reveal religious insight.)

4. To offset the brevity of a 31-syllable poetic form, Japanese poets resorted to strategies of complexity available through double meanings, word association, allusion, and resonance to make these poems more meaningful. From among the poems presented, identify examples of each of these techniques.

5. How do these poems reflect humankind's relationship to the natural world? Notice that the poet does not try to give us a detailed or objective description of nature; rather, with a zoom lens focus, he picks out details that reflect the poet's feelings at the moment.

Izumi Shikibu
The Diary of Lady Izumi Shikibu

Students will find this diary account of a love affair very accessible. While some of the conventions of Japanese courtly love may seem exotic (soaking one's sleeves with tears until they rot away, for example), most of the issues that concern these lovers are universal. In this case, we see the lovers' concern for discretion. In the beginning, at least, they cannot flaunt their relationship. When the Prince comes one night to visit Lady Izumi and finds someone else's carriage parked in front of her house, we can immediately share his disappointment. We see over and over the uncertainty and misgivings expressed by each partner. Neither wants to make a commitment to the relationship without first being sure that the other partner is equally committed. At other times we see the compulsion that draws these two together despite their doubts.

One obvious approach to this text is to compare the courtship rituals found in this account to the courtship practices we follow today. One can also find a wealth of comparisons between courtly love as it was practiced in Japan and courtly love in other cultures. One might look at the stories of Marie de France, for example, or, for sharply contrastive modes of self-analysis, Augustine's or Rousseau's Confessions.

Although little has been written in English to provide interpretation or commentary on Lady Izumi Shikubu's diary, there is a wealth of other diaries by other Japanese court ladies. These include Richard Bowring's translation of Murasaki Shikibu: Her Diary and Poetic Memoirs (Princeton, 1982), Ivan Morris's translation of As I Crossed the Bridge of Dreams (New York, 1973), and Edward Seidensticker's translation of The Gossamer Years (Rutland, VT, 1964). For general background on the mores and customs of Japanese court society see Ivan Morris, The World of the Shining Prince (New York, 1994).

The passage presented here does not celebrate the fulfillment of a love relationship, but rather deals with the difficult and uncertain process involved in bringing the lovers together. Consider the problems these lovers need to overcome. In the first place, he is already married and although this is a polygamous society, the Prince's involvement with Lady Izumi causes a strain in his relationship with his wife. In the second place, he is the Crown Prince and of much higher rank than she, and therefore some regard the relationship as inappropriate. His old wet nurse advises that he simply make Lady Izumi his servant and then he can do with her as he will, rather than treat her with the more exalted status of lover. In the third place, he believes (mistakenly perhaps) that she has other lovers and so is cautious about making a commitment that may not be reciprocated. She, for her part, feels considerable chagrin that she has a reputation to live down—a reputation as a promiscuous and fickle woman.

It is also useful to consider the images of love expressed in this diary. The moon is often seen as being emblematic of the Prince. In a variety of ways Lady Izumi makes this association in her poems. The mournful cry of the wild geese crossing the autumn sky is emblematic of separated lovers. This is an association that goes back to a Chinese legend of a man being held prisoner in a far northern country who sent a poem of love to his wife by tying it to the leg of a migrating goose. Dipping salt water at the seashore at Sode is an expression of the salt tears of grief that soak her sleeves. Sode is a place name, but another word, sode, means sleeves.

It is worth noting that Japanese love poetry only rarely expresses the enthusiasm that lovers experience when they are in each others' arms. For the most part, the poems express the melancholy of separation. Either the lovers are apart, yearning for each other, or, if they are together, the poems anticipate their imminent separation. This notion that love is grief and separation rather than joy and fulfillment comes from the Buddhist notion that the nature of human existence is suffering and that all relationships are transitory. Japanese literary lovers never live happily ever after.

Questions for Study and Discussion:

1. What are the frustrations the woman feels in this courtship? For one thing, her role is fairly passive. The Prince comes to visit her—or he does not come to visit her, or some other man comes to visit her, but she cannot go to visit him. If he does not come, the only thing she can do is write to him and express her disappointment and hope that he will be moved by her entreaty. On one occasion he shows up unexpectedly and she is embarrassed because she is not prepared to receive him. On another occasion, he arrives late at night, but the servants are slow to answer the door and he goes away. She can't get up and answer the door herself although she is eager to

do so. In the end she attracts him through her displays of decorum, refinement and sensibility, but this only works if he recognizes these qualities in her.

2. We might ask why Prince Atsumichi is attracted to Lady Izumi? We are told that she was a beautiful woman and an excellent poet. She had also been his older brother's lover. Is there any evidence in this passage that he is merely curious to sample his brother's one time lover? Does she express any concern that he may only be interested in her out of curiosity rather than true affection?

3. The lovers' feelings are often intimately tied to nature and the passing of the seasons. What examples do we see of this? At one point when the endless, dreary rain falls, dampening her spirits and apparently keeping her lover from visiting her, she gazes out at the rain and feels melancholy. The Japanese word nagame, which means "to gaze vacantly," is a near homophone of nagaame, which translates as "a long or endless rain." Through this sort of wordplay the author ties her feelings and responses to the natural cycle.

Murasaki Shikibu
The Tale of Genji

The Tale of Genji deals with the twin issues of political competition and amorous competition at the Japanese court. Although we have presented only two chapters of this massive work, they are key chapters. The first goes far in outlining the heroic yet problematic destiny of Prince Genji. The second shows consequences of his many amorous entanglements. This long romance can also be read as a detailed psychological study as we follow the career of Prince Genji and watch him come to terms with himself and the meaning of his own life. This most perfectly endowed of all men turns out to be vulnerable in all sorts of ways. This work can also be read as a novel of manners depicting for us in great detail what life was like in the Japanese court of the eleventh century. Finally, this tale can be read as a guidebook showing the finest examples of what it meant to be a courtier or a court lady within that society.

In the tradition of Japanese literature we can see another example of life at court in the Izumi Shikibu Diary. For comparable texts in other cultures, see the Lais of Marie de France and The Thousand and One Nights, where an enclosed world of women is controlled by aristocratic men.

For further background on the customs and mores of the Japanese court, see Ivan Morris, World of the Shining Prince (New York, 1994). For commentaries and interpretations of The Tale of Genji see Norma Field, The Splendor of Longing in The Tale of Genji (Princeton, 1987), Haruo Shirane, The Bridge of Dreams: A Poetics of The Tale of Genji (Stanford, 1987), and Amanda M. Stinchecum, Narrative Voice in The Tale of Genji (New York, 1980). In order to see how The Tale of Genji served as a source for the No theater see, Janet Goff, Noh Drama and The Tale of Genji (Princeton, 1991). For a study of the phenomenon of spirit possession see Doris G. Bargen, A Woman's Weapon: Spirit Possession in The Tale of Genji (Honolulu, 1997).

Questions for Study and Discussion:

1. How are the two themes of amorous love and political competition outlined or established in the first chapter? When Lady Kiritsubo, a lady of low rank, is raised to inappropriately high status as the Emperor's favorite, she incurs the jealous wrath of other ladies. More significantly, because her relationship with the Emperor, by its nature and intensity, is beyond reason, the very moral balance of society is disrupted, a dislocation that cannot be corrected in less than three generations.

2. In the first chapter, many allusions are made to the Chinese story of the beautiful courtesan Yang Kuei Fei, whose analogous love affair leads to revolution and the collapse of the state. Consider comparisons between these two texts.

3. Lady Kiritsubo has replaced Lady Kokiden in the Emperor's affections. Does Lady Kokiden feel threatened and how does she respond? There is an implicit suggestion that she is behind the torments aimed at her rival Lady Kiritsubo. After Kiritsubo's death, Kokiden refuses to observe mourning and instead plays music far into the night, showing her contempt for the dead lady. Kokiden also takes steps to insure that her own son is not displaced from his position as Crown Prince.

4. One of the functions of the first chapter is to establish Genji's credentials as a heroic figure. What evidence is there of this? He is set apart from others not only by his personal beauty and talents, but also by the fact that he has never known his mother's love. Also, his future—a paradoxical one—is predicted by a visiting Korean sage and verified by both Indian and Japanese fortune tellers.

5. In the "Evening Faces" chapter we have two of Genji's loves contrasted: the beautiful, proud, and powerful Lady Rokujo versus the beautiful, timid, and vulnerable Lady of the Evening Faces. What comparisons do we see between these ladies and the rivalry seen earlier between Lady Kiritsubo and Lady Kokiden?

6. Genji deserts Rokujo in favor of Evening Faces only to lose her, too. What do we learn of Genji's character from this episode? What does Genji learn about himself? Genji pursued Rokujo precisely because she is older, above his station, and beyond his reach. Having succeeded in winning her love, his interest in her fails. What is there about Rokujo that causes Genji to turn away from her? Why does Genji find Evening Faces an attractive alternative? At the end of this chapter Genji has lost both women; does he seem to realize that he cannot control his own destiny, much less that of others?

7. The death of the Lady of the Evening Faces comes at the hands of her jealous rival, Lady Rokujo, who has been betrayed and abandoned by Genji. Consider the victims in this affair. Certainly the meek Evening Faces is a victim, but so is Rokujo—a victim of Genji's indifference and also a victim of her own jealous rage. Is it surprising that Genji, who caused all this grief, does not appear to pay a price?

8. Genji is a married man at the time of his affairs with Lady Rokujo and the Lady of the Evening Faces. Does he face any consequences as a result of his multiple adulteries? What does this tell us about marital relations in courtly Japan?

9. One of the lessons Genji learns much later in the tale is that no matter how privileged he may be, he cannot hold on forever to those things he cherishes most. Is there any evidence that Genji has even a flicker of this awareness at this point in his life?

10. As a romantic hero, Genji is endowed with everything a person could want: wealth, power, talent, and beauty. Paradoxically, he fails to possess those things he most cherishes: a mother's love, a wife's love, an enduring lover, political power. Consider this aspect of his tale.

Kamo no Chōmei
An Account of My Hermitage

At one time or another everyone dreams of getting away from everything. Chōmei's essay allows us to consider that possibility. Students faced with the demands and cares of daily life, many of them on their own for the first time, find this work appealing in much the same way that Thoreau's Walden is appealing. Chōmei was a sophisticated and intelligent man who lived in an age of great turbulence, but who was nevertheless able to find a life of peace and serenity. His essay is an invitation to examine our own lives and reconsider our own ambitions and values.

Chōmei is certainly not alone in celebrating the simple life. His essay can usefully be compared to the work of Bashō, Tao Q'ian, Montaigne, and Henry David Thoreau. Within its immediate context of Japanese literature this essay can also be contrasted to the Tales of the Heike, where we see the fruit of unbridled ambition, competition and strife. Or it can be read alongside The Tale of Genji, where Prince Genji frequently speaks of renouncing the world for a life of religious simplicity, but never goes through with it because his world is simply too beautiful to abandon. For an important source to Chōmei's essay, see the Vimalakīrti Sutra.

For an interpretation and commentary on Chōmei's essay, see William LaFleur's, The Karma of Words (Berkeley, 1983). For a general background to the period see Donald Keene's, Seeds in the Heart (New York, 1993).

Questions for Study and Discussion:

1. Consider the trade-offs Chōmei has to make by choosing a life of seclusion. Does he seem to have any regrets or misgivings about the life he leaves behind? Does he recomend his simple lifestyle for everyone? Does he suggest that society would be a better place if all people made the choice he has made?

2. The disasters Chōmei cites which bring grief to men's lives are all natural phenomena and beyond the control of men to prevent or avoid. Chōmei contrasts these disasters with the pleasures of music and poetry. Is his argument persuasive? Can music and poetry be meaningful without an audience?

4. Throughout his essay Chōmei links men and their dwellings, the dwelling being the measure of humankind's success in the world. In Japanese the term *ie* refers both to the house one lives in and also to the family that lives in the house. What are the implications of this dual meaning for Chōmei's argument in favor of seclusion?

5. At the end of his essay Chōmei makes a reference to "the abode of the honorable Yuima." Yuima is the Japanese rendering of Saint Vimalakīrti, and the reference here is to the Vimalakīrti Sutra. Consider Chōmei's argument in light of the message of the Vimalakīrti Sutra. According to the sutra, the conflict caused by duality can only be resolved by silence, not debate.

6. By invoking Yuima (Saint Vimalakīrti), Chōmei not only undercuts his own argument in favor of a life of seclusion, but challenges the whole notion that truth can be expressed in words or through words. Contrast this with the notion expressed in the Gospel of John that "In the beginning was the Word, and the Word was with God, and the Word was God," where "the [w]ord" (logos) is given a primacy that makes it equivalent to God.

Tales of the Heike

Tales of the Heike is one of the world's great war epics and can be usefully compared to The Illiad, The Rāmāyana or to the Norse Sagas. At the same time, this work displays features uniquely expressive of Japanese culture. The accounts of the war told in these narratives were originally recited orally by blind, itinerant priests much like the troubadours of medieval Europe. Because these narrators were priests, the work has a distinctly religious tone. We see, for example, in the opening lines a homily that is illustrated over and over in the subsequent accounts. The message of the homily is that those in this world who are great and powerful will surely be brought low and become as dust before the wind. Consider how each character in these passages, Lady Gio, Tadanori, Koremori, and Lady Kenreimon'in, have experiences which reflect the truth of this homily.

Tales of the Heike not only chronicles the fall of the Taira (Heike) family, but in a broader sense laments the loss of culture—the loss of all that is good and beautiful in the world as the forces of brutishness and violence prevail. In this light, comparisons can be made with the Arthurian tales of the loss of Camelot and parallels can be made with Gone with the Wind, both of which mourn the loss of similarly elegant cultures. Comparison might also be made with the struggle depicted in the Ramayana, and to the Shāh-nāmah, which, like Tales of the Heike, ends tragically.

For the literary and historical context of this work see Donald Keene, Seeds in the Heart (New York, 1993), particularly the chapters "Tales of Warfare" and "Medieval War Tales." For other Japanese war tales see Helen McCullough's translations of The Taiheiki (New York, 1959) and Yoshitsune (Stanford, 1966). For background on the construction of this literature of warfare see Barbara Ruch, "Medieval Jongleurs and the Making of a National Literature," in John Whitney Hall and Toyoda Takeshi, Japan in the Muromachi Age (Berkeley, 1977). For a general history of the age see George Sansom, A History of Japan (Stanford, 1963).

Questions for Study and Discussion:

1. The civil war that provides the basis for these tales marks the beginning of samurai culture in Japan. What do these accounts tell us about the characteristics of the ideal warrior?

2. Consider how the experiences of Lady Gio, the dancing girl, serve as a microcosm for the entire work. What parallels can we draw between Lady Gio in the opening chapters and Lady Kenreimon'in at the conclusion of this long work?

3. Buddhism teaches the futility and evanescence of human endeavor. Knowing this, the heroes of this work nevertheless commit themselves to worldly glory and to experiencing life to its last full—and often bitter—dregs. What motivates Sanemori, an old man, to go into battle and contend with younger adversaries? What does he accomplish?

4. Tadanori and Koremori are both poets and warriors. Discuss how each is depicted in these episodes, looking specifically at how they compare to one another and how they compare to warrior heroes in other traditions. Consider in each case what are their most cherished values and their deepest ambitions.

5. Buddhism teaches that there are six paths or levels of sentient existence: the realm of heaven, the realm of mankind, the realm of hungry spirits, the realm of the asura kings, and the realm of the hottest hells. There is also the realm of animal existence to which Lady Kenreimon'in does not refer. Normal progress would be from the lower regions to the higher. Discuss how Lady Kenreimon'in's life trajectory has followed an opposite course.

6. The retired Emperor Go-Shirakawa survived the war with his status intact. When he comes to Ohara to visit Lady Kenreimon'in, he represents a mirror which reflects the worldly power and glory which she has lost. Can he be considered a winner in this context or a loser? Why?

Nō Theatre
Atsumori and Aoi no Ue

To more fully understand the literature in this section of the text, it may be useful to walk the students through the setup of a Noh stage. The stage is a bare platform with a walkway approaching from stage right. The only setting is a pine tree painted on the back wall. There is no curtain. The musicians enter the stage in silence and tune their instruments. Following this, the chorus enters from a small side door and takes its place at stage left. The secondary actor enters and introduces himself and the play to the audience. At last, the main actor enters and the play is enacted. Afterwards, the actors leave, followed by the chorus and the musicians, so that all that remains at the end is the empty stage the audience saw at the beginning—along with the memory of the play that was performed.

Noh theater has often been compared with classical Greek theater. It may be useful to compare a Noh play with a Greek drama, focusing on the respective roles of the chorus, the notions of protagonist and antagonist, and the concepts of conflict and resolution in each. Toward this end, students should be directed to Euripedes's The Bacchae in this anthology. Alternatively, Atsumori can be usefully compared to episodes of conflict in the Tales of the Heike. Students will notice how the Noh plays—written two centuries after the events described in the Heike—reflect a more developed sense of the samurai ethic of Medieval Japan. There are also interesting links between these examples of Noh theater and the Kālidāsa. Finally, students might also be asked to consider the influence of Noh theater on two hugely important modernist writers in English, William Yeats and Ezra Pound.

For more examples of Noh plays, see Karen Brazell's Twelve Plays of the Noh and Kyogen (Ithaca, NY, 1988) and Donald Keene's Twenty Plays of the Nō Theater (New York, 1970). For a comparative study of Noh and Greek drama, see Mae J. Smethurst's The Artistry of Aeschylus and Zeami (Princeton, 1989).

Questions for Study and Discussion:

1. The introduction to these plays mentions that the Noh theater does not have a protagonist and antagonist as we see them in Western theater, and that the plays generally do not end with a clear statement of victor and vanquished. Given these differences, what is finally resolved in these plays?

2. In Atsumori, the encounter between the two former warriors is presented only as a memory, and this distance from reality privileges elements of refinement and elegance. As the values of the warrior society developed historically, it became imperative to balance the necessary brutality of the samurai warrior's work with sensibility and refinement. What example of these characteristics do we see exhibited by the warrior Atsumori?

3. A Noh play is often constructed around a central metaphor. In Aoi no Ue, that central image is the wheel; in Atsumori, it is the flute. How do these key metaphors enrich each play, or do they merely distract from the story being enacted?

4. Both plays presented here involve the intercession of a Buddhist priest. What roles do they play? (Note that in Aoi no Ue, we get a glimpse of the religious diversity of Japan. A shamanistic medium is used to summon the malignant spirit, but a Buddhist priest is required to confront the spirit and negotiate a resolution. In Atsumori, by contrast, the priest both summons the restless spirit and negotiates the resolution—making him directly responsible for the spirit's grief. Indeed, the whole encounter between priest and warrior may only be taking place in the remorseful memory of the priest. From this perspective, the priest may be seen as subduing his own demon.)

5. In both plays we have characters who have suffered grievous wrongs. Is it possible to identify a victim in either play?

6. Vengeance is a common theme in world drama. Consider how the idea of vengeance is treated in these two plays. Lady Rokujo, it will be seen, seeks vengeance on her rival in love, but the resolution of her resentment lies within herself. For his part, Atsumori seeks revenge on the man who killed him, but comes to realize that such vengeance will only restart the cycle of revenge. Only by helping each other can each man find his own salvation.

Korea in the Middle Period
Hyangga, Cho'oe Ch'i-Won, Songs of Flying Dragons, Hwang Chin-I, Hŏ Nansŏrhŏn

The poems in this section span a variety of genres. Songs of Flying Dragons could be read with any of the epics we have included, especially the Odyssey and the Aeneid. Hŏ Nansŏrhŏn's "A Woman's Sorrow" would work well with Ovid's "Dido to Aeneas" (one of the Heroides) or Pope's Eloisa to Abelard. In units on genre, or poetic form, the sijo (described below) of Hwang Chin-I might be read with Japanese haiku, to which form it is often compared. There are similarities, but there are also striking differences in the ways both forms produce their effects. The Buddhist sentiments of the Hyangga work well as illustrations of any of the works that are imbued with Buddhism in this anthology, such as The Dream of the Red Chamber.

Hyangga means, literally, "native songs." The twenty-five extant hyangga were found in two different prose narratives. Scholars are still debating the connection, if any, between the narratives and the poems. While many of the themes are Buddhist, as in the Requiem and the devotional poem included in our selections, other themes, not necessarily Buddhist, are articulated in elegies such as the Ode to Knight Chukchi. Since little is known of the authors of these poems or the circumstances of their composition, students should be encouraged to let the poems' elegant simplicity speak directly to them.

The poems we have included from the Songs of Flying Dragons come from what Peter H. Lee has called the Iliadic cantos and the cantos of remembrance of this long poem. These Iliadic cantos praise the unusual physical powers and skill of Yi Song-gye, and his "huge arrow" will immediately remind Western readers of the prodigious ashen spear of Achilles, or the unstringable bow of Odysseus. The cantos of remembrance emphasize Yi's virtuous, Confucian behavior in administering the state. Together they form a picture of the ideal Confucian hero: the soldier-statesman whose heroism and benevolence bespeak his election to rule with the Mandate of Heaven. Students should be apprised of the fact that, while the majority of the cantos of the poem are in praise of General Yi, the whole poem encompasses the deeds of four ancestors and the first (Yi) and third kings of the Yi dynasty, hence the plural "Dragons" of the title.

Hŏ Nansŏrhŏn, here represented by "A Woman's Sorrow," was an extremely gifted poet who lived a short, tragic life under the extreme subjugation of women practiced by the Confucian Choson Dynasty. This poem was written as a kasa, a new genre of vernacular verse which appeared toward the middle of the fifteenth century. It consists of words written to a pre-existing melody, and was meant to be sung with a set number of drumbeats, hand-claps, and elaborate regulations governing its phrasing. While its immediate subject is Hŏ Nansŏrhŏn's abandonment by her faithless, playboy husband, it can also be seen as a lament for all the injustices suffered by women, especially those of extraordinary sensibilities, in such a man-centered world. In both cases, it is a poignant example of what is known in Korean as han, the pure distillation of long accumulated and lingering bitterness and sorrow.

In contrast, Hwang Chin-I, despite being a woman, enjoyed favored status as a kisaeng, or professional poet-entertainer. She wrote in that most popular and characteristically Korean form, the sijo (or shijo). This form consists of three lines and six phrases. There is a strong pause in the middle of each line. The first line declares the theme, the second reinforces it, and the third usually introduces a jarring twist, or counter-theme, which casts the main theme in a new light. Peter Lee has likened its effect to that often produced by the final couplet of a Shakespearean sonnet. The English translations of the sijo that we have included in our anthology are rendered in six rather than three lines, with each line representing one of the six phrases of the original Korean poem.

Kichung Kim's An Introduction to Classical Korean Literature: from Hyangga to Pansori (Armonk, NY, 1996) is a general and highly accessible overview of Korean literature. Peter H. Lee's work, especially his Korean Literature: Topics and Themes (Tucson, AZ, 1965) and Songs of Flying Dragons: A Critical Reading (Cambridge, MA, 1975), are highly recommended. See also In-sob Zong, A Guide to Korean Literature (Elizabeth, NJ, 1982).

Questions for Study and Discussion:

1. Discuss the images and uses of nature in the Hyangga selections.

2. How do the first two poems (lines 1-8) of <u>Songs of Flying Dragons</u> relate to the poem as a whole? What is the "tree"? What is the "stream"?

3. The last lines of <u>Songs of Flying Dragons</u> is an admonishment to future monarchs. Why do you suppose the poet(s) tell any future kings to "beware"?

4. Compare the qualities of the Confucian hero, as you understand them from <u>Songs of Flying Dragons</u>, with the qualities of a Greek or Roman hero, as you understand them from either the <u>Odyssey</u> or the <u>Aeneid</u>.

5. What do you see as a common theme running through the <u>sijos</u> of Hwang Chin-I?

6. Compare the sentiments expressed in Hŏ Nansŏrhŏn's "A Woman's Sorrow" with another story of tragic love you have read. What poetic devices do the authors use to tell their story?

Augustine
Confessions

Students respond to Augustine with great interest if he is presented as an observer of the late Roman empire rather than as just a Christian thinker. Once the book has captured their interest it can be made more exciting by discussing Christian ideas in their ancient context. It works well with the ancient works that influenced it, like the Bible and the <u>Aeneid</u>, but also with medieval works it influenced, like Bede, Abelard and Heloise, Dante and Chaucer. As an autobiography—the first in the Western tradition—it works well with Abelard, Montaigne and Rousseau. Non-Western works that might be taught with it include the Japanese autobiographical works by Izumi Shikibu and Kamo no Chōmei (who writes an explanation of his withdrawal from the world) and Bashō; and from modern China, Shen Fu's <u>Six Records of a Floating Life</u>.

As autobiography, the <u>Confessions</u> has a typical narrative dynamic that students find interesting: there are two Augustines, the young one who is growing, wandering and questioning, and the mature one who is writing the book. It is not always clear whose voice we are hearing. As the book progresses, the two come closer together, and at the moment of his conversion they finally merge. Only at that point do we realize where the narrative has been leading, and why it has been structured the way it has. It turns out to be a falling away from his mother and from God, from the religion of his childhood, and a return to it—the story of a prodigal son.

Most students are startled by the importance Augustine seems to attach to the pear-tree episode, a trivial adolescent prank. Many will remember similar pranks of their own. For Augustine, it is the occasion to analyze sin and human nature; its seeming triviality makes it all the more dramatic a case. Is a minor theft any less wrong than a major one? In context, the episode substitutes for the steamy sins of adolescent sex; and some will spot the parallel with Adam and Eve taking fruit from the forbidden tree. Symbolically the episode is a replay of the

Original Sin. The essence of sin turns out to be that it is irrational, and it is also social: there was no reason for this sin, and he would not have committed it alone. Society is essentially corrupt. For Augustine, God is truth and truth is reason; un-reason (letting the lower faculties rule the higher) is one definition of sin. The gladiator episode can be analyzed very like the pear-tree: Alypius "falls" in the social atmosphere of the arena. The episode is riveting as a story of daily life in the Roman Empire, but also contributes to Augustine's theory of human nature. It is human nature to fall.

The conversion takes place under another tree: it is a Christian commonplace that we fall by one tree and rise by another (the cross). Here in another garden, Augustine struggles with a single problem: can he give up sex? It is a problem because he wants to do it, but cannot seem to. Students will recognize the issues of habit and addiction. Most of us make resolutions but cannot keep them. Why? Augustine believes human beings are free to choose, but finds himself bound by something within himself. Note the fascinating visions his imagination conjures up: continence (virginity) appears as a woman, and paradoxically a mother; and he hears the voice of a child telling him to "take and read." Is it his mother? Is it the voice of his own childhood?

Students will have heard of Augustine's theory of original sin, and his negative attitude toward sex. He may appear more interesting if they are told he is the champion of human free will, and understands that no one is perfect. Even if they dislike his culture's values, they may come to appreciate his honesty: he has nothing to hide, since God can see right through him.

Teachers and students who want to learn more about the Confessions should see Peter Brown's excellent biography of Augustine, Augustine of Hippo: A Biography (Berkeley, 1967), also a beautiful introduction to the late Classical period. Elaine Pagels' book, Adam, Eve and the Serpent (New York, 1988) is a highly authoritative, readable (and brief) introduction to Augustine's theory of sexuality, by a respected scholar who blames him for many of the ills of Western civilization.

Questions for Study and Discussion:

1. Why does Augustine steal the pears from his neighbor's tree?

2. Why does he take this prank so seriously?

3. Why do you think he chose this particular sin to illustrate his depravity and to explore the nature of sin?

4. Do you trust Augustine as a narrator? Is he honest with us, and with himself? How can you tell?

5. What are we being taught about human nature by the story of Alypius at the arena?

6. Is there a point to the story of Alypius in the marketplace, besides the interest of the dangers of everyday life in a Roman city?

7. What is Augustine's struggle in the garden all about? Why does he want to give up sex? Why can't he just do it? Why are the "chains of habit" so important to him?

8. Why do you think Continence takes the form of a woman, a chaste mother? Whose voice does he hear over the wall? Is it a vision, a hallucination, an angelic voice, an inner voice?

Bede
"[The Parable of the Sparrow]" and "[The Story of Cædmon]"

These two short passages can teach a lot about the Middle Ages, and especially about the clash of cultures that takes place when a new religion appears—in this case, the clash between native Germanic values of northern Europe, and Christianity, which came to England from the Mediterranean in the seventh century. There are other reasons for including them in a syllabus, however: the first is a memorable parable, a short allegory which borders on myth; and the second records a culture's passage from orality to literacy, and from official to vernacular literature. Both are excellent classroom texts because they appear quite simple at first, but contain fascinating complexities when examined more closely.

The parable of the sparrow can profitably be compared with the Plato's <u>Allegory of the Cave</u>, and with the parables of Jesus in the Gospel of Mark; also to Asian parable-like texts such as the Upanishads and the <u>Dharma-Door of Nonduality</u>. In the modern period, one might compare Kafka's <u>Imperial Message</u> or Borges's <u>Borges and I</u>. Like these, the sparrow parable is mind-expanding, because it casts the essential facts of the human condition into a very simple (but somehow puzzling) narrative. To the Germanic peoples, the universe appeared essentially chaotic; though human life may be happy, it is brief and meaningless. As this tiny narrative unfolds it becomes clear that the hall in the storm is not really a spatial image—an oasis of order in a chaotic universe—rather, the hall represents the time of a man's life from birth to death, and the storm outside represents the unknown eternity that precedes birth and follows death. Parables usually have twists of this sort to tease the brain. Notice that the speaker has no idea what Christianity really is, he has simply been led suddenly to see the meaninglessness of life in the Germanic world view. At least this is how Bede tells the story—and one must remember he is a Christian. The conversion of the Anglo-Saxons was, of course, not this simple; this story presents it as a miracle, part of a longer narrative filled with miracles demonstrating God's plan for a Christian England.

The story of Cædmon documents not only the borderline between oral and literate culture, but also between official and vernacular language. As a divinely-inspired cowherd, Cædmon is something of a mythical figure validating the use of the vernacular for sacred subjects normally restricted to Latin. It is sometimes difficult for students to see why Cædmon's poem, so short and simple, should prompt such astonishment in those who heard it. Most students have little awareness of the distinctions between official and vernacular language, or orality and literacy. You might compare the shock of mixing "high" and "low" culture in this story to the shock of a jazz symphony or a rock opera, or a concerto for electric guitar. Closer to the point of the story would be Christian rock music.

Are these stories "true"? They seem so simple and transparent that they are easily taken as history; but they are very polished and literate, and may be Bede's inventions. How are we to understand the miracle at the center of the Cædmon story? Miracles are the essential feature of a special literary genre, the saint's life—and this story is an episode in the life of St. Hilda.

Students or teachers who want to go deeper into this text should turn first to the surrounding contexts of these stories in Bede's <u>History</u>. The whole story of Edwin will make the parable of the sparrow more interesting; and the life of St. Hilda will put the story of Cædmon in context. A beautiful discussion of Bede and the principles underlying his narratives can be found in Charles Jones's book, <u>Saints' Lives and Chronicles in Early England</u> (Hamden, CT, 1968).

Questions for Study and Discussion:

1. Why does Coifi, the chief priest, accept the new religion? What does he want from the new religion?

2. What is the allegorical meaning of the king's hall in this parable? What does the sparrow signify? The winter storm?

3. Why does Cædmon leave the hall? Who is the visitor in the barn?

4. Why is everyone so astonished by Cædmon's little song? What it is about the song that makes him so famous?

Abelard and Heloise
The Letters

These letters between the most famous lovers of the Middle Ages work wonderfully well in the classroom. They might be included in units on biography and autobiography, or love and romance, or the history of women writers. They work especially well with a number of Western works: other love stories, like that of Aeneas and Dido in Virgil's <u>Aeneid</u>, Ovid's retelling of that story from Dido's point of view in the <u>Heroides</u>, and Christine de Pizan's version in the <u>City of Ladies</u>; with autobiographies like Augustine's and Rousseau's <u>Confessions</u>; with monuments of the romantic love tradition that developed from these letters, including the romances of Marie de France and the sonnets of Petrarch; and with Alexander Pope's verse adaptation of Heloise's letters. The only other letters in the anthology are those of Mme. de Sévigné. Asian works that can be usefully taught with it include the history of Sima Qian (the Chinese historian who, like Abelard, tells the story of his own punishment by castration), Kalidasa's <u>Sakuntala</u> (a drama of tragic love from classical India), <u>The Diary of Izumi Shikibu</u> and <u>The Tale of Genji</u> (a Japanese woman's autobiography and a romance contemporary with Abelard and Heloise), Yuan Zhen's <u>Story of Ying-ying</u> (a medieval Chinese story of an abandoned woman), and the Korean poem <u>A Woman's Sorrow</u>.

The introduction to the letters in the anthology hints at a productive classroom strategy: students are very likely to find Abelard cold, unfeeling, selfish, and exploitative, not only in his seduction of Heloise, but in his subsequent act of forcing her into the life of a nun. His prose is dry and offputting, lacking any passion except self-pity. Students will be quick to find the most offensive passages. They will be interested to learn that in the twelfth century it was an unquestioned assumption of European culture that not only priests but also philosophers (i.e., professors) must be celibate. They may find Abelard more interesting when they learn that intellectually he was an avant-guard radical, who was condemned by the Church for championing the use of reason. A quick trip to an encyclopedia by interested students will open up the interesting issue of the relation of his philosophy to his personal life. It is also worth remembering that Abelard's long autobiographical letter is not addressed to Heloise, but—ostensibly—to a friend whom he was attempting to console by telling of his own misfortunes. It is a public letter.

Heloise, on the other hand, is heart-wrenchingly passionate in her letters, and will remind students of Juliet or the tragic heroines of Bronte novels. Even as they sympathize with her, however, they are likely to be horrified by her unwavering adoration of the moralistic, priggish, domineering Abelard, who abused and victimized her so badly. The class will need to be reminded that Abelard, when he wrote his letter, had long been castrated; his unromantic tone is hardly unexpected. And Heloise, when she wrote hers, had risen to a powerful position as abbess of her convent and spokeswoman for religious women throughout France.

These dynamics alone can create a lively discussion, but can be further complicated by reminding the class of medieval Christian attitudes, which are quite the reverse of our modern ones. Heloise's passionate outbursts only reinforced the medieval stereotype of women as fleshly and irrational, while Abelard's calm, rational self-condemnation struck the medieval audience as moral and exemplary. It is amazing to think that their letters were written to be published publically. It is a clue to how different medieval attitudes are from modern ones, that they could discuss such extraordinarily private matters so openly. Privacy as we know it today did not exist in the Middle Ages—which is one of the things that makes the story of their secret life together so interesting historically.

Ironically, Heloise was often quoted as an antifeminist in the Middle Ages, because of her powerful arguments against marriage; until recently modern scholars suspected that she did not even write her letters, but Abelard forged them to strengthen his own postion—patriarchal scholarship thus silencing one of the most brilliant female voices of medieval Europe. Heloise is a complicated woman, and our responses to her are equally complicated. Students might come to understand that their own initial responses were hasty and stereotypically modern, even if they disagree with the dominant values of Heloise's own culture. They will not be pleased to learn that in the end Abelard won the epistolary debate: the later correspondence only concerns the religious instruction of Heloise's nuns. In any case, students are as moved as they are confused by this memorable first-person account of love in the Middle Ages.

There are a number of accessible treatments of the Abelard and Heloise story, including an elegant (and fairly brief) historical analysis by the eminent medievalist Etienne Gilson, and a Hollywood movie version, <u>Stealing Heaven</u> (1988). A more scholarly essay by Peter Dronke—in his <u>Women Writers of the Middle Ages</u> (Cambridge, 1984)—demonstrates that Heloise's letters are more than just passionate outbursts, but are deeply learned and rhetorically elegant compositions owing much to the classical learning Abelard had given her. As a writer, she is absolutely his equal.

<u>Questions for Study and Discussion</u>:

1. Describe Abelard's motives in seeking out and falling in love with Heloise.

2. Why does Fulbert have Abelard castrated? Why does the marriage not satisfy him?

3. Why does Abelard send Heloise to the convent, and why does she agree to it?

4. What does Heloise seek from Abelard in her letters? What are her arguments against marriage, and why does she make them? Who does she blame for their tragedy? Who do you blame?

5. Do you sense a growth or change in Heloise's attitude in the course of her correspondence with Abelard?

Thomas More
Utopia

More's Utopia is a fixture in introductory literature courses because of its tremendous cultural importance, and because of its immediate and great interest to young people even with little historical background. Reading Utopia stimulates instant discussion and debate among students about what they think an ideal society might look like, and how problematic the idea of an ideal society is. Can anyone describe a perfect society in which he or she would actually like to live?

It is worth noting that this anthology presents the Utopia as part of the medieval Latin tradition, but it is easily linked to other utopian works, especially Plato's Republic and Christine de Pizan's City of Ladies, and to other texts of its period, such as Marco Polo's Travels (another book of fantastic travels), Montaigne's Of Cannibals (another humanistic treatment of the discovery of the New World), and Shakespeare's King Lear (with its themes of natural man and natural law). Machiavelli's The Prince, Shakespeare's The Tempest and Swift's Gulliver's Travels are also relevant, though they are not contained in the anthology. The one utopian vision from Asia in the anthology is the Chinese Peach Blossom Spring, which may be useful for highlighting the utopian theme by contrast.

The Utopia practically teaches itself. The teacher can keep the discussion focused and elevated by supplying historical and cultural background, and pressing students to read between the lines. Most students are initially charmed by the idea of a society devoted to peace, social harmony, tolerance and equality, without the evils of money or private property. One might start with the question, then, "Would you actually like to live in Utopia?" It is important to bring out that, for all its serious themes, the work is very playful and humorous, as in the whimsical account of golden chamber-pots, and the joke about the foreign ambassadors who are taken for fools by children. But how seriously are we to take such ideas? The entertaining tone disguises extremely negative, cynical elements in the book—like pervasive state terrorism, and the fundamental intolerance of difference. This last is especially interesting in the discussion of marriage: students may at first find the idea of pre-marital inspections amusing; but note how the practice reduces human beings to the status of horses chosen merely for their flesh, it being assumed that a hidden physical flaw makes a person an unfit spouse. Divorce may be allowable (if difficult) in Utopia, but adultery is punished by death; there is no freedom of speech; and the Utopians' practice of euthanasia will certainly engage students' attention—how could the Catholic saint and martyr have written that? Similarly, the Utopians may seem tolerant in religious matters, but basic beliefs in God and the afterlife are required, because it is assumed that without these beliefs people would be immoral, seeking only their self-interest and pleasure. Students can be set searching for these and other negative elements in the book, and they will always find them intertwined with seemingly liberal ideas. Which of these are More's genuine attitudes, which are ironic, and which are satiric of European practices? It is this slippery quality of the book that makes it so fascinating, and which makes it appeal to so many different political and social movements over the centuries.

Historically, the Utopia is on the borderline of the Middle Ages and the Renaissance. Though it is often thought of as a monument of progressive Renaissance humanism, in many ways it is a deeply conservative, medieval work. Utopia is modeled on the communal values of the monastery, and can be seen as a reaction to the new Real-Politik of the Renaissance, embodied in Machiavelli's The Prince (which appeared in the same year); it is also opposed to the new commercialism which was destroying England's traditional small farming villages—thus More's attack on money. One might compare the problem to the American small farm today.

For extra reading, one should recommend first of all the rest of the Utopia. Book One, not included in our selections, deals with the question of whether a wise man should enter government service, which Hythloday claims is by nature corrupt. Students could try to answer the question, "What is the relation of the two parts?" A classic biography of More by E. K. Chambers, though old, is informative, exciting, and very readable. Students with an interest in the period can look at the life of More written by his son-in-law William Roper, one of the first biographies in English (London, 1935). And of course, there is the excellent movie of More's life and death, A Man for all Seasons (1966), which is based largely on Roper's life. Students who see the movie might be set wondering how the author of Utopia could be the same man—he is highly principled and inspirational, but hardly a satiric wit, or a model of tolerance and free thinking.

Questions for Study and Discussion:

1. Characterize the narrator, Raphael Hythloday. How seriously are his opinions to be taken? Find examples of his editorial remarks that make you wonder.

2. Why do you think Utopia is created as an island? In what other respects do you imagine it might resemble (or contrast with) More's England?

3. Can the Utopian moral philosophy be called hedonistic, or Epicurean?

4. In the end, what are More's (not Hythloday's) objections to the Utopian system? How seriously do you take his objections?

Old Norse Literature

Western culture is rooted about equally in the Biblical, Classical, and Germanic traditions. The most conspicuous Germanic contribution to the culture our students live in is our conception of the strong, silent warrior hero whose fate is to go down fighting—familiar in films set in the American West, in heroes like John Wayne and Clint Eastwood. This Germanic heroic tradition is represented in the anthology only by these eight pages. Lack of space prevented the inclusion of the more familiar Beowulf, but this short entry is an extremely powerful substitute. In some ways these two short texts are even more purely Germanic than Beowulf, since they are relatively uninfluenced by Christianity. Even Bede's parable of the sparrow, which is a Christian depiction of the Germanic world view, cannot capture the tragic bleakness of vision we find in this story. Snorri has given us a synopsis of an epic, which might very usefully be taught in conjunction with other primary epics in the anthology, especially Gilgamesh, the Odyssey, and for contrast the Persian Shāh-nāmah. The Indian Mahābhārata and the Japanese Tales of the Heike also have provocative resemblances to the Edda.

These two texts offer easy access for classroom use, since they complement each other so neatly. The poem expands upon one moment in the prose narrative. Reading the poem first, one should try to grasp the dramatic situation, which is only implied. Here is a nice example of a text close to oral tradition; the poet feels no need to tell the story, which the audience already knows fully. Can students figure out the relationships among the characters whose voices we hear? The key is in noting who is related to Gjuki: Gudrun's brothers have killed her husband, in spite of having sworn oaths with him; and she is now in the awkward position of cursing her own brothers. Brynhild makes an appearance as "the other woman." The details are unclear, but the emotional force of the lament is unmistakable. One theory of the origin of epic is that short poems of this sort were woven together into longer and longer units and finally embedded in a unifying narrative.

Snorri's retelling of the whole tale reveals the context of the poem. In every way the prose version is opposite in genre: it is all plot, and all the emotions are implied rather than stated. Several key moments in the plot are represented by poems like The Lay of Gudrun. Snorri's summary is no more than a summary; it has an extremely understated tone, which is actually quite appropriate to Germanic heroic narrative. This culture reserved lyric poetry for the expression of emotion, which is typically left unexpressed in narrative. In this case this understatement may seem comical to students, because it is so extreme—like the brief plot summaries of soap operas in TV Guide. Is it possible that Snorri intended this effect?

The key perception to aim for in teaching Snorri's text is that its violence has no profound source, and little if any moral significance. The unbroken chain of cause and effect begins with the god Loki amusing himself by killing an otter with a fish in his mouth—hardly an Original Sin. This trivial accident, a joke, begins a chain of events that will consume generations and whole nations in increasingly horrible disaster. There's little sense that the consequences ever reflect punishment of wrong behavior; rather, as in tragedy, punishment seem far in excess of fault. It is a tragic vision of life and history. Occasionally one glimpses a fault, like Loki's final demand on Advari, Hreithmar's final demand on Othin, or Fafnir's greed. But when the curse descends on Sigurth, it's not clear what his fault might be, besides being in possession of the cursed gold. Does this gold symbolize anything? Hard to say. Does Sigurth treat Brynhild wrongly when he first meets her? The narrative refuses to tell us. Is he wrong to change shape with Gunnar to woo Brynhild later? Ditto. The women's jealousy is trivialized (realistically?) by the question of who will wash her hair upstream of whom. Why does Brynhild have Sigurth killed, and why does she kill herself? Is this romantic love? She seems to love and hate him at the same time. Although Gudrun hates her brothers for killing her husband, when her second husband kills them (is this not her plan?) she kills him to revenge them! At this point one wonders if Brynhild had killed herself to revenge Sigurth's death, paradoxically, on herself. The plot revolves around such twisted conflicts and contradictions of duty. Fate, perhaps, is no more and no less than the grip of conflicting obligations of revenge, which inevitably lead to tragedy.

Those who want to do further reading related to this text might first of all look at the rest of Snorri's Prose Edda, which includes a myth of creation as well as Ragnarok, the end of the world. This latter story is especially relevant, since it captures the fatality of the Nibelung story in ultimate cosmic terms: the world just ends, with no sense of a moral lesson, the forces of order and chaos having all killed each other in a final battle. Many students will already know Beowulf, which contains a digression referring to the Nibelung story. The story is also the basis of the beautiful Laxdaela Saga, available in a Penguin paperback. Perhaps the most obvious text for the ambitious student who wants to explore this story in a paper is Wagner's Ring.

Questions for Study and Discussion:

1. In The Lay of Gudrun, how are the many characters related? Who is Gjuki, and who are his children? What relation do Gudrun and Brynhild seem to have to Sigurth and Gunnar? Why is the poem so unclear about the narrative situation?

2. What causes the horrible chain of events in Snorri's tale of the Nibelungs? What lessons are we supposed to learn from it? Do you detect irony or humor in Snorri's account?

3. What does the gold symbolize, if anything?

4. Why does Brynhild kill herself? Is she in love with Sigurth? Is this romantic love as we know it?

5. Why does Atli kill Gudrun's brothers, and why does Gudrun kill her children and her husband?

Provençal Poetry

The great attraction of troubadour poetry is that it is the original love poetry of the modern West. In it we can see the first glimmerings of "romantic" love, with its quasi-religious rituals of adoration, idealization, secrecy and fatality; and yet in this earliest form of the tradition the poets' voices are surprisingly edgy and realistic, frankly erotic and adulterous. The Provençal lyrics, and thus the whole Western love tradition, were strongly influenced by Arabic poetry from Spain; it is therefore quite pertinent to read the two poems of Ibn Hazm and Ibn Zaidūn in the anthology. More distantly, one can compare these love poems to the courtship songs in Inanna, The Song of Songs in the Bible, Sappho in ancient Greece, Catullus in ancient Rome, and the Old Norse Edda, to see what is new in them; and to the courtly love of the Lais of Marie de France and the poems of Petrarch to see how the tradition will develop after them. They are roughly contemporary with the Sanskrit anthology of Vidyakara, and the love poems in the Diary of Izumi Shikibu and the Tale of Genji. They should take center stage in any thematic treatment of love in the anthology.

My own classroom strategy with these poems, as with much love poetry, is to discern an ideology of love in them; then, once the students see that love is not an entirely natural phenomenon, but takes different forms in different cultures, to prompt them to articulate the ideology of love they themselves inhabit. These are the earliest poems in the romantic love tradition, and in this case the ideology might be summarized,

> Each day I am a better man and purer,
> for I serve the noblest lady in the world,
> and I worship her . . . .
>
> But this torment I endure
> could not make me turn away from loving well,
> although it holds me fast in loneliness . . . .

Love is a purifying force in a man's life; the beloved is "set on a pedestal," as students say; and loving her is a form of religious devotion. True love involves the heart-breaking torment of rejection, but is steadfast even when impossible, and leads to self-knowledge. Many students today think such love pathological; the idealization of women is a strategy for denying them any authentic selfhood; and this sort of lover sounds a bit like a stalker.

On the other hand, these first remarks do not really describe the attitudes in Arnaut's poem. He is obviously being witty, ironic, and comical; he makes fun of himself and of the very conventions of love, going so far as to lampoon the beloved for her cruelty. He recognizes these new romantic love conventions as being nothing but conventions of behavior and of poetry, and he plays with them.

The interest of the second poem is quite different, and is discussed in the headnote. It is totally shocking in content and tone, revealing the dark underside of the courtly warrior's life. The third poem shows the same world, but from the woman's point of view. The most unexpected part of it is the sexual frankness of it all; the twelfth century may be Christian, but not puritanical.

There are two classic treatments of the Western love tradition: C. S. Lewis's Allegory of Love (London, 1938), and Denis de Rougement's Love in the Western World (Princeton, 1956). Lewis treats medieval love traditions with great respect, outlining their features and their paradoxical relationship to religion. Courtly love adopts the language of religion, but is subversive of religious ideas. De Rougement shocked Europe and America fifty years ago by his claim that Western love is bound up with a love of death. Romeo and Juliet and Tristan and Isolde are the classic cases. Another fascinating approach can be found in Montaillou (New York, 1978), a famous account of everyday life in a Provençal village in the twelfth century by LeRoy Ladurie. In several chapters on sex and marriage, especially "The Libido of the Clergues," we can see the nitty-gritty historical reality behind the poetry. This is great "research" for students writing papers. The great debate about courtly love, which developed quite directly out of the troubadour poetry, is whether it bears any resemblance at all to reality, or was an elaborate social fiction. Of course we can ask the same question about love as it's portrayed in movies and songs today.

Questions for Study and Discussion:

1. What are the most prominent features of the idea of love in Arnaut's poem? How does love in these poems compare with the ideal of love in modern America (for example, in movies and songs, and in student life)?

2. Discuss the tone of Arnaut's poem. Is his idea of love complicated by irony, or humor? How seriously does he take the conventions of romantic love?

3. What is the relation of Bertran's poem to the "extra stanzas"? What are these extra stanzas, and what thematic link, if any, do you see between them and the rest of the poem?

4. Compare the attitude toward love in Beatritz's poem with that in the two men's poems. What are the most surprising features of her poem, given the common understanding of the Middle Ages we find in stories like King Arthur, or Robin Hood?

Marie de France
Poems

    Few texts are so charming as Marie's lais, and students have been prepared to enjoy them by the many medieval fantasy movies that imitate their style. Ladyhawk, for example, has the stylistic features and many of the motifs of Yonec. (That's not a recommendation to show it, though even bad films can be useful.) Marie's lays are the quintessence of medieval romance, and they have the advantage of being short—the three pieces anthologized here can be assigned for a single class. They can be taught in conjunction with other texts about love (obvious choices would be the Indian drama Śakuntalā, Abelard and Heloise, and the Provençal poets), especially those from a courtly ambiance (Izumi Shikibu's Diary and the Tale of Genji are near-contemporaries from Japan—and both are by women), or fantasy literature (the Arabian Thousand and One Nights, for example), or women authors (several of the foregoing, and also Christine de Pizan and the Indian poet Mīrābāī). A syllabus with all or several of these texts would certainly win the hearts of students! The next time I teach the middle term, I will adopt these texts as a unified syllabus; they are connected in many ways, and each throws light on the others.

    The short introduction by Marie is included primarily so we may hear Marie's voice. Compare the introduction by Christine de Pizan, who had not read Marie; it is important to note that there is no developing tradition of women's writing, but every woman writer in Europe has to solve the same problems of establishing her own voice. The king Marie addresses is Henry II, whom some students will recognize from the movies as the king who killed Thomas Beckett, and whose marital squabbles with Eleanor of Aquitaine are portrayed in The Lion in Winter.

    It is Yonec that will take most of our attention. Notice that although the story is named after a man, it is really about a woman, as so many of Marie's lays are—though she and all the characters except Yonec remain oddly nameless throughout. Though the tale is wonderfully imaginative in its plot, its characters are paper-thin (as in romance typically), and little attention is given to scene or realistic action. (How surprised we are to discover the husband can install razor-bars on the window without the lady knowing; the lady can escape by simply jumping out a window; the knight has a magic ring that makes her husband forget all that has happened; she has brought the sword to the fair under her cloak, though she was not expecting to find her lover, etc). In romance, the exigencies of the fantastic plot usually determine all other features—unlike epic, where profound characterization generally predominates, detail abounds, and plot can be quite minimal.

    Yonec is dreamlike in its fantasy, filled with impossibilities, contradictions, and unexplained images. I think we enjoy such tales, in spite of their bizarre qualities, precisely because they deliver the familiar and comforting world of our sleep. Many of the tale's dream-images are clustered in the heroine's fantastic journey: the hill with a bloody tunnel through it, the paradisical meadow, a flotilla of arriving (not departing) ships whose sails are numbered, an empty and silent city made all of silver, a palace with a sleeping knight in each chamber. There is no harm in posing the meaning of these images for imaginative commentary. Students are likely to identify the tunnel as a birth image, and the city as the otherworld; the sleeping knights resemble a common image in science fiction: bodies frozen in suspended animation, awaiting rebirth. Is there a consistent overall meaning to the narrative? If we read the two Middle English poems that follow Marie in the anthology, we find the wounded knight-lover begs to be interpreted as Christ, and the lady as the soul; but it's very hard to make such an identification work, given the adulterous sexuality of the story—and yet God seems to bless their union.

Class discussion can proceed along these lines: what are the surprising inconsistencies of the plot? What are the meanings of the strange images? What do we learn about the characters? (Nothing—not even their names.) What does the poem say about the nature of love? What is its attitude toward religion and the Church?

The tiny Chevrefoil has some of the same mystery—what exactly does Tristan do to the hazel tree? Amazing coincidence that she spots his sign! What did he write on the hazel? Did Tristan really write the lay?—but these odd details take a back seat to Marie's portrayal of love, the construction of a beautiful parenthetical moment of tender stolen love in the middle of what we know is a tragic affair.

Students who want to do further work on these poems should first of all read another lay or two by Marie, such as Eliduc or The Nightengale. The same books I recommended for the Provençal poems are even more appropriate here: C. S. Lewis's Allegory of Love (London, 1938) and Denis de Rougement's Love in the Western World (Princeton, 1983). Also, Andreas Capellanus's Art of Courtly Love (New York, 1941) provides a guide to the doctrines of love, written by a cleric in the court of Eleanor's daughter. Capellanus's attitudes are very contradictory, and perhaps ironic, and remind us of the ambiguous role of the Church in Marie's tales.

Questions for Study and Discussion:

1. Try to characterize the doctrine of "courtly love" as it is exemplified in these two stories.

2. What are the lovers' names in Yonec? What city does she travel to? Who are the sleeping knights?

3. What are the most surprising, improbable, or contradictory elements in the plot of Yonec? Which elements are most dreamlike?

4. In Chevrefoil, what does Tristan write on the hazel? What elements of this story are found in Yonec also? Characterize the mood, or tone, of the story; what is its "point"?

Two Middle English Lyrics
"Quia Amore Langueo" and "The Corpus Christi Carol"

It is difficult to date these two lyrics; the first is probably fourteenth century, the second may be as late as the sixteenth, though both have folkloric roots that go back earlier. They have been placed after the Provençal lyrics and the romances of Marie de France in the anthology because this group of short texts forms a very attractive thematic unit. In these two poems we see the romance tradition's potential for religious development, as the figures of the knight-errant and courtly lover are made powerful symbols of Christ. In both poems we find the wounded knight-lover, strongly reminiscent of the one in Marie's Yonec. Once we see the Christian version of this image, should we read Yonec with allegorical overtones? In either case, we want to be aware of this powerful configuration of symbols, so prototypically medieval.

The confluence of the literature of love and the literature of religion goes back ultimately to the biblical <u>Song of Songs</u>. That collection of love-songs was included in the Bible probably on the grounds that it was an allegory in which the bridegroom was God, and the bride Israel. Christians interpreted it as the marriage between Christ and the Church (or the individual soul). This allegory legitimizes the language of erotic love as a metaphor for religious love; and also the adoption of religious language for erotic love. Christ as lover may seem a bit blasphemous today, in our puritanical culture, but it is not hard to find contemporary examples of the lover who worships his beloved like a goddess. Interestingly, in <u>The Song of Songs</u> and these poems it is the lover, not the beloved, who reflects the divine. The same idea can be found in medieval India, in the poems of the <u>bhakti</u> poet Mīrābāī, who sings love songs to the god Krishna; and the Arabic poet Rumi also blends erotic and spiritual themes.

"Quia Amore Langueo" is a good text for discussing allegory. In this case the allegory is a fully-developed parallel between the doctrine of courtly love and the Christian doctrine of the incarnation. Christ is the ultimate courtly lover. Even students who claim to dislike religious literature will be impressed by the wild imagination of the poet, who has found an extremely sexy approach to theology, and who seems to recognize no limits. Christ is gradually transformed from male to female, and late in the poem offers his breast to his lover, who has now become his baby. The governing idea is that God is love, and that love endures all; God suffers for our love, even as a courtly lover suffers for his lady's love. He suffers for the same reason, because his love is unrequited; but he continues to love us in spite of our rejection of him. We have broken God's heart, but he remains steadfast.

The first line of the poem is an open invitation to a psychological reading: the action of the poem takes place "in the vale of restless mind." It is most likely a dream vision—which may account for the surreal and fluid imagery. His lover is "my sister, man's soul": for this and many other images in the poem, <u>The Song of Songs</u> is the source and guide. This poem shows how the Middle Ages read that book of the Bible. The knight's beloved is quickly revealed to be the worst imaginable incarnation, unsurpassingly cruel; she is humanity as medieval Christianity understood it, cruel enough to kill even its own helpless and innocent god; alienated, we might say today, from the Creator and his creation.

"The Corpus Christi Carol" is technically a carol, which means that its opening refrain, "lully lullay," is repeated after each little stanza; and like carols today, medieval carols were strongly associated with Christmas. This poem too is dreamlike, as each stanza brings us closer to the mystery of the dead knight. The stone identifies the knight in the last line; the "may" weeping by his bier is most likely the Virgin Mary, or according to the symbolism of the first poem, man's soul. Is he really dead? His wounds continue to bleed, perhaps because Christ's blood is the continuing sacrament of the Church. The image recalls the burial of Christ before Easter, a pietà. I show Michelangelo's pietà to the class, pointing out the startlingly youthful and placid Mary, who hardly looks like the mother of the dead man on her lap. It is easy to see the scene as a disturbing variation on the familiar madonna images of Christmas, and this association may help us understand the poem as a macabre Christmas poem.

Students who have read King Arthur literature will wonder if the poem isn't possibly about him; and yes, the romance imagery is strong in the poem. King Arthur doesn't really die, you remember, he goes off to Avalon with the mysterious ladies, and he may one day return. Another strong association is with the Grail legend; perhaps this is the Grail king, or Fisher king, whose wound will not heal until we ask the right question. In some versions of that story, the grail is a stone, rather than a cup. In any case, whoever the knight is, he is the mystery of mysteries in this poem. The headnote to the poem outlines several readings, the last of which is a real surprise: this may be a political poem having to do with the divorce of Henry VIII. If so, we have to imagine a medieval poem about the dead Christ and the sacrament, as well as the Arthurian legend, which was adapted in the sixteenth century for a political cause; a traditional song which suddenly took on new meaning when Henry wickedly put aside his wife and the Catholic church together.

Questions for Study and Discussion:

1. What imagery in "Quia amore langueo" has been taken from The Song of Songs?

2. Trace the transformation of the lamenting knight throughout the poem. Are the images of the bridal chamber, the nursery, and the nursing mother grotesque? What effect do they have on the reader, and why would the poet have chosen them?

3. If you think you know who the knight and the lady are in the "Corpus Christi Carol," who or what is the falcon?

4. What relation can you see between this poem and the chapel scene in Marie's Yonec? Could that story be a religious allegory, or at least resonant with religious themes?

Marco Polo
The Travels

Marco Polo is critical to our anthology because he was one of the first bridges between East and West. His description of travels across Central Asia to China was extremely popular and won a wide readership throughout Europe. Nevertheless, it must be noted that his influence was entirely one way—no notice of his presence in China has yet been found in any Chinese record and it is likely that he was a much less significant participant in the Chinese world than he leads us to believe (certainly he was not governor of Yangchow as he claims!). But his writing did capture the imagination of many Europeans and has continued to find an avid Western readership down to the present. A good place to begin a discussion of Marco Polo is to ask students to describe and respond to him as a travel writer—that is, what kinds of things does he notice, what are his prejudices, does he seem reliable, etc.? Student response to this broad question may tend to be highly critical of Polo. It is then useful to begin to contextualize him—that is, to remind students that he traveled to Asia as an easily impressed young man, that he was a merchant who was mainly interested in the world of surfaces and was not necessarily well-educated, and that he lived in a Europe that felt itself threatened both by those "who worship Mahomet" and the Mongolian "idolaters." One can note, for example, that Marco Polo tends to identify people more according to religion than to race. He notices skin color, to be sure, but this is far less important to him than religious belief.

Marco Polo should be compared to the great Moslem traveler Ibn Battutah. The latter is more urbane. He assimilates into the Moslem communities of the regions where he travels and thereby becomes much more of an insider than Marco Polo. He also seems to have a better grasp of the political worlds in which he travels. But Marco Polo probably excels Battutah in his descriptions of the physical world—his account of the "Desert of Lop" (=the Taklamakan) being one prominent example (pp. 1305-1306). Moreover, Marco Polo's accounts of the customs of the people in the regions where he travels are unexcelled and provided Europe with some of their first detailed reports of the "exotic" peoples of the East (see, for example, his description of the cremation rights of the "Idolaters" on p. 1307).

One cannot discuss Marco Polo without somehow broaching the controversial question of reliability. There is a great deal about his record that is troubling, particularly the fact that it was written down long after his initial travels and only then by the hand of the romance writer Rustichello, who undoubtedly embellished the account considerably. Moreover, Marco Polo seems easily impressed—everything he sees is the "greatest" or the "biggest," and he frequently reminds us that he is telling the truth. Students can be asked directly if they find him believable. In responding, they will almost certainly seize on one of his miracle stories, like the stone in the church of St. John the Baptist (p. 1304) to discredit him, but most of these stories can be explained either by his own gullibility or by Rustichello's desire to further exaggerate what Polo must have told him. Still, Marco Polo remains a controversial figure down to the present day, with some skeptics still arguing that he never really traveled to China. Thus, he becomes an excellent springboard for a discussion of the problems presented by any piece of travel literature that purports to be "fact": can we ever see the other clearly, particularly when our own sense of identity might be at stake? does travel writing that seeks a broad audience inevitably shade into fictional presentation?, and other such provocative and difficult queries.

While the R. E. Latham translation in the Penguin Series is excellent, the standard scholarly work, with an extensive commentary, is Sir Henry Yule, The Travels of Marco Polo: The Complete Yule-Cordier Edition, two volumes (1903, 1920; New York, 1993). For the latest attack on the reliability of the text, see the highly readable work of Frances Wood, Did Marco Polo Go to China? (Boulder, 1996).

Questions for Study and Discussion:

1. Despite his obvious interest in religion as a means of categorizing people, Marco Polo tells us nothing of doctrinal or theological issues. How do you account for this?

2. What are Polo's priorities in describing others (religion, language, etc.), and how do you think these would compare to those of a typical modern traveler?

3. How do you account for the continued popularity of Marco Polo, a popularity that has not lessened even though we have later reports that are more detailed and accurate?

Dante Alighieri
The Inferno

Many teachers insist on teaching "whole works" instead of "just excerpts," which is perfectly understandable. Yet teaching the whole Inferno is still only teaching a third of the Divine Comedy; and even this much is overwhelming if read quickly as part of a World Literature course. Reading selections from the Inferno does not lessen its impact in this setting. The World of Literature contains a third of the Inferno, including those portions which modern readers find most memorable and instructive. There are no explanatory notes, which would be essential in a more advanced course; but those coming to Dante for the first time will not find the poem too impenetrable or intimidating without them—though hardly a cake-walk.

The most obvious syllabus context is the great epics, including the standards in Western literature courses, the Odyssey, the Aeneid, and Paradise Lost. Less familiar but just as effective for comparison are Gilgamesh (or the Descent of Inanna, another descent into Hell), the Persian Shāh-nāmah, and the Indian Mahābhārata or Ramayana. In China and Japan the nearest thing to these epics is perhaps the great novels, Dream of the Red Chamber and The Tale of Genji. All these "heavies" are an effective core for a World Lit sequence, but the Inferno fits comfortably in any number of other syllabi. For example, as a religious/metaphysical poem from the Christian tradition it could be compared with Job, the Bhagavad-Gītā, and Asvaghosha's Buddha-Karita. Like Marie de France or Chaucer, Dante can represent the European Middle Ages in any syllabus.

Here we suggest discussion topics for each canto in turn; the introduction suggests more general approaches, such as the crucial distinction between Dante the Pilgrim and Dante the poet.

Canto I is the perfect opportunity to discuss allegory. Even beginners can see that the dark wood, the valley of death, the sunrise, and the three animals are symbolic, even if the meaning of the animals remains opaque. Virgil is identified clearly, but students need to be told what he means to Dante: he is the master-poet, "the font that pours so overwhelming a river of human speech." His role in the Divine Comedy is limited by the fact that he was not Christian.

In Canto II Virgil's role is explained further. He is in particular the poet of the Lower World, in Book VI of the Aeneid (see the excerpt on pp. 666-67), and the poet of the foundation of Rome, which was to become the capital of the Church after St. Paul ("the Chosen Vessel") arrived there. In Canto II we also meet Beatrice, and the allegory of Dante's inspiration becomes more complex: both Virgil and Beatrice are his muses, the one serving the other.

Canto III opens with the most famous words of the poem; students might compare Pinsky's "Abandon all hope, you who enter here," with the aphoristic "Abandon hope, all ye who enter here," to consider issues of poetic style and translation. As Dante is singled out by Charon as the one living person going to hell, and the only good one, students may sense for the first time Dante's immense arrogance, portraying himself as elect, worthy of this vision. And yet, he portrays himself as so shocked by his own election that he faints from fear.

Canto IV depicts Limbo. In Oregon, at least, many students need basic Christian ideas explained, such as the Harrowing of Hell, Christ's liberation of the Old Testament figures after his death on the cross. Here Dante's arrogance becomes an issue again, as he is welcomed by the great poets of antiquity: "that fair company then made me one among them." He also parades his classical learning, naming the heroes and heroines of Greek and Roman literature, and the ancient philosophers. What we see as arrogance is Dante's claim to authority to write the poem.

When students forget everything else about the Inferno, they are likely to remember Canto V. Here we see for the first time how "the punishment fits the crime." For teens who consider passionate love a virtue rather than a sin, Dante's renunciation of courtly love (including perhaps his own early poetry) is a show-stopper. And yet, as only the first stage in his downward journey, the circle of lovers presents the least serious of the sins according to the medieval scheme—the inverse of the American scheme, which sees pride as a virtue and lust as a synonym for sin. In the Middle Ages, pride is the worst because it is a perversion of the higher faculties—the intellect—and lust is merely a perversion of the lower ones. Note the role literature plays in the seduction of Paolo and Francesca—Dante's criticism of the Romance genre

The portraits of Farinata and Cavalcante in Canto X are the subject of Auerbach's great essay on Dante's realistic characterizations in <u>Mimesis</u>. This canto has been included especially so teachers can take advantage of that essay.

The speech of Ulysses (Odysseus) in Canto XXVI is one of Dante's most original inventions. Like Virgil, Dante sees Ulysses as the perfidious enemy of the Trojans (Romans), rather than as the clever hero of the Greeks. He transforms Homer's Odysseus, who thirsts for home, and Virgil's Aeneas, a figure of duty and filial piety, into a figure of infinite ambition, thirsting for the unknown. Though such ambition is clearly sinful in Dante's medieval world, it is easy to see as a precursor to the ambition of Renaissance humanism and modernity in general; Tennyson celebrates it in his dramatic monologue, "Ulysses" (an excellent classroom supplement).

Canto XXXIII presents the piteous tale of Ugolino. Though he is in hell for political betrayal, it is his heart-rending story of being starved to death with his children that we hear. His dying children's plea that he save himself by eating them has spiritual overtones, as Christ offers his body to the faithful; our admiration for the children and pity for their father turn to horror as Ugolino confesses (or does he?) to cannibalism. Dante's refusal to clarify this point leaves the reader in confusion. If we pity Ugolino, we have failed Dante's test of moral maturity.

Canto XXXIV has a number of surprises for beginning students, not the least of which is that Dante knew the world was round, and imagines the problem of gravity reversing at its center. More important, though, is the surprise that the murderers of Julius Caesar are identified (along with Judas) as the worst of all sinners. For Dante betrayal is the worst of sins.

<u>Questions for Study and Discussion</u>

1. What is the symbolism of the dark wood? The sunrise? The animals?

2. How does Dante portray himself? Does this portrait change during the <u>Inferno</u>?

3. Why is Virgil in particular his guide? Who sent him? Why?

4. How grievous is Paolo and Francesca's sin? What is their excuse?

5. Campare the characters of Farinate and Cavalcante. Why are they punished together? Explain the odd limitation on their knowledge of events.

6. Does Dante admire Ulysses's ambition in sailing for the unknown? What is his sin?

7. What is Ugolino's sin? Why does he tell the story of his imprisonment? Why is Dante so cold and unpitying?

8. Why are Brutus and Cassius in Satan's mouth? Explain the pilgrims's turn-around at the end of the last canto.

Francis Petrarch
Rime

Petrarch is the preeminent love poet of Western literature, and can be taught effectively with other love lyrics, like those of ancient Egypt, the biblical Song of Songs, Sappho and Catullus, the Sanskrit poems of Vidyakara's Treasury, the Chinese Book of Songs, Japanese court poetry, including the poems in Izumi Shikibu's Diary and the Tale of Genji, and the poems of Baudelaire. Petrarch can also be seen as the culmination of the romantic love tradition that begins with Abelard and Heloise, and develops through the Provençal lyrics, Marie de France, and the Middle English lyrics. He is also an effective representative of the European Renaissance, especially in tandem with Dante, who can be made to represent the Middle Ages by contrast, even though the two poets are near-contemporaries. Petrarch is especially useful in the syllabus because important insights can be gained from these eight short poems in a single class period.

Students can be drawn into a discussion of the conventions of Petrarchan love by comparing it with our contemporary love conventions—which inform popular love songs, and which students have thought about a great deal. In class I exaggerate that most of our modern notions of romantic love were invented by Petrarch, including love at first sight, love as a deep mystery, love as psychological torment, love as addiction, the total idealization of the woman, bottomless despair over rejection, and the sublimation of sexual frustration into art or worldly success. Many of these features are from the earlier courtly love tradition, of course. Students want to fight when you stereotype their attitudes toward love and sex. Many find Petrarch objectionable because he seems to have no interest in the real Laura, but idealizes or objectifies her; because his relentless pursuit seems little more than what we now call stalking; because he's obsessed; because he's self-absorbed, using Laura only as a vehicle to fame; etc. These objections can be used to stimulate class discussion and close reading of the poems, which should be the real goal.

Of the eight poems here, the first one and the last two frame the sequence from what seems like a mature transcendence of the passion that rules the ones in between. There is nothing youthful about #1, which concludes from his experience of love that "from my vanities comes fruit of shame," and "worldly joy is a quick passing dream." Number 365 asks God to forgive "all my shameful, wicked errors" in loving Laura rather than God. But is this a genuine resolution? In the sonnet right before it, #333, he adopts Dante's solution, converting Laura into an angel who is drawing him toward heaven; but in the context of the whole cycle, these three poems may not be totally convincing.

The five poems in between display the emotional tumult and contradictions that characterize most of the 366 poems in the cycle, and the many Petrarchan imitators. In #3 he tells of falling in love at first sight in church on Good Friday, when he was particularly vulnerable because off guard. Laura herself was not smitten by love. The association of this one-sided event with Christ's death marks Petrarch's love as particularly woe-ridden. Saying "all my misfortunes began in midst of universal woe" he audaciously identifies his love-sickness with Christ's passion.

Number 16 is a moment of self-pity, as he compares himself to an aged religious pilgrim looking for her image in the world. The last words reveal how inappropriate the religious simile really is: his own goal is not as spiritual as he sometimes pretends.

Number 61 displays the fervor of his obsession, as he declares how much he loves his own agony and his wounds of love—and his poetry, for here he reveals how his love has become first and foremost a literary mission.

Number 132 is a classic catalogue of the features of Petrarchan love, a tangle of contradictions: "O living death, O pleasurable harm." What is love? Who can say? It is beyond reason and understanding. Some students will recognize the experience of love here, and some will dismiss it as romantic clap-trap. It is an interesting debate, how realistic Petrarch's vision of being in love is. What are the functions of romantic love in society? Why do so many love stories follow this formula? Do people in love really feel "so light of wisdom, so laden of error, that I myself do not know what I want"? Does "love" rule you when you are in love, against your will?

Laura died about half-way through the sonnet sequence. Number 319 reveals that Petrarch's love is strong enough (or self-absorbed enough) to survive even this rebuke. Does he succeed in transferring his love from her worldly memory to her spirit? He is obviously struggling to free himself from his obsession, but he seems too much in love with his own love to succeed. Dante's success in moving from worldly to spiritual love nicely illustrates what makes him a medieval poet; and Petrarch's inability, which leaves him hanging in unresolved ambivalence, nicely characterizes the "modern" view of uncertainty in human life.

The topic of love may be the easiest way into these poems, but in doing close readings it is useful to stress that they are sonnets, and that sonnet form is clear and logical enough to be usefully analyzed. Paraphrasing each stanza in a single sentence will usually show the inner structure. Number 1 might be paraphrased, "Reader, behold the errors of my youth. If you've ever been in love, you'll pity and forgive me. I have become an object of public scorn. Now, aware of my own vanity, I see that joy is illusory." Writing such a simple paraphrase forces the reader into closer contact with the poem.

Questions for Study and Discussion:

1. Who is Petrarch addressing in his first sonnet? What has he concluded from his experience of love?

2. When did Petrarch fall in love with Laura? Why is the timing appropriate? What was her reaction?

3. Petrarch compares himself to a religious pilgrim. How appropriate is the comparison?

4. What exactly is Petrarch's "sweet agony"? Why is it an agony? Why is it sweet? Is this love, or self-pity?

5. Itemize the contradictions of love in #132. Is this view of love Petrarch's personal peculiarity, a set of social conventions, or a universal phenomenon of human nature?

6. What is Petrarch's response to Laura's death? What has he learned from his experience of love and death?

7. In # 333 the poet seems to be struggling to make sense of his experience in religious terms. How convincing is his argument? Do you find him sincere and honest? Is he self-aware or self-deluding?

8. Who is he addressing in the final poem? Paraphrase this sonnet and the first one, reducing each stanza to one simple sentence.

Geoffrey Chaucer
The Canterbury Tales

Chaucer's <u>Pardoner's Tale</u> is among the most popular classroom texts in the anthology, and for good reason. Among Chaucer's tales (and European medieval literature generally) it stands out for the vividness of its psychological realism—the Wife of Bath and the Pardoner are the most "modern" of Chaucer's narrators; like Shakespeare's characters they seem to have complex personalities complete with unconscious motivations—modern subjectivity. In this case we have the classic self-portrait of the sinful preacher. It is a stereotype well known to Americans, since the Puritan impulse is to expose the preacher's hypocrisy, from <u>The Scarlet Letter</u> to <u>Elmer Gantry</u> to today's televangelists (parodied in movies like Steve Martin's <u>Leap of Faith</u>). Yet students are not prepared for the complexity of the Pardoner or the moral problems he presents.

Among the texts in the anthology, the letters of Abelard and Heloise—the fallen monk and nun—are an obvious choice for comparison, having some of the same themes and complexities. Dante and Petrarch are Chaucer's great contemporaries. But it is difficult to think of close analogies to the combination of philosophical irony, dark comedy and unreliable narrator before Dosteyevsky's <u>Notes From the Underground</u> or Borges's <u>Pierre Menard</u>.

It is important to stress the excitement and attractiveness of the tale immediately, because students coming to Chaucer's Middle English for the first time need a strong incentive. It is a rare student who does not have a lot of trouble with the language—more than he or she will admit. In a World Literature course there is no time to conquer this problem, but most libraries have recordings that can alleviate the panic somewhat. Also, generations of students have memorized the first eighteen lines of the <u>General Prologue</u>; if they can pronounce them with fair correctness they will able to read the rest aloud with improved comprehension.

I divide the tale into its four obvious parts, and discuss them separately. First there is his Prologue, in which he confesses his own sins. His most amusing and confusing feature is his seeming honesty, as he openly confesses his dishonesty. How should we take this? (See question #1 below.) Lee Patterson calls this part "a theatrical self-representation of evil so extravagant that it necessarily calls itself into question." Over-the-top elements include his happily cheating a widow with starving children of her last penny; and—in spite of his questionable masculinity—his boast of having a wench in every town. His outrageousness suggests he is an extremely unreliable narrator, pulling the rug out from under our easy moral judgments. Starting in l.106, the Pardoner insists over and over again that in spite of the actual good his preaching may do, his one and only intent is to cheat his victims. Avarice is his sole motive for preaching against avarice. How are we to take this? (See study question #2 below.)

The second section, the "Tale" up to l.342, where he finally says "now wol I telle forth my tale," appears to be a straitforward sermon on the three "tavern sins." Many readers mistake this for Christian doctrine, and find it powerful in spite of the fact that the Pardoner himself embodies all of the sins he preaches against. (Remember, he's actually preaching this sermon in a tavern, drinking!) As rhetorically powerful as the sermon is, however, it is quite at odds with the Bible and Christian doctrine. He reduces human life to the purely physical, and declares man no more than a disgusting animal, with no hint of the spiritual. "O wombe! O bely! O stinking cod, / Fulfild of donge and of corrupcioun!" (ll. 217-18) Another typical excess of the sermon is his claim that Adam and Eve fell from grace because of gluttony, whereas the Church understands their sin as pride.

The third part is the memorable exemplum of the three rioters who try to kill Death. Note their characterization: they are Dumb, Dumber and Dumbest, drunk and totally literal-minded. If they represent the Pardoner's view of Man, it is a darkly comic vision at best, cynical and nihilistic at worst. The mysterious Old Man, easily overlooked by first readers, can profitably be made the focus of the tale's interpretation. The Old Man wants to die, but cannot—and yet he knows where Death can be found. Recent critics sense that the Old Man may represent the Pardoner's own anguished despair. In the medieval Church, despair is the conviction that one is too evil to merit God's mercy; thus the sinner refuses to repent, plunging ever deeper into sin in order to assure his damnation. (See study question #3 below.)

The fourth part is the short epilogue starting at l.587, in which the Pardoner attempts to sell the pilgrims his phony wares. Why does he do this? (See study question #4 below.)

The key in all these suggestions is that the Pardoner's performance has a slick surface, but closer reading reveals complicating undercurrents and a host of perhaps unanswerable questions. What could Chaucer mean by leaving these questions so unanswerable? My own conclusion is that it is not our place to judge the Pardoner, it is God's. Our job, hard as it is, to "love the sinner but hate the sin," as St. Paul says. The tale poses quite a moral challenge to the reader.

Two brilliant and not unsimilar interpretations of the Pardoner and despair are in Marshall Leicester's The Disenchanted Self (Berkeley, 1990) and Lee Patterson's Chaucer and the Subject of History (Madison, WI, 1991). Harold Bloom summarizes some of their ideas in elementary form, stressing characterization, in The Western Canon (New York, 1994).

Questions for Study and Discussion:

1. Is the Pardoner in control of his own behavior, or is he driven to confess, like the Ancient Mariner? Is he tricking his listeners with fake honesty? Is he an amiable and comic con-artist, or a loathsome horror? What is Chaucer's attitude toward him? Is Chaucer lampooning the Church, or only the betrayal of Christian values he believes in? Is the Pardoner deformed, or gay? a predator, or a victim of medieval social attitudes?

2. In his opening confession does the Pardoner protest too much? Is he striking a pose at his own expense? Why? Though he is sinful, aren't his victims virtuous for giving him money? Is their gullibility a moral fault, or merely innocence?

3. Who is the Old Man who guides them to their death? If he represents the Pardoner's own despair, does this analysis affect our judgment of the Pardoner? Does it make him a more serious or sympathetic figure?

4. Why does the Pardoner try to sell his wares to the pilgrims? Is he crazy? Does he imagine he has them under his spell? Has he gotten so wrapped up in his sermon that he's forgotten where he is? Is it a test of his own skill? Or is he just asking for it? He calls down on himself the Host's savage attack; why is the Host so incredibly angry? Has he taken personal offense? Is he homophobic? Or does he hate the Pardoner for making a mockery of the Church, religion, salvation, and every social norm?

Christine de Pizan
The Book of the City of Ladies

The Book of the City of Ladies begins as the narrator, Christine, sits in her study reading. She happens to read The Book of the Lamentations of Mathéolus, a lengthy poetic tirade against women written in Latin about 1300 and translated into French in the late fourteenth century. Christine uses this misogynist tract to begin her defense of women, first comparing the concrete example of her own life with the generalizations about women made in Mathéolus. Dramatizing the powerful effects literature can have on our self-image, and in this case an internalized self-deprecation, the despairing narrator is visited by three female allegorical figures: Lady Reason (in the French, Raison), Lady Rectitude (Droitture), and Lady Justice (Justice) who counsel her to abandon her despair and work to right the wrong of misogyny. The argument in defense of women is furthered by an allegorical structure, as each account of good women functions like a brick in a walled city that will, once completed, provide a haven for "good women" and a defense against misogynist attacks.

The title, The City of Ladies, alludes to St. Augustine's City of God, but other classical and medieval texts have had the greatest influence on Christine's argument and on her material, probably most importantly Boccaccio's De Mulieribus Claris (Concerning Famous Women) and Dante's Divine Comedy, both readily available in English translations. Boccaccio's individual stories of famous women are interesting to compare with Christine's. While Dante places Semiramus and Dido in the second circle of hell, and while Boccaccio is disturbed by the two mythic figures' sins, Christine makes Semiramus the founding brick for her city and reads Dido quite differently from either Dante or Boccaccio. Because of the incest Semiramus commits with her son, students will likely find Semiramus a strange cornerstone for a city of virtuous ladies. An excellent discussion of Christine's apparent strategy is found in Maureen Quilligan, The Allegory of Female Authority: Christine de Pizan's Cite des Dames (Cornell, 1991), especially chapter two. Quilligan argues that Christine quite purposefully locates the founding cites for her tradition of female virtue and cultural contribution in Babylon and Carthage rather than in Rome, Troy, or Florence. Both cities, feminized and reviled in classical and religious narratives, are reclaimed as foundational for a woman's tradition. The incest taboo does not exist, Christine claims, until after the origins of written laws; she imagines a state of Nature before laws, one such as St. Augustine had posited in The City of God (see section 15.498 in The City of God).

The allegorical framework that provides the impetus for all the arguments and short tales about women that form Christine's examples is worth study. Readers should know that Christine borrows from genres familiar to late medieval audiences: the philosophical dialogue, allegory, elements from the dream-vision genre, among others. Many medieval narratives can be found in this genre, including Dante's <u>Divine Comedy</u>. Often, the late medieval dream vision invites psychological readings as well as allegorical ones. Guide-figures frequently counsel the dreamer-narrator and help him, in this case her, understand puzzling or disturbing questions. In the anthologized selection from the <u>City</u>, 1.9.2 (our pp. 1373-1374), Christine wonders why famous thinkers and writers often have such poor regard for women. She also wonders about the dissonances in Ovid, the first-century Roman writer whose works were well-known to the European Middle Ages, and why he "attacks women so much and so frequently." Christine's account of Dido and Aeneas (pp. 1383-1384) provides students with a perfect opportunity to compare Christine's readings of myth with Ovid's (pp.687-962).

The story of Saint Christine provides readers with a very short version of a saint's life, a genre extremely popular throughout the European Middle period. Because the writer-narrator is named after Saint Christine, this hagiography holds considerable importance. The name links the writer with the saint and both with Christ. The power of Saint Christine's voice to make an idol crumble, to sing and mock her enemies (even while being tortured), and to inspire the conversion of masses of people hold special valence within an argument written by another Christine who works to challenge culturally authorized assumptions about women and make them tumble and convert.

While students may be surprised at the sophisticated strategies of revision and argumentation present in Christine de Pizan's defense of women, they might also benefit from considering the conservativism that powerfully shapes her vision of a city. Sheila Delany's article "'Mothers to Think Back Through': Who Are They? The Ambiguous Example of Christine de Pizan," in <u>Medieval Texts and Contemporary Readers</u>, edited by Laurie Finke and Martin Schichtman (Cornell, 1987), provides a powerful critique of simple feminist readings of Christine de Pizan. At the conclusion of the <u>City</u>, not found in the anthology selection, Christine writes: "And you ladies who are married, do not scorn being subject to your husbands, for sometimes it is not the best thing for a creature to be independent." She notes that women with good husbands are lucky; that women with average husbands should praise God for not having severely vicious husbands and "should strive to moderate their [husband's] vices and pacify them"; and that women who have brutal husbands "should strive to endure them while trying to overcome their vices and lead them back, if they can, to a reasonable and seemly life. And if they are so obstinate that their wives are unable to do anything, at least they will acquire great merit for their souls through the virtue of patience." (These citations are from <u>The City of Ladies</u>, translated by Earl Jeffrey Richards, page 255. This is the same translation as our selection.) Delaney especially criticizes Christine for her reinscriptions of social class structures and for her essentialist views of women.

Questions for Study and Discussion:

1. What kind of person does Christine de Pizan construct for herself as the narrator in the opening scenes of the selection?

2. What strategies of argumentation does Christine de Pizan use in the selection to make her defense of women and encourage readers to reconsider some of the common and authorized assumptions about women?

3. Why would Christine make Semiramus the "corner-stone" of her city?

4. Compare Christine's depiction of Dido and Aeneas with Ovid's found earlier in the anthology.
How does Christine shape the mythic material to her own purposes?

5. Because the story of Saint Christine calls attention to the author's namesake, what parallels between the work of the saint and the work of the woman writer are suggested?

Michel de Montaigne
"Of Cannibals"

As the headnote to this selection indicates, this justly famous essay engages (among other important ideas) myths of a Golden Age and Noble Savage, re-working both; Ovid, More, and Rousseau are therefore excellent companions to set alongside Montaigne. Travel narratives, like those of Ibn Battutah and Marco Polo, are also extremely compatible with this text, which treats tales of "wild" people with wit, skepticism, and insight. Kamo no Chōmei's An Account of My Hermitage makes a further interesting comparison piece; like Montaigne and other writers in this anthology (Bashō, Tao Q'ian), Chōmei invites readers to enter a process of self-examination that begins in productive solitude.

Surely the most striking thing about "Of Cannibals" is the way it disappoints the expectations of luridness suggested by the title. This is purposeful, and figuring out why Montaigne couches his essay in a strategic disappointment of readers' expectations is a first step toward understanding and appreciating it. What is at stake is a definition of civility, cloaked in a discussion of barbarism. And this definition, while it has something to do with the Brazilian tribes—the "cannibals" of the essay's title—is principally concerned with a reexamination of European cultural insularity. Having begun by asking students what the title of the essay leads them to expect, a good way to proceed is by then asking them to describe (paragraph by paragraph, at least for the first part of the essay) what they discover instead. The step-by-step approach helps students separate out the main point of Montaigne's paragraphs from the details they don't understand. So, for example, in the first paragraph, the idea that received opinion is often mistaken as the main point that students need to see; the fact that they may never have heard of Pyrrhus is incidental.

When, some way into the essay, Montaigne at last turns to the indigenous Americans ("Now, to return to my subject . . ."[1391]), he has thus already dashed readers' certainties about the concept of barbarism, besides deflating their expectations of hope for a bloody account of cannibalistic gore. By aligning nature with what is wild, and artifice with what is distorted from nature (students can visualize this point by thinking of organic and irradiated foodstuffs), Montaigne moves the cannibals toward the positive end of a contemporary European scale of values. When the cruel practices of the cannibals are finally introduced, they are decidedly and purposefully anticlimactic: the cannibals are only so-called cannibals because, having adopted the far crueler vices of the "people from the other world"—i.e., the Europeans, who "were much greater masters than themselves in every sort of wickedness"—they no longer even practice the shocking vice for which they are known (1394). What we learn from Montaigne of cannibals, then, is that they are, in ways that are as flattering as they are humbling, no different than ourselves. Thus we are returned from criticism of the Other to self-criticism: the "boundless country . . . worthy of consideration" to which Montaigne refers at the beginning of his essay being as much a reference to the unexplored topography of the New World as it is to the unexamined interior world of our own attitudes and beliefs.

There are several good resources for study of Montaigne. Of these, the most accessible include From the Perspective of the Self: Montaigne's Self-Portrait (New York, 1994), by Craig B. Brush and Montaigne's Essais (London, 1987), by Dorothy Gabe Coleman. Students will appreciate Coleman's excellent second chapter, entitled (in part) "How to Read a Page of Montaigne." Teachers preparing one or more classes on Montaigne may find Approaches to Teaching Montaigne's Essays (New York, 1994, in the MLA series of teachers' guides), edited by Patrick Henry, a valuable resource.

Questions for Study and Discussion:

1. Why does Montaigne cite traditional European authorities so frequently in this essay?

2. What keeps Montaigne's view of indigenous peoples from being a simple precursor to Rousseau's idea of the Noble Savage?

3. How would you characterize the tone of the last sentence of the essay? Why do you think Montaigne includes this sentence?

4. Montaigne writes: "We ought to have topographers who would give us an exact account of the places where they have been." What rhetorical topographies are mapped in this essay? That is, having analyzed the essay, what are the previously unexplored possibilities it brings to light?

William Shakespeare
King Lear

The most obvious works to teach with Shakespeare's tragedy are the other dramatic works we have selected, from Euripides's Bacchae to Noh drama, Kālidāsa's Śakuntalā and the Ring of Recollection, and the modern absurdist Happy Days by Samuel Beckett. Different visions of human potential and destiny are expressed by the variations in cultural forms represented in these plays. Both Euripides and Shakespeare, for example, share the European concept of tragedy that befalls a heroic individual blinded by arrogant self-assertion, while types representing conflicting principles are the central focus in Indian drama. By the time of Samuel Beckett's postmodern plays, the possibility of tragedy is rendered impossible by a meaningless universe.

The story of Job in the Hebrew Bible is an early predecessor to the crushing injustice we encounter in King Lear, and it similarly raises the question of whether there is any ultimate justice in the universe. A very different, quietly contemplative response to old age and disappointment is presented in "On Encountering Sorrow" by the ancient Chinese poet Qu Yuan. Also King Lear's terrible journey of self-realization can be usefully contrasted to Bashō's deliberate pilgrimage away from civilization and its discontents in The Narrow Road to the Interior. Both the tragic English king and the Zen poet test their values in the natural landscape, with different initial motives and final realizations as death nears. For Lear, heroic anguish gives way to identification with the most humble of beings but bursts forth anew when his virtuous daughter Cordelia is murdered. Bashō understands from the beginning of his journey that self-consciousness and ambition stand in the way of genuine communion with the spiritual essence of the natural world. Other similarly instructive contrasts can be made with Dostoyevsky's Notes from Underground and T.S. Eliot's bleak vision in "The Waste Land."

King Lear is such a well-known play in the Western tradition that students will in some ways feel on familiar ground. They should quickly grasp the tragic movement of Lear's rejection by his cruel daughters and the sub-plot concerning the Earl of Gloucester's disastrous misreading of the characters of his sons. The play's language will be challenging for most students, but if they are assured that context will gradually open up the basic meanings of words, they can relax and come to feel comfortable. Videotapes of performances and films of King Lear can be helpful in introducing students to the dramatic qualities of the play. Lawrence Olivier's 1984 film version of the play is widely available, and Japanese filmmaker Kurosawa's 1986 adaptation, Ran, offers a vividly illuminating contrast which changes the old king's daughters to sons and sets the action amidst bloody samurai warfare.

Close attention to the conflicts and responses of characters in the opening scene will help to orient students to the themes that dominate the play. Edmund's illegitimacy and his father's callous jesting at the beginning introduce the problem of parent-child relationships, ambition, and sexuality which become blatantly obvious when Lear demands testimony of the love his daughters bear him and then explodes with rage when his expectations are foiled by Cordelia. Look closely at the declarations of the three daughters in I.i, with Cordelia providing choral commentary on the emptiness of her sisters' claims. Kent's determined honesty stands with Cordelia's as a contrast to Goneril and Regan, and the ending of the scene makes explicit the villainy that will gradually overtake the king. Students can easily follow the unfolding of the Gloucester subplot in I.ii, but they will need help in seeing that Edmund's soliloquy is not meant to be reasonable, in spite of how plausible it may sound to modern ears. Any character who speaks so cynically in Shakespeare is sure to prove a villain.

Lear's colloquy with his Fool marks a crucial psychological awakening in I.iv, and it is important to point out that Court Fools or Jesters were granted a special dispensation to mock and tease those in authority, pretending to be simple-minded or tricksters whose irreverence entertained. With this persona, the Fool can probe the King's errors and bring him to understanding through riddles. Then in Act II, the King is gradually deprived of his authority, and Gloucester's decent son is exiled in a parallel treachery.

Act III brings the critical turning point of the play. First we have a report of Lear's exposure on the heath, and then in III.ii Lear himself appears, howling at the storm and the gods. His awakening and humbling proceed intertwined with the madness that deranges his sense of identity. Thus by the end of scene ii, he sympathizes with the Fool, and by scene iv finally realizes that a man is "but a poor, bare, fork'd animal" like "Tom O'Bedlam," the mad beggar whom Edgar pretends to be. Poor Tom becomes his new teacher, a Natural Fool who takes the place of the Court Fool who soon disappears from the play. By scene vi of Act III, Lear has completely lost touch with the literal reality around him and instead plays out a symbolic restoration of justice by acting out the arraignment of his wicked daughters in Gloucester's barn. Edgar, still disguised as Poor Tom, provides a summary of the scene's meaning in his closing soliloquy. But worse is to come, as fiendish sadism is visited upon Gloucester by his guests in Act III, scene vii. This scene of Cornwall's gleeful blinding of the old man is one that offers an extreme vision of evil as an active force in the play. Asking students to connect this bodily violence to contemporary examples in television and film can stimulate lively discussion about the ethical and psychological effects of the subplot, and its function in intensifying the significance of Lear's mental anguish.

Act IV brings the two suffering old men into contact with each other and provides a powerfully ironic conversation between the mad, but oddly wise old king and the insightful though physically blind Gloucester. Close attention should be paid to Edgar's rescue of his father and his strange performance of the imaginary "fall" from the cliffs of Dover in IV.vi, which brings Gloucester to an acceptance of his fate. Immediately afterward, Lear appears, mad and crowned with flowers. Students should work through Lear's pronouncements to see what kind of symbolic wisdom he seeks to share. As Edgar exclaims, this is "Matter and impertinency mix'd, / Reason in madness," and Shakespeare uses it to present a fierce condemnation of social corruption. Weaving in and out between the scenes dealing with the principal tragic heroes are episodes chronicling the increasing discord and suspicion among the treacherous usurpers of the old men's roles and properties. These need to be examined with students, to be sure the basic plot business is clearly understood.

The final act of the tragedy has been a controversial one through the centuries. Cordelia's defeat and death seemed too horrible and unnatural to Neoclassical sensibilities in the late seventeenth century, so that in 1681 Nahum Tate revised the play to provide a happy ending that held the stage for a century and a half. Students can debate the issue of the surprise catastrophe in an effort to understand why Shakespeare chose to reverse the possibility of justice and restoration, instead contriving a meaningless accident which destroys one of the purest exemplars of virtue in the world of the play. The ending can be related to the Holocaust of World War II and more recent acts of genocide in Africa, Central America, Southeast Asia, and the Balkans.

For general background on Shakespeare's theatrical world, The Bedford Companion to Shakespeare (New York, 1996) offers a wealth of up-to-date information and copies of relevant documents from his milieu. An older but still helpful introduction to the play is Maynard Mack's King Lear in Our Time (Berkeley, 1965). Stanley Cavell's essay, "The Avoidance of Love: A Reading of King Lear" in his Disowning Knowledge: In Six Plays of Shakespeare (New York, 1987) is a strong, more recent reading. Stephen Greenblatt's essay, "Shakespeare and the Exorcists" in his Shakespearean Negotiations:The Circulation of Social Energy in Elizabethan England (Berkeley, 1988) is a classic of New Historicist criticism. A feminist approach is provided by Coppelia Kahn's "The Absent Mother in King Lear" in the anthology Rewriting the Renaissance: The Discourse of Sexual Difference in Early Modern Europe (Chicago, 1986), edited by Margaret W. Ferguson, Maureen Quilligan, and Nancy J. Vickers.

Questions for Study and Discussion:

1. What problems and conflicts emerge in the first scene of King Lear? Look closely at the opening conversation between the Earls of Gloucester and Kent, and the reaction of Gloucester's illegitimate son Edmund to their banter. Look closely at the speeches of King Lear's three daughters and decide which are truthful. Notice the use of the word "nothing," and compare it to Lear's use of the word at the play's end. Why does Kent defy the King, and what do we learn from Cordelia's suitors? Where are we by the end of the scene?

2. What kind of a person is Edmund? What is the definition of Nature produced by his soliloquy in Act I, scene ii? Remember that soliloquies in Shakespeare follow the conventional understanding that characters always speak the truth when alone and addressing the audience.

Edmund's reasoning may sound justified to a modern audience, but how does it look when placed beside the actions he performs during the rest of Act II?

3. Can we believe the charges brought against Lear by Goneril in I.iii? Examine Act I, scene iv closely to see what their relations seem to be, particularly in light of Goneril's instructions to her servant Oswald.

4. What is the Fool's role in Act I, scene iv? What are the purpose and effect of his riddling speeches to Lear in this scene?

5. In Act II, scene ii, why does Kent insult Oswald, and what symbolic purpose is served by his being placed in the stocks? Shakespeare uses this situation to powerful effect when Lear appears outside Gloucester's castle and sees his servant thus humiliated.

6. How does Edgar's disguise both protect him and communicate a central truth about the whole play?

7. In Act II, scene iv, what is the effect of Lear's quarrel with Goneril and Regan and their decision to reduce his train of knights? What is Lear's state of mind by the end of the scene? Notice through these early scenes, and throughout the play, how often the word "fool" appears; in fact, you might make a list of its uses.

8. What does King Lear learn in Act III? Identify two or three speeches that are especially revealing. The turning point of Shakespeare's plays usually occurs in Act III; does that happen here, and if so, where and why? What has happened to Lear's mind by the end of Act III?

9. Why does Shakespeare add the blinding of Gloucester to the traditional stories about King Lear? How does it function in relation to King Lear's situation?

10. Is Gloucester's "suicide" in Act IV plausible? How do you think it would work on stage? Why does Edgar take his father through this imaginary suffering?

11. When Lear and Gloucester meet in Act IV, scene vi, what do they see in each other? What is the symbolic function of this scene, and what are we to learn from Lear's mad speeches?

12. What is the purpose of Lear's reunion with Cordelia? What is his state of mind?

13. Why does Edmund repent in Act V? Is his change of heart believable?

14. What is the effect of Cordelia's death in Act V? What is the meaning of Lear's response, and how are we to take the final speech of the play? What happens to Kent?

Cervantes
Don Quixote

Given Cervantes's purpose of satirizing the sentimentalized medieval conventions of the Romance tradition, comparison of <u>Don Quixote</u> with the chivalric <u>Lais</u> of Marie de France is an important way to help students see what kinds of inappropriate fantasies the old <u>hidalgo</u> is indulging. One of the most obvious mistakes he makes is that of anachronism—expecting to find twelfth or thirteenth-century situations in sixteenth-century Spain. Changes in concepts of heroism can be explored by reading Cervantes with <u>The Epic of Gilgamesh</u>, Homer's <u>Odyssey</u>, Virgil's <u>Aeneid</u>, and such Asian narratives as the <u>Rāmāyana</u> and <u>Mahābhārata</u>, and Sima Qian's <u>Records of the Historian</u>. <u>The Shāh-nāmah</u> offers an interesting example of heroic literature from the medieval Persian world. Cervantes mocked the heroic tradition in order to demonstrate the need to turn away from ridiculous physical adventure to the moral dilemmas of ordinary life, and to question the role of narrative in addressing them. Useful texts to consider as alternative approaches to these issues are Murasaki Shikibu's <u>Tale of Genji</u> and Chōmei's <u>Account of my Hermitage</u>.

The opening chapter of <u>Don Quixote</u> is very important in its presentation of the essential situation and character of the rural gentleman who becomes Don Quixote de la Mancha. Some students may have experience of Spanish history and literature that can be brought into play to establish the plight of the <u>hidalgo</u> class of landed gentry being left behind in Spain's imperial development. The hero of Cervantes's novel is a member of this class, and its relation to the romance tradition of medieval chivalry is very important background. Even without knowledge of Spanish political and social history, however, students will be able to infer a great deal about "those gentlemen who always have a lance in the rack, an ancient buckler, a skinny nag, and a greyhound for the chase." Close examination of Quixote's habits and standard of living will reveal his poverty. Fantasies of an earlier era when this class might have been part of a glorious aristocracy are understandable reflexes in such a context. The possible names suggested for our particular gentleman are sly jokes on Cervantes's part: "Quijada" meaning jawbone, "Quesada" meaning "cheesy," and "Quejana" (from the verb <u>quejar</u>, to complain or lament) suggesting a whiner. Students can be asked to discuss the ways Quixote's reading is described and the effect it has on their own sense of the story, and of literature in general.

One of the most fruitful approaches to the old knight's adventures is to explore the sources of Cervantes's humor. Some are obvious, as when the armor is described as made of cardboard and the outmoded equipment of foot-soldiers, or the famous episode in which Quixote mistakes windmills for lawless giants. But more subtle questions can be asked about the common habit of mocking idealism in most societies, and the function Cervantes's exaggeration might have in pointing up both the absurdity of extreme ethical behavior, and also the way it dramatizes the meanness and selfishness of most people's behavior. Sancho Panza is as famous as his master, and the contrasts between this earthy character and his deluded master are important to discuss. It is interesting to speculate on the ways the two characters could be seen to satirically represent social classes, and the wry light Cervantes seems to cast upon unequal social bonds. Sancho Panza's practicality does not prevent him from getting caught up in the delusions of his master, and students can be asked to comment on how fully they think he shares Quixote's view of the world. Students can trace the influence of this comic pair in popular media of our own century.

The standard biography of Cervantes is William Byron's Cervantes, A Biography (Garden City, New York, 1978). A briefer introduction to the life and works is provided in the Twayne Cervantes by Manuel Duran (Boston, 1974). Louis A. Murillo offers a thorough interpretive grounding in A Critical Introduction to Don Quixote (New York, 1988), while a more focused scholarly study is Stephen Gilman's The Novel According to Cervantes (Berkeley, 1989).

Questions for Study and Discussion:

1. What sort of a man is the old gentleman described as at the beginning of the story? His possessions, dress, and eating habits tell us a great deal about his status.

2. Why does Don Quixote read so much? Exactly what kind of literature attracts him most, and why? Who are his heroes?

3. What do we learn about Quixote's state of mind when we read about the way he outfits and names himself in preparation for chivalrous adventures?

4. Does Don Quixote learn anything from his adventure with the windmills? What is Cervantes's satiric point? Why does the innkeeper indulge the old man's fantasies?

5. Contrast Don Quixote with his squire Sancho Panza. How do they differ, both physically and mentally? What qualities or values might each represent?

6. What is the nature of Don Quixote's devotion to Dulcinea del Toboso? What is it that he loves in her, and how does he seek to prove his love? Does this behavior have anything to do with reality?

7. What kind of spell does the story of Don Quixote and Sancho Panza finally cast on you as a reader? Has it changed your understanding of the purpose of fantasies, or the light that illusions can shed on ordinary experience? Think of one example of how your thinking has been changed.

Naguib Mahfouz
"Zaabalawi"

From his early historical novels, Mahfouz has returned again and again to representing fate, and that is surely one of the elements to be considered in this short story. He also turned early on in his career to the streets of Cairo, where a plethora of characters and situations easily give rise to the colorful everyday life that forms a more or less realistic social backdrop for the narrator's quest. Belonging to a category of modern urban literature, the depiction of Cairo might be usefully compared with other descriptions of modern cityscapes found throughout the modern section of the anthology. But students might also be encouraged to consider whether what appears to be realism might have its own forms of "conventionality," and whether a kind of valorization of the ordinary forms, therefore, a tension with the very commonplace setting it tries to express.

As the headnotes mention, the narrative chastises the technological and scientific advances of the Western twentieth-century because they have blinded the West to the common humanity of the entire global community. Students might find Mahfouz's Nobel acceptance speech useful in considering the short story. (The speech is readily available.) A concern with the powers of technology and science does not mean, however, that Mahfouz longs for a former time or that he simply opposes technology or science; instead, a careful reading of his corpus suggests that he thinks science may hold important gifts for humanity, but he worries that its misuse may empower some at the expense of others. Mahfouz has been extremely outspoken, criticizing governments, fanaticism of all sorts, and has even been censored for producing too blasphemous a narrative in his novel, Awlad Haratina (Children of Gebelawi, the book's English title). The book incited extremists to issue a fatwa against the author, not nearly as well-publicized as the fatwa issued against Rushdie. To date, the novel has not been published in Egypt as a complete text. (It was originally serialized between September and December of 1959.) Awlad Haratina represents God as a human figure and offers up an allegorical version of history from Genesis to the twentieth century, representing Jewish, Christian, and Muslim religious figures, not as divine prophets but as social reformers. Science, represented as Arafa, a character who might offer the alley people of Cairo some benefits, quests after Gebelawi (the allegorical figure of God), but accidentally kills Gebelawi's house servant and indirectly causes Gebelawi's death from grief. The story is more complicated than this brief glimpse affords, but suggests the persistent attraction Mahfouz has for allegory set within realistic alley and market life.

If Mahfouz's thinking sometimes borders on the iconoclastic, his prose style is somewhat traditional. It refuses the colloquial dialects of Cairo's spoken Arabic (called 'āmmiyyah) and prefers the cultivated and elite language of literary Arabic (called fushā). This pull in his work—between Western forms of stream-of-consciousness, realism, and genre on the one hand, and Arabic literary traditions of allegory, dream, quest and stylized literary language on the other hand—create some of the haunting qualities of his art. Students can benefit from examining the pulls of allegory and realism within the short story included in the anthology.

In addition to background provided by the Cambridge History of Modern Arabic Literature, edited by M. M. Badawi (Cambridge, 1992), other texts that may prove useful include: Naguib Mahfouz: From Regional Fame to Global Recognition, edited by M. Beard and A. Haydar (Syracuse, NY, 1993); Sasson Somekh, "Zaabalawi — Author, Theme and Technique," Journal of Arabic Literature, 1 (1970):24-35; Trevor Le Gassick, editor, Critical Perspectives on Naguib Mahfouz (Washington, DC, 1991); Mona N. Mikhail, Studies in the Short Fiction of Mahfouz and Idris (New York, 1992); and Samia Mehrez, Egyptian Writers Between History and Fiction (Cairo, 1994). Mahfouz's Nobel Prize acceptance speech is reprinted in Matti Moosa's article, "Naguib Mahfouz: Life in the Alley of Arab History," Georgia Review 49.1 (Spring 1995): 216-30.

Questions for Study and Discussion:

1. Why does the narrator go on the quest for Sheikh Zaabalawi? What are the contours of this quest? Do the figures the narrator encounters resemble guide figures in other quest narratives found within the anthology?

2. How would you characterize the narrator in the short story? What sort of person tells the tale? What elements in the text build, for you, a sense of who this narrator is?

3. What purpose does the dream have for the narrator?

4. The narrator thinks, at the end of the text, "yes, I have to find Zaabalawi," but did he succeed? What possible ways of reading the text seem reasonable? What is the effect of leaving such an open ending?

5. What tensions seem to emerge from the contrary impulses in the text: one toward allegory and the other toward realism? Where do the cues that one is reading allegory arise? What elements seem more allegorical and what elements seem more realistic? Why?

Salwa Bakr
"That Beautiful Undiscovered Voice"

  This story takes place in the domestic realm of Egyptian women's lives, so that its scope is limited by the conventional roles and private sphere assigned to women in traditional Islamic society. Thus the closest literary examples from other world cultures will be circumscribed feminine realms like that of Lady Murasaki in the medieval Japanese Tale of Genji or the Chinese family compound of The Dream of the Red Chamber, or in more recent times the predominantly feminine enclaves of Jane Austen's novel Pride and Prejudice. By Austen's day, however, women and men socialized together in domestic settings, as they do also in the late Victorian milieu of Virginia Woolf's To the Lighthouse. Bakr's story can be compared in fruitful ways with these works, with special attention paid to the range of activity and possible expression for women in these different worlds. James Joyce's "Eveline," William Faulkner's "That Evening Sun," and Ángela Hernández's "How to Gather the Shadows of Flowers" all present situations of entrapment for women protagonists that resonate with the plight of Bakr's Sayyida. In each case, the shaping of the character's predicament and the impossibility of escape dramatize the human tragedies endured by many women. Marie Lazarre of Louise Erdrich's "Saint Marie" is an instructive contrast—a very different kind of young woman who insists on determining her own destiny in spite of severe social restrictions. Bakr's use of the mysterious voice seems a technique drawn from the kind of Magical Realism Gabriel García Márquez uses in "The Handsomest Drowned Man in the World" or Toni Morrison uses in describing Shadrack's hands in Sula.

  The title of this short story is a key to its unraveling. Students can move immediately to question what kind of a voice suddenly bursts forth from the protagonist, and what it might mean within the severely ritualized, restricted round of daily activities Sayyida is accustomed to performing. If close attention is paid to the opening paragraph, with its recital of the cleaning rituals and afternoon news tuned to the required low pitch, then Abdul Hamid's uneasiness about his wife's behavior sets the reader's attention upon his wife's edgy behavior. Abdul Hamid's expectations and plans for punishing his wife make an interesting contrast to her inner experience. Students should look closely at the dynamic interchanges between husband and wife as Sayyida tries to explain the voice that has taken possession of her. What possibilities the voice represents can be seen in contrast to the crisis that returns her life to "normal" by the end of the story.

For a brief historical context of Salwa Bakr's work, describing the history of Egyptian women's writing in the modern era, Marilyn Booth's Introduction to My Grandmother's Cactus: Stories by Egyptian Women (London, 1991) is useful.

Study and Discussion Questions:

1. What do the rituals at the beginning of the story tell us about the main character's life, and what function do they have as the story continues?

2.. Does Abdul Hamid see his wife as a companion, or simply as a servant? How would you describe their relationship by the end of the story? Has it proved to be dynamic or is it frozen by habit?

3. How does Bakr define the voice that suddenly pours out of Sayyida? Notice the kinds of songs she yearns to sing, and try to decide what the voice represents.

4. What do we learn about Sayyida's world as she struggles to find a receptive listener to her story about the mysterious voice?

5. Why does Sayyida lose the "beautiful, undiscovered voice"?

Fadwa Tuqan
Poems

These poems range from more secular and historical concerns, such as those expressed in "The Aging City" and "Face Lost in the Wilderness," to love poetry, to the more spiritual poetry of "I Found It." Although Fadwa Tuqan has lived on the West Bank most of her life, her poem "The Aging City" features a Palestinian refugee, a persona often featured in post-1948 Palestinian literature. The poem begins in London and expresses, in italic passages, memories of Nablus, where the poet was, herself, born, as well as the speaker's interpretation of her relationship to the urban London cityscape. The speaker remembers Aisha's letter, sent to her from a prison in Palestine, where Aisha holds fast to her own memory of the landscape despite the guard's claim that "the trees have fallen." The speaker in the poem also calls attention to her alienation from other London city dwellers, like the man who makes a pass at her and the old woman walking her dog: "We remain on the surface, touching nothing" (l. 84). The poem, with its sense of disconnection and alienation, resembles Eliot's "The Waste Land." The speaker finds herself alienated from Londoners, from the urban masses, and separated by time and space from her life as a young girl in Palestine and from her friend, Aisha, whose letter from prison bespeaks only another form of alienation and discontinuity. Just as Aisha refuses the guard's information about the landscape, so the speaker refuses the sexual advances of a man she encounters on a park bench. The speaker's sense of alienation runs deeper, however, as she chastises herself for having "learned not to disturb the path of traffic" (ll. 17-18). Her sense of having betrayed her parents (figuratively sold in the London slave market) and of having betrayed the souls of the dead who, she imagines "cursed me / as I gave way for a tank to pass" when she was a child, suggest the chasm caused by the Palestinian diaspora. But where she obeys the traffic lights in London streets and where she stepped back away from the tanks in the streets of Nablus, she now refuses to join London's loose "hippie" culture. Her connection is with Aisha, the one imprisoned but determined to remember, and fiercely dream another world.

By way of contrast, "In the Flux" describes the intimacy of a love affair. Imagery in the poem is particularly worthy of study. Students may want to consider to what extent the imagery resembles love poetry of the medieval Middle East and to what extent it seems to borrow from a European tradition. "Face Lost in the Wilderness" may be read along with Amichai's poem, "Jerusalem, 1967" to explore ways both poets—one Israeli, one Palestinian—read the city. "I Found It" is not a complicated text, but it does demonstrate the continuing tradition of religious writing and resembles some of the medieval Islamic poetry included in the anthology.

Few resources exist which focus exclusively on Fadwa Tuqan's poetry, but Carmen Sue Cross has written a short Master's Thesis available through interlibrary loan: "The Impact of Political Conflict on Contemporary Arabic Feminine Literature: A Study of Fadwa Tuqan" (Columbus, Ohio: Ohio State University,1996). More general surveys of modern Arabic literature may also prove useful, including: Barbara M. Parmenter's book, Giving Voice to Stones: Place and Identity in Palestinian Literature (Austin, TX, 1994). A book useful for a Palestinian perspective is Khalid A. Sulaiman's Palestine and Modern Arab Poetry (London, 1984); it includes brief discussions of Fadwa Tuqan's poetry and more extended discussions of Ibrahim Tuqan's verse. (He is her brother.) The Cambridge History of Arabic Literature: Modern Arabic Literature, edited by M. M. Badawi (Cambridge, 1992) provides an extensive background for any discussion of modern Arabic literature.

Questions for Study and Discussion:

1. Consider the poetic techniques and images in Tuqan's poems. Although the poet represents herself as one extremely alienated from the England around her, do the images and techniques assist that representation or pull against it?

2. What meanings seem to emerge from the speaker's recollection of a letter from Aisha?

3. Whereas the speaker tries to remain separate from the flux in "In the Aging City," in the next poem, "In the Flux," she seems to relish fusion with the other. How do you explain the difference? What images help the poet represent her evening with her beloved? Are these images common in other love poetry in the anthology? How does this poem compare with the love poetry of Ibn Hazm or Rumi's poem, "When you display that rosy cheek?" With Petrarch's rime #3?

4. What image of Jerusalem comes through in Tuqan's poem, "Face Lost in the Wilderness"? How does that compare with Amichai's images of the same city in his poem, "Jerusalem, 1967"?

5. What does the poet find in her poem, "I Found It"? How does this poem compare with other spiritual quest poems of the medieval Middle East?

Yehuda Amichai
"Jerusalem, 1967" and "Tourists"

Modern Israeli poetry, developing since the founding of the modern state of Israel in 1948, negotiates a number of influences upon its forms, its perspectives, its themes and its language. Late twentieth-century Hebrew poetry emerging from the Middle Eastern state of Israel reveals the influence of biblical literature, orthodox Jewish literature and thought, modern Israeli nationalism, the holocaust in Europe that contributed significantly to the shape of the modern Israeli state, the ongoing political and cultural effects of European imperialism in the Middle East, and the influence of European and American writing. But this influence is not simple. In some of Israel's early generations of writers, a rejection of, or resistance to, the spiritual and cultural world of the Eastern European Jewish diaspora creates interesting tensions where fathers or ancestors who survived the holocaust are uneasily rejected in favor of a commitment to the new Jewish state. The past haunts the younger generations, as writers are both attracted to and alienated by the worlds of their fathers and mothers. Addressing a writer's convention in 1968, Amichai said, "Words are a new beginning with the stones of the past. No matter how small these stones or how broken they are the new building will be stronger. Influential people and rabbis have never understood this: words are not a defense of deeds, they are not a hard shell. Words are a living kernel, not versions and not formulas, but life" (his speech was published as "Dorot ba-aretz," Lamerhav, May 3, 1968). He was also keenly aware of his creative weaving of past and present together in his poems. In an interview with Esther Fuchs, he noted: "Every word we use . . . reverberates through the halls of Jewish history. Coming from a religious background, the spoken language I use still retains for me the original traditional flavor. In my poems I work with both levels, the new and the old, simultaneously. In my poems I try to recreate and reinterpret. In this sense my writing is genuinely Jewish" (see Encounters with Israeli Authors, ed. Fuchs. Marblehead: Micah Publications, 1982, pp. 86-92).

The poem "Jerusalem, 1967" is organized loosely as a dramatic interaction of God, Jerusalem, and the poet's lyric "I." In Hebrew the word "city" ('ir) is grammatically feminine, but poetic language here also casts Jerusalem as a woman who can be cruel, vain, stubbornly contrary, self-indulgent, or benevolent; who can be protector, mother, and beautiful lover; who can be besieged and vulnerable as well as warring and triumphant. The relationship of persona with city is one key element students can fruitfully explore in the poem. Relationships between God and Jerusalem, and God and the poet are equally crucial elements in Amichai's poem. As the persona returns to the city over and over throughout the poem cycle, a parallel begins to emerge between the discontinuous past of the poet (uprooted from Europe and transplanted in Israel) and the multicultural history of the city (which, over the centuries was passed around among a group of conquerors). Jerusalem, often romanticized in other Israeli poetry written right after the 1967 war, is not simply praised and worshiped in Amichai's verse. The city's history intertwines with war and crisis, and its identity is no more constant than the poet's: it is now Yerushalayim (Hebrew), now Al-Quds (Arabic), now Aelia Capitolina (Latin), and so on (see lines 92-99). Its uneasy present day is apparent in the persona's fears of future wars: "a light warning remains in everything, / like the movement of a light veil: warning" (26-27).

Amichai's poem "Tourists" asks readers to see the voyeurism of tourism and ways it encourages a romantic objectification of place, as well as ways it encourages a blindness toward the present and toward the human inhabitants of historical spaces. Its movement from poetry to prose reinforces the poem's desire for tourists to rethink and re-envision their relationship to other people's present and other people's cities and landmarks.

Resources for studying Amichai include: Glenda Abramson, The Writing of Yehuda Amichai (Albany, 1989), which contains an extended interpretation of the poem, "Jerusalem, 1967", and Abramson's more recent book, The Experienced Soul: Studies in Amichai (Boulder, CO, 1997); Modern Hebrew literature, ed., Robert Alter (NY, 1975); Amichai's book, Poems of Jerusalem: a bilingual edition (New York, 1988) offers teachers and students fluent in Hebrew opportunities for exploring translation issues; Points of Departure: International Writers on Writing and Politics, interviews by David Montenegro (Ann Arbor, MI, 1991); Joseph Cohen, Voices of Israel (Albany, NY, 1990); Edward Hirsch, Responsive reading (Ann Arbor, MI, 1999); Haim Chertok, We are all Close: Conversations with Israeli Writers (New York, 1989); Chana Kronfeld, "'The Wisdom of Camouflage': Between Rhetoric and Philosophy in Amichai's Poetic System," Prooftexts: A Journal of Jewish Literary History, 10. 3 (September) 1990: 469-91.

Questions for Study and Discussion:

1. Although a translation, what elements in "Jerusalem, 1967" appear to be echoes of biblical literature? How do these echoes function?

2. Why does Amichai repeat the word "illuminated" in section 3?

3. How would you characterize the depiction of the city of Jerusalem in Amichai's poem?

4. What kind of relationship does the persona in the poem have to the city? To God? Do these relationships help us understand what the poem is about?

5. How are tourists described in Amichai's poem on the subject (p. 1534)?

6. Why does "Tourists" move from poetic verse in the first stanza to prose in the second?

7. How and why does the persona ask tourists and their guides to reconceive an understanding of Jerusalem in the second stanza? What are the two conceptual frameworks around tourism that the persona plays with? What are the effects of this playing with frameworks?

8. Compare Amichai's sense of place and time in "Jerusalem, 1967" with Fadwa Tuqan's "In the Aging City," T. S. Eliot's "The Waste Land," and Szymborska's "The Century's Decline."

9. What implications does this poem have for studying any text in world literature?

Léopold Sédar Senghor
Poems

Like so many other writers represented in this anthology, Senghor stands between two cultures—in his case, West African and French. He is perhaps unique, however, in the degree of influence and status he exercised in both of his cultures. Widely admired in France, where he became in 1983 the first black African elected to the prestigious Académie Française, he also served his native Senegal as president from its independence in 1960 until 1981. This cultural duality is an essential feature of his poetry. He is very much in the tradition of his older French contemporaries Paul Claudel (1868-1955) and Saint-John Perse (1887-1975), who wrote a lengthy poetic line inspired by biblical verse and frequently filled with an aura of myth and mystery. At the same time, he is very much aware of the oral tradition of the <u>dyali</u>, the troubadour of Western Africa, who used only "the golden red stylet of his tongue" (see "The Return of the Prodigal Son," line 12). Moreover, the historical and mythic references that dot his poetry often derive from the African tradition: the Mali Empire, that dominated West Africa from the eleventh to the seventeenth centuries, the noble <u>guelwar</u>, who descend from the conquering Mandinques, the kings who reigned in the southwestern region of Senegal known as Sine, etc. It is important to note that Senghor sees his two cultures as necessarily linked, as "joined by the navel" (see "Prayer to Masks," line 12) and yet he believes that the cultural spirit of each is radically different from the other. In an essay written in 1939 ("Ce que l'homme noir apporte"), Senghor wrote that "African reason does not impoverish things, it does not mold them into rigid schemes, eliminating the juice and sap; it flows into the arteries of things, it feels all the contours so as to lodge in the living heart of the real. European reason is analytical through utilization, African reason is intuitive through participation."

The difficulty of Senghor, and he is a poet as difficult in his own way as Rilke is in his, derives both from the complexity and richness of his mixed cultural world and from the emotionally ambivalent position he obviously occupies between these worlds. Although students and teachers will no doubt find his work sometimes perplexing, one critical message should come through quite clearly: Senghor longs for the sensuality, the earth, the night, and even the spiritual presence of his dead ancestors in his native land. The teacher can engage the students in a discussion of whether Senghor's poetry, as represented here, celebrates his bicultural status or bemoans it. "Is the movement between two cultures represented here by Senghor, a condition that is becoming more and more common in our modern world," we might ask, "as much a loss as a gain?" "The Return of the Prodigal Son," written in the late 1930's after a long sojourn in Europe, for all its difficulty, is a particularly poignant statement of this problem. Senghor returns once more to "the fresh bed of childhood," but unlike the biblical Prodigal Son, he departs again: "Tomorrow, I shall take again the road to Europe" (line 76). Some Africans, Wole Soyinka among them, have taken issue with what they perceive as Senghor's essentially assimilationist art, an art which they believe consists of a dialogue between an African past and an European present.

It is essential to approach Senghor as a poet of feeling who is trying to take the reader into another world. His frequent use of African words might frustrate us, but it also reminds us of the fluidity of language and of the fact that languages, in this case French, can expand to include new worlds of experience. Senghor writes his poetry against the backdrop of colonialism, under which his own "Fathers . . . allowed contempt and derision . . . prohibitions and segregations" ("The Return of the Prodigal Son," line 44), but there is little bitterness in his poetry precisely because his own goal, which some labeled naive, was always universality. The tensions and even contradictions inherent in the work of this great poet, if anything, have gained relevance as the years have passed. He presents the teacher with a particularly good opportunity to explore the ironies and challenges of multicultural life.

In addition to the translations of John Reed and Clive Wake included in the anthology, one might also consult Léopold Sédar Senghor, <u>The Collected Poetry</u>, translated and with an introduction by Melvin Dixon (Charlottesville, NC, 1991). Dixon's introductory essay is particularly interesting. A biography that says much about the cultural and political complexities of Senghor's life is Janet G. Vaillant, <u>Black, French, and African: A Life of Léopold Sédar Senghor</u> (Cambridge, MA, 1990). On the rather difficult issue of "negritude," see Sylvia

Washington Ba, The Concept of Negritude in the Poetry of Léopold Sédar Senghor (Princeton, 1973).

Questions for Study and Discussion:

1. "Nuit de Sine" is one of Senghor's most often anthologized poems. It takes the reader into a highly intimate world that is distant from one's own immediate experience. How does it work then (or does it?) as a more general statement with which we all can identify?

2. The black woman is a recurrent theme in Senghor's poetry. What does she seem to represent? How do you respond to this treatment of the "feminine?"

3. "Prayer to Masks" is really a prayer offered to the ancestors who are represented in West African ritual by masks. The poet's prayer turns in this poem to Europe. What might be the crisis in Europe of which he speaks and what can Africa provide?

4. Consider Senghor's use of the biblical story of the "Prodigal Son" (Luke 15:11-32). How does his attitude both resemble and differ from that of the biblical character?

5. Judging from these two poems, how successful was Senghor's attempt to, as he put it, "assimilate without being assimilated?"

Grace Ogot
"The Bamboo Hut"

Stories of mysteriously separated twins occur in narrative traditions around the world, a fact that might provide an interesting beginning for class discussion. Why might this be? "The Bamboo Hut" is based as well on other familiar folk motifs such as that of the abandoned baby who reappears in a fateful way, the king or tribal leader who has no son to succeed him, and the young man who unwittingly falls in love with a close relative. Grace Ogot's charming story can be taught with the Biblical stories of Moses, Abraham, and Joseph, in which these motifs are played out in a similar tribal world of patriarchs and clever mothers. The story of Joseph treats the notion of abandonment from a very different perspective and shows another way an unrecognized sibling can intervene in brothers' lives. The Greek myth of Oedipus is another obvious link, and although we have not included Sophocles's tragedy in the anthology, the story is a familiar part of Western popular culture and thus can be contrasted to Ogot's when discussion begins. Certainly Euripides's Bacchae offers a radically different situation for the meeting of relatives who fail to recognize each other; the mother's treatment of her child in this play is a horrifying alternative to Achieng's.

Students should have no trouble understanding the clear, direct style of narrative in "The Bamboo Hut." The problem with which the story begins opens out into a mystery that brings a surprising climax and reversal. Kinship arrangements in this Kenyan village world are so different from American nuclear families that it is a good idea to discuss them at the outset, being sure that students understand housing arrangements in a family compound where co-wives have their own huts within the walls or fencing that protects the entire patriarchal "house" or homestead. A wife's status has much to do with her ability to produce the sons needed to insure the father's lineage, hence the importance of the title in establishing the status of the bamboo hut which Achieng achieves. The irony is her anguish in living for so many years in this favored place, knowing that it was achieved at the price of abandoning her daughter. Achieng's motives in leaving her baby girl at the well is an issue that can open up the whole story. Owiny's character and Awiti's are similar, in spite of the fact that they were raised by different parents; exploration of this point can also be a subject of student discussion. Father-son tensions, as well as the painful lack of a mother-daughter relationship are also dramatized in the story. Finally, Chief Mboga's reaction to his wife's revelations at the end reveals the wisdom and compassion characteristic of an effective leader.

Grace Ogot is one of the first indigenous African women to publish fiction in English, with short stories coming out in the early 1960s. She was one of the founding members of the Writers' Association of Kenya, and she has been prominent in other fields, working as a broadcaster for BBC Overseas and representing Kenya at the United Nations. Even so, she has received little critical attention in comparison with her male contemporaries. For basic biographical information, the Dictionary of Literary Biography (Vol. 117) is a useful source. Another is "Grace Ogot: A Creative Writer's Contribution to Cultural Development and Women's Emancipation," Writers' Forum 1 (March 1992): 73-80.

Questions for Study and Discussion:

1. What does the architecture and arrangement of Mboga's homestead tell us about the family arrangements of the Luo people?

2. Why does Achieng abandon her baby daughter?

3. What kind of a person is Owiny, and why is he attracted to Awiti?

4. How would you describe the values that lead Achieng to confess to her husband that Awiti is their daughter?

5. What are the community precedents for dealing with a woman who abandons a child, and how does Mboga reconcile the conflicting demands of public and private loyalties?

Chinua Achebe
Things Fall Apart

Chinua Achebe's novel Things Fall Apart is regarded as the first English language novel from tropical Africa and has become a classic. It is the second volume of a tetralogy dealing with the history and experiences of the Ibo people of Nigeria during a seventy-five year period when they first came into contact and accommodation with European cultures. The other novels in this series are Arrow of God, No Longer at Ease, and A Man of the People. Although Achebe was raised in a Christian family and writes in English, he has striven in his works to give expression to the traditional culture of his people so that it might be recognized and legitimized even as it is disappearing under pressure from outside influences.

The cultural conflict resulting from the exposure of indigenous cultures to European influences is a common theme in modern literature. Indeed, the break between tradition and the modern is, for many people, the very definition of the modern. Other versions of this confrontation can be found in the work of Natsume Sōseki of Japan and the story by Rajee Seth of India. The writing of Toni Morrison, Léopold Sédar Senghor, and Irena Klepfisz—all represented in this anthology—provide excellent companion pieces for Achebe's text, as well.

For further background information on the author, see David Carroll's biography, Chinua Achebe (Basingstoke, England, 1990). For a discussion of his fiction see G.D. Killam, The Novels of Chinua Achebe (New York, 1969). For a broader context of the author and his work, see Achebe's World: The Historical and Cultural Context of the Novels (Washington, D. C., 1980), by Robert M. Wren.

Questions for Study and Discussion:

1. Consider how family dispute is handled. Each party is represented by family members and each argues his case in the presence of the entire village as well as in the presence of the ancestral spirits. Although it is the spirits who pass judgment, their decision represents the consensus of the community.

2. We see a grave court case and a festive wedding ceremony in the selections presented here. Both reflect the life of an assured and stable community. Once contact is made with Europeans, however, a cloud of doubt and uncertainty begins to form. Identify some of the causes for this disquiet.

3. In the discussion on the nature of god between Mr. Brown and Akuma, who is presented as being more tolerant and broad-minded? Give examples to justify your case.

4. What are the advantages provided by Mr. Brown's school? The disadvantages?

5. Why is Okonkwo distressed by the "progress" that has taken place in Umuofia while he was in exile?

6. Why is Mr. Smith so hostile to African culture?

7. What does it mean when Enoch is called "The Outsider who wept louder than the bereaved?"

8. Compare Enoch and Okeke as examples of Christian converts.

9. Euro-American literature has many stories about the white man confronting black "savages." Consider how Achebe reverses traditional literary accounts and thereby challenges the stereotype of the black African. .

Wole Soyinka
A Scourge of Hyancinths

A Scourge of Hyacinths is a relatively recent work by Soyinka that is not well known but which speaks eloquently to the plight of many people in developing countries around the world. Franz Kafka might have been looking into a crystal ball when he described the baffling decrees and sudden, motiveless arrests of ordinary citizens in his novels The Trial and The Castle. The Kafka story, "A Country Doctor," which we have included among our selections shares the nightmare atmosphere of these novels and the impossibility of effective action against mysterious forces which trap and confound the main character. Soyinka's play applies such fictional techniques and themes to the political situation of Miguel Domingo, who is like so many who have been targeted for harassment or elimination because of bureaucratic mistakes or simply because they are too independent-minded to be tolerated in a repressive society. This is a distinctly modern vision of political injustice which can be fruitfully contrasted with the preceding selection, Achebe's Things Fall Apart. Achebe's novel describes an earlier stage of African history in depicting a man who cannot adapt to the changes to traditional tribal life brought by English colonial occupation. Soyinka's play is set in the confused urban environment which developed after the departure of colonial rulers, where older tribal values coexist with Europeanized modernist popular culture and technology. Interesting comparisons can be made also with Lu Xun's "Story of Ah Q" which uses comedy to focus on a different kind of political confusion in the life of a fatuous man disastrously swept up in political revolution. Both Toni Morrison and Ángela Hernández also write stories of ordinary people destroyed by disruptions of their young lives, though Morrison's Shadrack is a victim of war, while Hernández's Faride is undone by the more common problem of betrayal in love. More ancient precedents for such psychic horrors exist in underworld travels by Mesopotamian heroes like Inanna and Gilgamesh.

Soyinka weaves the theme of the African diaspora ironically through A Scourge of Hyacinths, playing the idea of slavery enforced by European colonial masters against the political slavery imposed by native African governments upon their own people, including those of African descent who have returned to the motherland in search of their roots and independence. Students should examine the treatment of Miguel's Cuban ancestry in his conversation with his mother. Also his political cynicism can be discussed in contrast to his mother's passionate belief in honesty as the central family value instilled by the patriarch who returned his family to Africa in flight from the heritage of slavery in the new world. These clashing values resonate strangely within the absurd political nightmare that engulfs Miguel. Attention should also be paid to symbolic elements like the grandfather's whip and the hyacinths that choke the waterways around the prison. Students could discuss the perspectives of the three men who sit together in the prison talking of their situation, and note the various walks of Nigerian life they represent.

For further information on Soyinka, Obi Maduakor's Wole Soyinka: an Introduction to his Writing (New York, 1987) is a good basic resource. Also the 1993 Twayne study, Wole Soyinka Revisited, by Derek Wright is a more recent study that provides an overview of his career. More specific critical studies of earlier works can be found in Critical Perspectives on Wole Soyinka, edited by James Gibbs (Washington, D.C., 1980).

Questions for Study and Discussion:

1. What kind of a world do we find ourselves in at the opening of this play? Why does Soyinka introduce us first to the prison Superintendent, and how are we to interpret his treatment of Miguel Domingo?

2. Who are the men with whom Miguel shares his cell? Why has Soyinka assembled this particular group?

3. How does Miguel's conversation with his mother establish major themes of the play? What do slavery and gambling have to do with Miguel's plight?

4. What is the role of traditional African religion in this play?

5. What is Miguel's crime?

6. How are the water hyacinths connected to the human world in this play?

Rabindranath Tagore
"The Hungry Stones"

Tagore was a man of such talent and sweep that it is exceedingly difficult, if not impossible, to give students a full appreciation of his significance. He was a poet, novelist, dramatist, painter, philosopher, educator, political figure, and much more. As a writer, he shaped his native Bengali language in a way reminiscent of the way Shakespeare shaped English. During his long and active life, Tagore had fruitful exchanges with some of the greatest minds of his time—Albert Einstein, Y. B. Yeats, Ezra Pound, Bertrand Russell, and, of course, Mohandas Gandhi. India's first prime minister, Jawaharlal Nehru, put Tagore alongside Gandhi and said that he rated them above all other human beings "not so much because of any single virtue but because of the toute ensemble." While much of this information is not necessary to a discussion of "The Hungry Stones," it is important to recognize that Tagore is a figure who will fascinate students, particularly if the teacher takes time to provide some information on his life and work (most students, alas, will never have heard of Tagore before). In fact, showing a picture of Tagore, whose often noted charisma is communicated even in photographs, is often sufficient to send curious students to the library to learn more.

There are many approaches one can take to this story. On one level it is a ghost story; on another it might be understood as a story about storytelling (note the reference to the Arabian Nights on p. 1597); and it also can be understood as a story about history and the way the past continues to haunt the present. As a ghost story, the narrative is doubly problematic. First, can we believe the storyteller? One of his listeners says he believes, whereas the other, who reports the entire event, disbelieves. Second, can we be sure, even if we choose to believe the storyteller, that the ghosts are anything more than the result of the storyteller's overly active imagination? A teacher might ask the students if the story grows from any wish they can identify with. Surely it is common, when entering an old building, to wish that "the walls could talk." In this story the stone walls literally breathe back the living energy they had absorbed centuries before. A common human fantasy is fulfilled, but the cluttering of the present with the past, and the confusion that results, can drive one mad!

On still another level, the story reflects the interest in questions of truth and illusion that can be found throughout Indian literature. There is, first of all, the problem raised above: whether the story is true or simply an elaborate lie. More importantly, the "collector of cotton duties," who tells the story of the hungry stones, comes to regard life in the haunted palace as more real than his mundane daytime duties: "Whatever belonged to the present, whatever was moving and acting and working for bread seemed trivial, meaningless, and contemptible" (p. 1599). Like Zhuangzi after his butterfly dream (see p. 359), the storyteller's sense of reality is profoundly unsettled. Moreover, the mad man, Meher Ali, who is the only person before the storyteller to escape from the hungry stones alive, circles the palace, crying out "Stand back! Stand back! All is false! All is false!" What is false, the world of the stones—i.e., the "dream of the past"—or the world outside the palace—i.e., that razor thin moment we call the present? Students of this story can easily be drawn into a discussion of the way this strange story turns around and around on itself raising all kinds of fascinating and disquieting issues.

For a good, recent anthology of Tagore's writings, which includes a detailed biography of his works, see Rabindranath Tagore: An Anthology, edited by Krishna Dutta and Andrew Robinson (London, 1997). A standard biography is Krishna Dutta and Andrew Robinson, Rabindranath Tagore: The Myriad-Minded Man (New York, 1996). The latter work includes a bibliography that will point the interested reader to numerous other sources.

Questions for Study and Discussion:

1. What kind of man is the "I" who narrates the frame story and reports to us what the man in the train said? How does the way he introduces "the man in the train" (p. 1594) influence our reaction to the story of the hungry stones?

2. What do you make of the fact that the man in the train is a "collector of cotton duties?" How might you connect this type of occupation with the sort of fantasies, if they are fantasies, into which he falls?

3. As he wanders in the palace, the collector feels as if he were following the "fragments of a beautiful story, which [he] could follow for some distance, but of which [he] could never see the end." What might be the significance of this statement? Does it in any way forecast the outcome of Tagore's story itself?

4. What do you think of Karim Khan's explanation of the events (at the bottom of p. 1600)? How might this explanation relate to what you know of Indian thought?

Rajee Seth
"Just a Simple Bridge"

This work represents a universal dilemma, the conflict between generations and their values and expectations. It also reflects the conflict of cultures when the younger generation moves away from home, whether to the big city or to another country. When the old certainties break down or are challenged, it is difficult to reach across the chasm that yawns to embrace the new. Yet when it is our children who embody the new, it perhaps becomes easier to embrace. When, as here, the gap is between both cultures and generations, the building of bridges becomes more difficult and more necessary. Any parent whose child has gone off to college and comes home at Christmas break knows he is receiving a new person. By the same token, any child who leaves home and returns learns that he cannot fully go home again. Still, the simple bridge of family love can keep that communication open across generations, across cultures, and across oceans.

For other accounts of cultural conflict in the modern world, see Chinua Achebe's Things Fall Apart and Natsume Sōseki's The Wayfarer.

Though not much is available concerning Rajee Seth and her writing, one can consult Women Writing in India, vol. 2: The Twentieth Century (New York, 1993). For a more general perspective see Jasodhara Bagchi, ed., Indian Women: Myth and Reality.

Questions for Study and Discussion:

1. Although Tilak Raj definitely wants his son to come home for a visit, he has reservations and misgivings. What are these and why does he have them?

2. In what way is Tilak Raj's household elevated socially by the return of their son?

3. Despite the warmth of reunion felt by both father and son, what sort of misunderstandings are apparent between them?

4. Despite the uncertainty Tilak Raj feels about his son's return, what is the gesture he makes to show his feeling for his son?

5. What disappointments do Tilak Raj and his wife experience after Ladi returns home? What disappointments does Ladi feel?

6. Consider the difference between how Tilak Raj relates to his son and how the mother does.

7. The dominant image in this story is the cooler. What does it represent?

Salman Rushdie
"The Courter"

For its verbal energy and sheer inventiveness, Rushdie's story can usefully be set alongside the writing of Gárcia Márquez, Naguib Mahfouz, Toni Morrison, Franz Kafka, Jorge Luis Borges, Virginia Woolf, and other writers in this anthology. With a focus on the specific postcolonial issues it raises, "The Courter" can be paired with texts by Gárcia Márquez (again), Rajee Seth, Chinua Achebe, Fadwa Tuqan, Léopold Sédar Senghor, Wole Soyinka, Louise Erdrich, and others who address similar themes in their work. A more playful pairing—and one that Rushdie himself would surely appreciate—is with the selection from The Thousand and One Nights. The narrator of "The Courter" has, after all, a baby sister with the association-begging name of Scheherazade.

"The Courter" is the last story in the collection East, West, part of a three-story section which is about, in various ways, crossings between East and West. Such crossings have not been a simple matter for Rushdie, who, as the headnote points out, was born in Bombay, raised in

Pakistan, and educated at Cambridge. In 1990, following the Ayatollah's fatwa against him, Rushdie re-embraced Islam, only to renounce his affiliation with the religion two years later. In this largely autobiographical story, the East-West crossings are generally, but not entirely, handled with humor. This is not to say that they are trivialized, but that the frame of the story—that is, the narrator's recollection of his 16-year-old self and family—seems to provoke a satirical playfulness in the author.

Perhaps the best way to help students appreciate the story is by focusing on its experiments with language. These, in turn, will illuminate the broader cross-cultural issues that the "The Courter" raises. What many students find most striking about the story is the "confused" beginning: the language bubbles up exuberantly on the page, but the referents (dwarfs, Hell, a tiger leaping from the roof) are so bizarre and the language (Certainly-Mary, ghats, filgrims,' Varanasi, Technicolor) so mixed that meaning seems to be held at one remove. An effective approach is to suggest to students that this verbal welter is purposeful, and to challenge them to figure out why. Once students begin to grasp the idea that the clash of language reflects a clash of cultures, they will move easily to other examples, such as the plethora of nicknames with which the characters are saddled, and so deepen their sense of what is at stake in the story.

Amid the superabundance of characters' names and period detail (the names of 1960s pop singers is one good index of this), it is interesting to note the relative void of the narrator's love-life. Rushdie effectively highlights the richness of the life around the young narrator—including the poignant alliance of Mixed-Up and Certainly-Mary—by contrasting it with his own, largely ineffectual, teenage crushes. Discussing the story, students will come to see that, although preoccupied with what the narrator refers to as "[his] own amorous longings," it is Mixed-Up Mecir's and Certainly-Mary's discovery of "a courtly wonderland of the ageing heart" that matters.

There are several good studies of Rushdie's writing. Of these, Reading Rushdie: Perspectives on the Fiction of Salman Rushdie, edited by M. D. Fletcher (Amsterdam, 1994), is highly recommended, although it predates East, West. James Harrison's Salman Rushdie (New York, 1992) provides a compact overview of the writer and his work. Catherine Cundy's Salman Rushdie (Manchester, 1996), while concentrating on the novels, includes some commentary on East, West. Her chapter called "Critical Overview" is particularly insightful in its discussion of the potentially restrictive labels "magical realist" and "postmodern" that are frequently attached to Rushdie's writing (and which he has specifically rejected). D. C. R. A. Goonetilleke's Salman Rushdie (London, 1998) is excellent. For those who are interested, there are also a number of books devoted to the so-called Rushdie Affair, of which The Rushdie Letters: Freedom to Speak, Freedom to Write, edited by Steve MacDonough (Lincoln, NE, 1993), is perhaps the best. It contains dozens of letters to the writer-in-hiding from contemporary authors, along with a brief response from Rushdie himself.

Questions for Study and Discussion:

1. In interviews, Rushdie has rejected the terms "magical realism" and "postmodern" that are sometimes applied to his writing, feeling that such labels are ultimately limiting. He favors, instead, the term "hybrid" as a designation for the kind of writing he produces. In what ways is "The Courter" a hybrid story?

2. Why do Mecir (a.k.a. the porter, the courter, Mixed-Up, Mr. Mxyztplk, Klptzyxm, Mishter Mikshed-Up Mishirsh) and Mary (a.k.a. our ayah, Aya, Certainly-Mary, Aya Mary, Jumble-Aya, Mary lady) have so many names? Who else in the story has an alternative name or names? What point is being made by this multiplicity?

3. The conclusion the narrator draws—that "Chess had become [the] private language" of Mecir and Mary—is significant in a story that is so much about language, public and private. What are some of the implications of this "private language" for these two characters, for the narrator, and for the larger issues raised by the story?

4. One's first experience of reading the beginning of this story is probably a frustrating, or a least a destabilizing, one. The names are bizarre, the references to dwarfs and Hell and a tiger statue are surprising, and the sprinkling of non-English words is puzzling. Can you think of reasons why Rushdie might have wanted to create this sense of confusion at the beginning of his story?

5. Why is it significant that the narrator alludes so frequently to pop music? How do these allusions serve the narrative?

6. What has the narrator learned by the end of the story?

Angkarn Kalayaanaphong
"Grandma"

Herbert Phillips describes the story "Grandma" by saying that it "is about the realities of nature and death, things to which the Thai have always given the most serious attention and about which their religion has provided the clearest, and also the most profoundly satisfying, understanding." Bearing in mind these basic connections is helpful as we encounter this rich and moving story.

Readers will want to know that in both the title and the text the word "Grandma" is intentionally misspelled by the author. This may be intended to depict the old woman as being without family ties, social station, or ego. Further, the misspelled word is a homophone for the Thai word for "grass" and may be intended to show the old woman's oneness with nature. Students can be challenged to provide their own explanations for this feature of the story.

As they draw connections between this and other selections in the anthology, students may be intrigued by attitudes towards death and nature. For other attitudes toward death, see Zhang Heng's "The Bones of Chuang Tzu,"Abū Nuwās's "Many's the noble face laid waste," and Al-Ma'arrī's "The days are dressing all of us in white." For other attitudes toward nature, see the section on Bashō, as well as Kawabata's story "Snow." One might also look at Ecclesiastes, where Qoheleth admonishes his listeners to live exclusively in the moment without thought of the past or of the future.

For a contextual look at Thai literature, see Herbert Phillips's Modern Thai Literature, With an Ethnographic Interpretation (Honolulu, 1987). For more Thai literature, see Geneviève

Caulfield's Three Thai Tales (Bangkok, 1961). For a study of Thai literature, see Wibha Senanan Kongkananda's The Genesis of the Novel in Thailand (Bangkok, 1975).

Questions for Study and Discussion:

1. Consider the attitude toward nature expressed in this story. Compare it to the notion expressed in the biblical book of Genesis that man is apart from nature and has dominion over it.

2. Consider the attitude toward death expressed by this woman. How does it compare with attitudes found in other cultures? In Ecclesiastes, for example, we find a protest spoken against the inevitability of death. Does anyone protest the old woman's death?

3. Consider the perspective the plants of the field have on human nature. Is there any other work of literature in which plants and trees critique human behavior?

4. The serpent here is the agent of the old woman's death. Is he demonized for taking the life of a harmless old woman?

Nguyen Huy Thiep
"Salt of the Jungle"

This story is a revealing modern comparison to the ancient Mesopotamian Epic of Gilgamesh in the way it demonstrates disastrous consequences of human arrogance in the natural world. Gilgamesh and Enkidu destroy the awesome cedar forest and kill its guardian Humbaba simply for self-aggrandizement. Mr. Dieu went hunting in the jungle to enjoy its delicate beauty brought by spring rain, and to forget the stresses of his daily life. But he too wished to prove his manly skill by killing a monkey. Thiep's story reveals the modern interest in the psychology of animals, and it also seems to imply an ecological message in Mr. Dieu's gradual realization of the monkeys' kindred feelings, and his own reduction to nakedness and humiliation. In a small way his experience is like that of King Lear on the heath in Act III of Shakespeare's tragedy, in which the arrogant king is reduced to humility and sees himself reflected in the plight of a naked, babbling beggar. A comparison could even be made with Kafka's "A Country Doctor," though the surreal qualities of that story are not linked to an encounter with the world of forest or jungle.

Because this story has a simple plot line, students can follow Mr. Dieu's transformation without difficulty. The stages in his hunting adventure can be defined, and particular attention given to the behavior of the monkeys and his increasingly close involvement with them. From the distant hunter with an impersonal, mechanical weapon to the man grappling on almost equal physical terms with his victims, Mr. Dieu grows more and more intimately involved with the primate family which takes over the story's emotional energy. Students should examine Thiep's descriptions of the jungle setting for these poignant events, as well as looking closely at the way the monkeys are characterized and made vivid physically for readers. Pointing out the contrast between Mr. Dieu's opening status and his situation at the end can help students determine the story's overall purpose.

Sources of background information are difficult to find for modern Vietnamese literature, because of strained relations between the United States and Vietnam after the war between the two countries in the 1960s and 1970s. Most discussion of Vietnamese literature remains untranslated.

Questions for Study and Discussion:

1. What is Mr. Dieu's purpose in hunting monkeys? What kind of man is he?

2. How are the monkeys first described, and what is Mr. Dieu's attitude toward his victim?

3. How do both Mr. Dieu's and the reader's views of the monkeys change, and why? What are some key moments in this process?

4. What are the differences between Mr. Dieu's state of mind and body at the beginning of the story and at the end?

5. What is the point of the story?

Cao Xueqin
Dream of the Red Chamber

    Dream of the Red Chamber, like several other works in this anthology, Don Quixote and In Search of Lost Time chief among them, must be read in its entirety to be understood and appreciated. At the same time, Dream is so lengthy and complex that it is virtually impossible to do the novel justice in a quarter or even a semester. Consequently, Dream is likely to remain largely untaught except in some excerpted form, even though almost any combination of excerpts is sure to leave the reader a bit confused. Our choices, like all others, are problematic. The connection between the first chapter of the novel, which we include, and what follows in chapters 27, 28, 97, and 98 may be important, but it is not at all apparent. This initial chapter does a number of critical things. First of all, it establishes the religious theme of the text and places the sometimes quotidian events that are to follow in a macrocosmic framework (indeed, the story is complete from the beginning, since it is already inscribed upon a stone when the novel "begins"). Second, the author attempts to position his work in relationship to the tradition of which it is a part. His words are a general critique of Chinese narrative, with its insistence upon an "artificial period setting" (see, for example, "The Story of Ying-ying") and a "social message." The author insists that he is doing something different from other writers of romance, but at the same time he alternatively gives the impression that his work is fiction and that it is actual history (on this problematic topic see Anthony Yu below), and he also insists that his text has as its "lesson" to encourage readers to give up "their vain and frivolous pursuits." Third, the story of Zhen Shiyin foreshadows what is to happen to Bao-yu. Within a short portion of one chapter Zhen experiences the disillusionment it will take Bao-yu one hundred chapters to experience, and Shiyin's poem (pp. 1650-51) reaches the same conclusion, albeit from an entirely different religious perspective, as the Teacher in Ecclesiastes, who proclaims: "Vanity of vanities! All is vanity. What do people gain from all the toil at which they toil under the sun?" (p. 155). Fourth, the first chapter of Dream, like the first chapter of other sweeping novels, is an attempt, admittedly somewhat awkward, to "get into the story." Narrative beginnings and narrative endings are always of interest precisely because they are so problematic. Cao Xueqin's beginning is oblique, to say the least. The mandarin who mysteriously appears at the end of the chapter, as the reader might guess, is Yu-cun, and he will provide a link in chapter two (not included here) to Lin Ru-hai, the father of Dai-yu. Dai-yu is orphaned and will be sent to her relatives, the Jia family (Yu-cun is a Jia) where she will meet her cousin Bao-yu and where the main events of the novel will take place! Fifth, the first chapter plays with the tangled relationship between "truth" and "fiction" that runs throughout the novel and finds expression in the very names of the two families introduced in this first chapter: zhen, the surname of Shiyin, means "true" and jia, the surname of Yu-cun and Bao-yu as well, means "false." Sixth, the first chapter introduces us to both Bao-yu and Dai-yu in their previous state as a stone and a flower respectively and indicates that the tears Dai-yu will shed in her mortal life are a repayment (a very strange repayment indeed!) for the fact that the stone was kind enough to water her during their premortal existence.

Dream of the Red Chamber, read on one level, is a tragic love story and the tragedy is foreseen in Dai-yu's poem in chapter 27 (pp. 1656-58), which is also filled with the self-pity that is so much a part of her personality. The fact that Bao-yu will be torn between his own emotional and "poetic" feelings, represented by Dai-yu, and good sense and family responsibility, represented by Bao-chai, is seen in his very name, which shares one syllable with the names of each of his cousins: Bao-(chai) and (Dai-)yu. Many students, particularly non-Chinese students, will find Dai-yu excessively emotional, but we must bear in mind that she is isolated in the Jia family as an orphan and thereby is isolated and vulnerable in a way that many of her cousins are not. She is also the most gifted poet of the cousins, a fact acknowledged by both Bao-yu and Bao-chai, and Chinese poetics posits a link between the purity of one's verse and the purity of one's character. For these and other reasons, Dai-yu has been much admired by traditional readers, who are all devastated when Dai-yu burns her poems in chapter 97 and then dies with Bao-yu's name on her lips in chapter 98. The burning of her poems is, of course, the very destruction of her soul, which she has consistently poured forth in her brilliant verse.

Bao-yu is tricked into marrying Bao-chai, an event that is likely to provoke students to condemn hastily the Chinese family and its power over the romantic lives of its members. But there is no doubt that Grandmother Jia, the powerful matriarch who arranges the marriage, loves Bao-yu profoundly and even indulges him excessively. It is her judgment, and the judgment of the family, that Bao-chai is more stable than Dai-yu and hence a better guarantee that the family will prosper. Bao-yu is the family's last hope for a reversal of its declining fortunes, and he needs sense (=Bao-chai) more than sensibility (=Dai-yu). That the family's action drives Bao-yu into madness for a time and eventually leads to his very rejection of this world proves that the family has tragically miscalculated, but their decision, given the dynamics of the family, is at last understandable. The teacher should also note that while what has happened is tragic from the "this-worldly" perspective, it completes the "disillusionment" of Bao-yu that was, at least judging from chapter one, the whole point of the stone's assuming mortality.

The five-volume Penguin translation by David Hawkes and John Minford is a brilliant piece of scholarship (for the full reference, see p. 2240). For less ambitious readers, there is an abbreviation which preserves the love story but trims away much else: Dream of the Red Chamber, trans. by C. C. Wang (New York, 1958). Since Dream is so complex, much of the secondary literature it has spawned is also complex and difficult. Perhaps most accessible as an introduction is C. T. Hsia's chapter on Dream in his important The Classic Chinese Novel (New York, 1968), pp. 245-297. Andrew Plaks' study opens up much of the symbolic significance of the story, including the way names reflect five-element cosmology—see his Archetype and Allegory in the Dream of the Red Chamber (Princeton, 1976). A more recent "reading" of the text is that of Anthony Yu, Rereading the Stone: Desire and the Making of Fiction in a Dream of the Red Chamber (Princeton, 1997).

Questions for Study and Discussion:

1. Given what seems to be the religious intent of the novel, at least as laid out in chapter one, are the subsequent events truly tragic or do they merely lead to "enlightenment?"

2. The Jias are a large, upper-class family whose compound is built around a garden. How is the life of this family portrayed in this novel? How does a nuclear family structure, which dominates today in the West and in China as well, both simplify and complicate family life?

3. The young cousins in this novel are obsessed with poetry. What seems to be the function of poetry within Dream?

4. From what you have read in the excerpts found in the anthology, why do you think the novel is referred to as a "dream?" Note that David Hawkes uses the alternative title Story of the Stone. Do you think anything is at stake in the discussion about which title should be used?

5. Discuss the character of Dai-yu. Is she, in your view, a sympathetic character? What is her appeal to Bao-yu?

Shen Fu
Six Records of a Floating Life

Six Records of a Floating Life is a remarkable text that can be seen as a culmination of a traditional Chinese aesthetic of the small and the common (flower arranging, burning incense, making miniature mountains, etc.). Shen Fu, plainly, can aestheticize almost anything—for example, imagining a swarm of mosquitoes flying through smoke as a flock of cranes soaring through the clouds. But even within the Chinese tradition, he is an unusual and extreme voice, and it is mainly this that has made him so popular among Chinese readers. Rarely has such a range of aesthetic experience been discussed so unabashedly, and rarely, too, has a Chinese written more tenderly and frankly of his relationship with his wife. His aesthetic sensitivity reminds one in some ways of what is sometimes encountered in Tale of Genji and other works of Japanese literature but which in the West sometimes gets branded as "decadence." Students are usually fond of Shen Fu and find his enthusiasms engaging, if a bit eccentric. He can, at moments, sound a bit like Martha Stewart, a comparison students find amusing, but his attention to refinement has little to do with impressing guests and a lot to do with a sense that since life is brief and beset by much difficulty that is ultimately beyond one's control (expressed well in several other chapters of this text), one is wise to take great care and find enjoyment in those small things that one actually can manage.

Six Records of a Floating Life is fundamentally autobiographical and might therefore be read alongside such texts as Augustine and Rousseau. Shen Fu, however, does not present his life in a strict chronological order but arranges events under broad topics. In a very general way, this structure might be shaped by a Chinese tradition of arranging material according to categories. For example, in traditional China there is even a type of book entitled leishu, which often gets translated as "encyclopedia" but literally means "book of categories." Such books attempted to arrange all important knowledge according to a scheme of interconnected categories. Shen Fu, in presenting his past, seems to follow such a structure. The point to stress with students is that a chronological presentation of one's life is by no means the only form autobiography can take—indeed, in some ways Shen Fu's approach to autobiography is reminiscent of certain twentieth century autobiographers who radically break-up the tradition of chronological presentation (Georges Perec is one example of such authors). Like so many works of Chinese literature, Six Records of a Floating Life is filled with nostalgia. It is written after the happy events recorded in the text have receded into the past (quite a different perspective than Augustine, who would discount his past as a mistake), and this surely influences his construction of the events he remembers.

From what Shen Fu tells us throughout his Six Records of a Floating Life, his wife Yün was a remarkable woman. She was literate, a capable poet (at least Shen Fu thought so), and participated fully in the intellectual circle Shen Fu gathered around himself. Certainly the story of women in traditional China, like in any other civilization, is an exceedingly complex and multifaceted one. Students almost all have a stereotype of the oppressed female in traditional China, and there is surely sufficient justification for this stereotype (as there is also in the West), but many women achieved remarkably and came to exercise considerable power both in public as well as private spheres. The examples of Yün, Li Qingzhao, and, to a lesser extent, Daiyü provide the teacher with an opportunity to conduct a somewhat more nuanced discussion of the position of women in traditional China (on this topic, see the book by Lisa Raphals noted below).

The best preparation for teaching Shen Fu is simply to read the entire text, which is exceedingly brief: Leonard Pratt and Chiang Su-hui, Six Records of a Floating Life (Harmondsworth, 1983). This translation also has an excellent introduction. Those with access to a sinological library might also want to consult Milena Dolezelova-Velingerova and Lubomir Dolezel, "An Early Chinese Confessional Prose: Shen Fu's Six Chapters of a Floating Life," T'oung Pao 58 (1972), pp. 137-160. On women in early China, see Lisa Raphals, Sharing the Light: Representations of Women and Virtue in Early China (Albany, 1998).

Questions for Study and Discussion:

1. Shen Fu is fascinated with finding or creating the "large in the small," the "real in the illusion," and the "illusion in the real" (see p. 1681). How would you describe this aesthetic? Can you find echoes of this way of thinking about beauty elsewhere in The World of Literature?

2. Since Shen Fu never was successful in the bureaucracy and did not come from a particularly wealthy family, he and his wife were forced to live very frugally. Discuss this text as a tribute to simple living and compare it to Kamo no Chomei's An Account of My Hermitage.

3. What kind of a philosophy is reflected in the things that were "forbidden" and the things that were "encouraged" at the Villa of Serenity? Do you find any irony in the fact that Shen Fu and his friends also played "examination" games?

Lu Xun
"Ah-Q—The Real Story"

Students typically read through "Ah Q—The Real Story" with a mixture of fascination and horror. In order to keep students from over-generalizing about China or Chinese, the teacher should provide the proper historical context. "Ah Q" was written at a time when many Chinese intellectuals, and certainly Lu Xun himself, had become profoundly disaffected with their native land. The gradual decline of the imperial system and the final fall of the Manchu dynasty in 1911 had fully disclosed China's weaknesses. The hopes that accompanied the founding of the Republic in 1912 soon turned to disillusionment as China fell into a period of warlordism and disunity. Thus, Confucianism, the imperial system, the civil service examination system, and other staples of the Chinese past had come to an end, but only political chaos and intellectual confusion had followed. An array of voices clashed, from anarchists to communists to political liberals to reactionaries who wished to restore the imperial system, and there was little clear sense of exactly what path China should follow. It was also apparent to many, Lu Xun among them, that Japan had succeeded at surging past China and moving into the "modern" world. A few decades later, after the communists came to power in 1949 and Mao Zedong proclaimed that China "had stood up," the mood, at least the official mood, had changed significantly, as the next story by Ding Ling indicates. But as Lu Xun penned "Ah Q" in the early 1920's, he was obviously making a very harsh statement about qualities he perceived to be crippling China at that particular moment. Of course, the story itself is set during the last years of the Qing Dynasty, perhaps in the first decade of the 1900's. And the character Ah Q becomes symptomatic of a "national disease"—he reinterprets every defeat as a victory, he is tragically self-deceived, and he is always quick to respond to being bullied simply by bullying others. In reflecting a general malaise through a single highly disturbing (and disturbed) representative, "Ah Q" bears comparison with the main character of Dostoyevsky's "Notes from Underground."

Of course, there are many obvious differences between Lu Xun's and Dostoyevsky's stories. The latter is a first person narrative and shows the obsession with "interiority" that had developed in the West in the nineteenth century and had influenced some of Lu Xun's writing, especially his "Diary of a Madman" (not included in this anthology). In contrast, "Ah Q," after the first-person "preface," is presented as a third-person narrative and satirizes a traditional Chinese literary form, the biography, that was familiar to every literate reader. Traditional Chinese biographies were always accounts of well-known people and were motivated to some extent by the Confucian desire to preserve the names of people of special significance. The notion of writing a biography of someone whose name is not even known and who did nothing of significance is ludicrous, and Lu Xun begins his story by playing on the humor of this situation. But on another level, Lu Xun seems also to be poking fun at the realist movement, which had come to China from the West and of which his own literature is a part—that is, he turns his attention in this story to a parody of a "common man" about whom no self-respecting Chinese writer of earlier times would ever have written.

"Ah Q—The Real Story" was originally serialized in the Beijing <u>Morning Gazette</u>. Halfway through the series, the tone of the piece seemed to change from satirical humor to a kind of tragic black humor. Up until Ah Q leaves Wei Village and goes to town, the story centers upon his "victories." Many traditional modes of thought are satirized here, including the idea, by no means unique to China, that "most . . . men would have become saints or sages a long time back—trouble is, they were done in by women" (p. 1699). When Ah Q returns to Wei Village at the beginning of chapter six, enriched by ill-gotten gains, the narrative takes a decidedly more political turn. Ah Q is attracted to revolution primarily because "there's a whole bunch of fuckers

I'd like to revolution clear out of this world . . . (p. 1712)." His attempt to participate in the revolution, a movement he never understands in the first place, ends tragically in his execution as a common criminal. In this second section he seems little more than the "poor schmuck" who is caught up in events that are quite beyond him.

For more translations of Lu Xun's stories, see A Diary of a Madman and Other Stories, translated by William A. Lyell (Honolulu, 1990). An excellent recent study of Lu Xun is William A. Lyell, Lu Hsün's Vision of Reality (Berkeley, 1990). C. T. Hsia's A History of Modern Chinese Fiction (New Haven and London, 1971) contains a useful chapter on Lu Xun (=Lu Hsün, pp. 28-54) and his important place in the larger context of Chinese literary history. For more on Lu Xun's position with regard to the Chinese Revolution, see Lu Hsün: Writing for the Revolution (San Francisco, 1976).

Questions for Study and Discussion:

1. What are some of the methods Ah Q employs to seize "victory from the jaws of defeat?" Do any of these reflect ways of thinking that might have characterized China's reaction to its own political problems at the time Lu Xun wrote?

2. What factions or groups might be represented by the Young Literati and the Fake Foreign Devil?

3. Why is Ah Q executed? What is the purpose of the final two paragraphs of the story?

4. Lu Xun was honored in China as a great revolutionary. What seems to be the attitude toward "revolution" reflected in this story?

5. Ah Q both bullies and is bullied. What might be the larger message in this theme?

Ding Ling
"When I Was in Xia Village"

In 1940, when Ding Ling penned this story, China was essentially divided between three political spheres. The Japanese, who had invaded China several years before, held the northeast and most of the seacoast. The Chinese Communists were dominant in the northwest, with their center in Yenan, and the Chinese Nationalists, under Chiang Kai-shek, made their headquarters in Chungking and held onto much of the southwest. Ding Ling was very much in the Communist camp and had already written some literature that was little more than political propaganda. But her relationship with communism (and, for that matter, authority in general) was always troubled. In fact, "When I Was In Xia Village" can be read as an attempt to find some essentially humanistic space between a political apparatus, represented perhaps by a character like Agui, who seems to want to impose a prefabricated interpretation on reality, and a village that continues, sometimes quite cruelly, to enforce the standards and categories of the past.

The fact that this story was written during wartime and in the politically charged atmosphere of Communist-held Yenan makes it ideal for a discussion of the relationship between politics and art and the degree to which the two are compatible. There is little question but that modern Chinese literature has tended to be sharply political, and sometimes has been condemned for this tendency. There are, however, other issues at stake in this story. One that students might discuss is the degree to which society demands outcasts to reinforce its own central values. Zhenzhen's crime, when all is said and done, is not so much that she might have slept with perhaps a hundred Japanese soldiers as that she refuses to display either shame or self-pity.

At the heart of this story is a tragic love story. Once again, as in Dream of the Red Chamber, the family has frustrated young love. In this case, the Japanese captured Zhenzhen, who was in love with young Xia Dabao, as she was fleeing from marriage to another man chosen by her parents. The recurrence of this theme in Chinese literature, both of the traditional and modern periods, indicates that it was a genuine point of tension in Chinese society. In this story, however, the theme of love takes an interesting and perhaps ironical twist when Zhenzhen, after returning to the village, rejects Xia Dabao even though he still loves her in spite of her "disgrace." Students might be asked why they think this happens and whether Ding Ling, at this point, is herself capitulating to "traditional values" or whether she is making some other point about female solidarity or the ultimate primacy of the Yenan-based political action which Zhenzhen, at the end of the story, seems ready to join.

A good selection of Ding Ling's work can be found in I Myself Am A Woman: Selected Writings of Ding Ling, edited by Tani E. Barlow with Gary J. Bjorge (Boston, 1989). Other pieces can be Miss Sophie's Diary and Other Stories, trans. by W. J. F. Jenner (Beijing, 1985). For a useful study of Ding Ling, see Yi-tsi Mei Feuerwerker, Ding Ling's Fiction: Ideology and Narrative in Modern Chinese Literature (Cambridge, MA, 1982).

Questions for Study and Discussion:

1. Are there any hints in this story that the narrator's relationship with her own political movement might be a complicated one?

2. What does Agui seem to want from Zhenzhen? Does her attitude toward Zhenzhen differ from that of the narrator? If so, how?

3. One cannot ignore the fact that Ding Ling is recognized as one of the greatest, if not the greatest, female Chinese writers of the twentieth century. Explore and discuss this piece as a work by a woman about women. What do you think is the significance of Zhenzhen's rejection of Xia Dabao in favor of going to Yenan to treat her disease and do some "studying?" (Do not forget that what Zhenzhen says about herself in her final speech to the narrator hardly indicates that she has a "healthy self-image," to use a current, shopworn phrase!)

4. Some have said that political ideology and art inevitably collide. Do you think this story works both as a political statement and as a work of art? If not, which of the two dominates?

Matsuo Bashō
Narrow Road to the Interior

In the spring and summer of 1689 the haiku poet and poetry master Matsuo Bashō made an extended journey through the northern provinces of Japan. Bashō's reasons for making this journey were complex. On the one hand, he saw life itself as a journey and wanted to live that metaphor and die on the road, which he eventually did. Another reason for the trip was to leave the bustle and competition of urban life behind and submerge himself in the simplicity of nature. Paradoxically, another purpose for the trip was to visit some of his many disciples who were scattered all over the country. Yet another reason for travelling was to spread the gospel of a new philosophy of haiku poetry which represented Bashō's own notion of what poetry should be. Finally, Bashō simply wanted to see those places which he had heard about but had never seen with his own eyes.

Bashō makes frequent allusions to Chinese poetry, and useful comparisons can be made with the work of the Tang poets and to the reclusive poet Tao Qian. Comparison can also be made to the work of Henry David Thoreau.

For further reading on Bashō, see the biography, Matsuo Bashō (New York, 1982), by Makoto Ueda, and Donald Keene's, World Within Walls (New York, 1976). For the context of Bashō's work, see William LaFluer's, The Karma of Words (Berkeley, 1983). For interpretations of many of Bashō's poems, see Makoto Ueda's, Basho and His Interpreters (Stanford, 1991), Haruo Shirane's, Traces of Dreams: Landscape, Cultural Memory, and the Poetry of Basho (Stanford, 1998), and Hiroaki Sato's, One Hundred Frogs, From Renga to Haiku in English (New York, 1983). For a general study of haiku poetry see Kenneth Yasuda's, The Japanese Haiku: Its Essential Nature, History, and Possibilities in English (Rutland, VT, 1958).

Questions for Study and Discussion:

1. Bashō is often regarded as a nature poet, and certainly one of the purposes for his trip through the north—the subject of the selection presented here—was to leave the city and experience nature. In confronting nature, however, Bashō does not try to make sense of the natural order, for to do so would presume to impose his intellect on the world. Instead, he seeks only to immerse himself within nature, to become one with it, and to understand it subjectively and intuitively. In this text we can see several places where he shrouds himself in nature. Consider his visit to See From Behind Falls at Nikko, his experience at Matsushima, and his night spent on Mount Gassan. In each case he is totally immersed in the waterfall, in the wind and clouds, and in the movements of the sun and moon. But Bashō is not always comfortable with nature. When he crosses the mountains at Dewagoe he is frightened by raw nature. Consider examples that reveal this uneasiness. Later, at Tako, he fails to go out of his way to see some famous wisteria. How do we account for this?

2. Another purpose of Bashō's trip was to visit historical sites. Consider his responses to the monuments to ancient warriors he finds at Sato Shoji, at Hiraizumi, and at Komatsu. Although from a samurai family himself, Bashō seems keenly aware of the futility of human endeavor as it is embodied in the warrior's heroic deeds. In light of this paradox, what does Bashō deem of lasting greatness?

3. Bashō, a man who has renounced all worldliness, spends the night in the same inn with a couple of courtesans at Ichiburi. How does he respond to this curious situation? Why does he refuse the next morning to help the two women?

4. A sophisticated man of the city, Bashō meets many ordinary people in the course of this trip. How does he respond to Honest Gozaemon at Nikko, to the farmer at Nasuno who lends him a horse, and to the farmer's children? What happens when the servant leading the poet's horse unexpectedly asks for a poem from the master? What is it about these people that he finds attractive?

5. Do we see humor in Bashō's account when he, the pilgrim on life's journey, receives guidance on his way from a horse? How about when he visits the Komyoji Temple and instead of worshiping the founder of the sect, he prays to the saint's clogs? When he recites a poem and uses the image of a fish's tears?

Natsume Sōseki
The Wayfarer

The hero of this passage, the nameless brother, is a tormented intellectual unable to find a strategy for coping with the demands of the modern world. Concerned for his physical and psychological welfare, his family encourages him to take a trip with an old friend. They also ask the friend to observe the brother's behavior and write them a candid description of his actions. The selection we have included here is that letter.

The brother and the friend constitute a familiar pair in literary works. Like Dr. Watson of the Sherlock Holmes mysteries, the friend in this case is a heavily built man of ordinary intelligence and perception, whereas the tormented brother is Holmesian—a thin, intense, highly cerebral and very troubled individual. The friend/confidant serves as a conduit and guide between us as readers and the brother's intellectual explorations.

Central to the arguments made here is the concept of the autonomous self. Although self-definition and self-responsibility have been key issues in Western philosophy since the time of Socrates, this was a new concept in Meiji Japan, and the implications were sometimes overwhelming. How could a person be autonomous and still function both effectively and morally in society? In confronting the anxiety and stress of the modern world, the brother proposes three possible choices: suicide, insanity, and religious faith. These choices are explored in this letter.

Perhaps the best selection with which to compare The Wayfarer is Chinua Achebe's Things Fall Apart. Like Sōseki's text, Achebe's is an account of a hero who also fails to accommodate himself to a new, alien—and, significantly, an inescapable—value system.

For biographical information and general interpretations of Sōseki's work, one can consult Edwin McClellan's Two Japanese Novelists: Sōseki and Toson (Chicago, 1969) and Beongcheon Yu's biography Natsume Sōseki. For more biographical and contextual information about Soseki's life see Donald Keene, Dawn to the West (New York, 1984). Masao Miyoshi, in Accomplices of Silence (Berkeley, 1974), has an insightful chapter on Sōseki. Another interesting source of information is Takeo Doi's The Psychological World of Natsume Sōseki (Cambridge, MA, 1976), in which a noted psychoanalyst gives his readings of Sōseki's works. Makoto Ueda's Modern Japanese Writers (Stanford, 1976) has a useful chapter on Sōseki's views on art.

Questions for Study and Discussion:

1. In the opening two chapters, Sōseki describes the circumstances of the travelers. Can we visualize from this description what it was like to live and to travel in Japan in the early twentieth century? Consider what it means to stay at a traditional inn where people would eat together and sleep together in the same room, and bathe together in a communal bath.

2. One of Sōseki's techniques of writing is to create suspense. Is he successful in doing this with regard to the letter? We are told of the recipients' anxious waiting in the first section. In the second, the author itemizes three conditions—difficulty, impropriety, and needlessness—that may keep him from writing, and yet he does write a long, detailed letter. What sort of expectation does this create in the reader? Is that expectation fulfilled or disappointed by the letter itself?

3. In section thirty-one we catch a glimpse of the brother's torment beneath his calm outward demeanor. What sort of statement is Sōseki making here about the nature of modern life? Seen against the certainties of the sleepy feudal period which Japan has abandoned, can we appreciate the stresses caused by the nation's drive toward modernization?

4. Wherein lie the insecurity and anxiety experienced by the brother? Are these real causes for concern or are they merely figments of his imagination?

5. What avenues of relief are suggested to calm the brother's feelings of anxiety and insecurity?

6. Think about our own lives. Do we accept the frantic pace and uncertainty of modern life with equanimity because we have mastered it, or because we are oblivious to it? Do we accept it?

7. Consider the passage in section thirty-four where God is discussed. The brother several times rushes forward and throws stones into the indifferent sea. What are we to make of this?

8. At the beginning of section thirty-nine the brother sees only three alternatives for himself: death/suicide, insanity, or religious faith. What are the implications of each of these? Are there perhaps other options as well?

9. In section forty-four the brother appears to make an argument for Western humanism, positing the notion that man is the measure of all things. Later he seems to argue the more Buddhist view that the egotistic self be submerged and become one with all things. Consider whether Sōseki is arguing for a Western or an Eastern philosophy of life here.

10. In sections forty-seven and forty-eight the brother is able to forget about himself momentarily while absorbed in his observation of crabs. How does this relief from self-consciousness serve as a possible vehicle for salvation?

11. In an age of rationalism, what does Sōseki have to say about rational intelligence as a way to solve modern humankind's dilemmas? Consider this in the context of the anecdote about Kyogen's enlightenment in section fifty.

Kawabata Yasunari
"The Pomegranate," "Snow," "Cereus"

Like Bashō, whose vision enabled him to select from a landscape just those elements which resonate in such a way that we can grasp some fundamental essence of the scene, Kawabata is an impressionistic writer. The images may all be familiar, but they are juxtaposed in suggestive ways that guide the reader to insight. These stories require reader participation, because what the author leaves unsaid may be as important as what is stated. The pomegranate, emblematic of female sexuality and left behind half tasted, invites us to share a young woman's pensive thoughts of love. A middle aged family man who chooses to celebrate a festive holiday in a locked room alone with his memories may leave us feeling charmed and troubled at the same time. The futility of human relationships expressed in all three of these stories reflects a truth taught by Buddhism, that all relationships are transitory, that meeting is the first step toward parting and separation. In the end, the characters are left to savor the bittersweet memories of past relationships.

Unlike the modern short story found in Western literature—the tight, sharp works of Anton Chekhov, Anatole France, or Ernest Hemingway, for example—these stories are as muted and suggestive as an ink wash painting. To appreciate their singularity, they might be set alongside examples of the Euro-American short story in this anthology—works by Kafka, García Márquez, and Faulkner, for instance. For a story that more closely resembles Kawabata's vision and technique, one might look at the work of the Thai writer, Angkarn Kalayaanaphong.

For further reading on Kawabata, see Masao Miyoshi, <u>Accomplices of Silence</u> (Berkeley, 1974) and Hisaaki Yamanouchi, <u>The Search for Authenticity in Modern Japanese Literature</u> (New York, 1978). For a study of Kawabata's views on literary art, see Makoto Ueda, <u>Modern Japanese Writers and the Nature of Literature</u> (Stanford, 1976). For a study of Kawabata's life, see Donald Keene, <u>Dawn to the West</u> (New York, 1984).

<u>Questions for Study and Discussion</u>:

1. The pomegranate is the central image in this story. What does it represent?

2. When Keikichi arrives at the house, why do you suppose the author tells us that Kimiko let her needle come unthreaded?

3. Notice the statement "Keikichi was going to war." Consider how this statement colors everything else that happens in the story, yet is tucked away so as to be almost unnoticeable in the middle of something else. What is gained or lost by such a strategy?

4. Consider the intensity of the counterpoint Kawabata creates between the strict formality that exists between Keikichi and Kimiko and the depth of feeling they have for each other. How would you describe the tension this creates, using evidence from the text as support for your claims?

5. Notice how Kimiko frowns, flushes, and becomes confused when her mother hands her the pomegranate. Why is this significant?

6. What are we to make of the scene where the mother combs her hair?

7. In the story "Snow," Sankichi imposes a number of layers between himself and the so-called real world. He closes the door, draws the curtains, climbs into bed, and brings down a blizzard of snow—and only then creates his dream world. Why is this layering important?

8. What are the implications of Sankichi erasing his sense of self, to the point where, as Kawabata writes, "The snowy landscape was all there was. Sankichi himself was not there"?

9. What can we make of the fact that all of the women are ones who had loved Sankichi, but none are identified as women he had loved?

10. In "Cereus" we see another example of a powerful yet unarticulated tension which runs beneath an outward formality (in this case, the formality of the gathering). Is this tension identical to that which exists between Keikichi and Kimiko?

11. What is left unspoken about Toshiko's response to the guests?

12. What is left unspoken about Sumiko's situation?

13. Why do you think this man would invite his estranged wife's friends to his home in the first place?

Abe Kōbō
"Stick" and "Red Cocoon"

In these early stories we find Abe using techniques of writing that he would employ throughout his career. One of these techniques is the use of metamorphosis to express his concern about how modern, urban society depersonalizes people and robs them of their humanity, transforming them into something else, something less than human. Abe sees this as the central issue for modern man. His concern is first of all that we should recognize our dehumanized condition and second that we should resist this and seek a more authentic way of life in the Heidegerian sense. Abe's fundamental notion is that when we experience disruption in our lives, our urge is to regain our old, comfortable way of being rather than to see the disruption as an opportunity for change and growth.

The most obvious comparison to make with Abe's work is that of Franz Kafka. Useful comparisons can also be made with the work of Dostoyevsky and T.S. Eliot.

For further reading about Abe see Hisaki Yamanouchi's chapter "Abe Kobo and Oe Kenzaburo: Search for Identity" in Modern Japan: Aspects of History, Literature, and Society, edited by William Beasley (Berkeley, 1977). For interpretations of these two stories see William Currie, "Abe Kobo" in Approaches to the Modern Japanese Short Story, edited by Thomas E. Swann and Kin'ya Tsuruta (Tokyo, 1982). For an overview of Abe's life and work see J. Thomas Rimer, "Abe Kobo" in Dictionary of Literary Biography, volume 182: Japanese Fiction Writers Since World War II (Detroit, 1997).

Questions for Study and Discussion:

1. Abe often uses very precise, realistic details in his stories to create the sense of realism and to set off the dream-like or nightmare-like quality of the main body of the narrative. In these stories what examples do we see of such realistic detail? How effective are these details in helping the reader accept the nightmare that follows?

2. Abe's landscapes are usually urban or wasteland or both. Is there anything in either of these landscapes that identifies it as being Japanese? In what sense can these stories be regarded as being Japanese literature?

3. As citizens of the modern world we often become so entrenched in familiar but meaningless routine that some sort of crisis in our day-to-day life is necessary before we can begin the search for a more authentic mode of being. What are the disruptions in these stories that lead to a new awareness of the characters' conditions? How do characters grow as a result of these crises?

4. The central character in "Red Cocoon" seeks a place of his own. What does he have to sacrifice in order to find that place? Is the sacrifice worth it?

At the time he wrote "Red Cocoon" Abe was a member of the Communist Party, an affiliation he later disavowed. Do you think Abe is making any sort of Marxist statement here about private ownership of property?

5. In "Red Cocoon" the character has two moments of self-awareness. At the beginning of the story he realizes he has no place of his own and ends up by remedying that situation. At the end of the story he realizes that he has no self to occupy his newly found place. Is this an optimistic or a pessimistic ending?

6. In "Stick" are we really supposed to believe that the man fell off the roof and turned into a stick, or was it all just a daydream? What is there in the story that might justify the conclusion that it was only a dream? If it was only a dream, does that make his awareness of his condition any less damaging?

7. In "Stick" the professor and his students are presented as being pretentious, conformist, and phony. What sort of statement do you think Abe is making here about the way in which social elites impose their judgments on the rest of society, if any?

Ōba Minako
"The Three Crabs"

This story was enormously popular in Japan when it first appeared in 1968 and had a profound impact on defining women's roles. Today, some parts of the story may seem dated—not just the references to the Vietnam War, but other aspects of the story, as well. The introduction of birth control pills and the legalization of abortion in the 1960s touched off a controversial sexual revolution, which in turn gave women a new sense of freedom and ownership of their own sexuality. Much that seemed revolutionary then may be taken for granted today. A central question students will want to consider as they engage the text is whether it addresses issues of gender relationships and personal choice that are still significant today, or whether it is merely an outdated reflection of an earlier age?

"The Three Crabs" can be usefully compared to Joyce's "Eveline," which recounts the story of a girl who tries to break free of a stultifying conventional life, but loses courage at the last minute. Similarly, it makes an excellent companion piece to Salwa Bakr's "That Beautiful Undiscovered Voice," a story about the entrapment of a modern Egyptian woman in a patriarchal society.

For further background on Oba Minako, see the entry on her in the Dictionary of Literary Biography. For more stories by contemporary Japanese women, see Noriko M. Lippit and Kyoko I. Selden, ed., Japanese Women Writers: Twentieth Century Short Fiction (Armonk, NY, 1991) and Yukiko Tanaka, Unmapped Territories: New Women's Fiction From Japan (Seattle, WA, 1991).

Questions for Study and Discussion:

1. What stereotyped images do we have of Japanese women? Does the author of this story merely challenge a stereotype of Japanese women, or does she challenge a universal image of women's behavior?

2. Is a part of Yuri's freedom to question traditional roles based on the fact that she is living in America? Is it conceivable that she could assert this sort of independence while living in Japanese society?

3. In thinking about this story, why does a mature housewife and mother choose to abandon family and friends in favor of a one night stand with a stranger?

4. In one memorable scene Yuri looks at herself in the bathroom mirror as she talks to her daughter. One might recall here the story of Snow White, where the queen looks repeatedly in the mirror to confirm her own sexual attractiveness—an attractiveness which is inevitably challenged and overthrown by her daughter's emerging beauty. In this light, would it be too much to say that Yuri's choice of a one night stand with Pink Shirt may be motivated by a need to reassure herself of her own sexual attractiveness?

5. The "Three Crabs" is the name of a seaside motel where Yuri and Pink Shirt spend the night. Is this image of three crabs symbolic of anything else in this story?

6. Yuri wakes up the next morning to find her world shrouded in fog. How is this emblematic?

7. We see Yuri in four contexts in this story: at home with her family, at a party with her friends, at an amusement park with a stranger, and (not described) at a motel with a stranger. How meaningful are each of these contexts for Yuri?

8. At the party, before the card game begins, the guests engage in sophisticated chit-chat. Some critics have suggested that this scene may have been influenced by T.S. Eliot's The Cocktail Party. Can any useful parallels be drawn? What does this comparison reveal about the sources of and influences on contemporary Japanese fiction? Can you think of any comparable instances of Japanese influences on modern Western literature?

9. Does Yuri feel repentant or remorseful after her one night stand?

Sonu Hwi
"Thoughts of Home"

This selection is a significant piece of Korean literature in at least two respects: as a short story, it participates in the most important genre in Korean fiction from the late 1920s until the late 1970s; and, in its underlying theme—the partitioning of the country—it addresses the single most important reality in post-war Korean fiction.

Upon a first reading, most students will see the protagonist and central figure of the story as Yi Changhwan's father, for it is he who lives out the reality of the conflict between the old ways of the North and the new ways of the South. With subsequent readings and discussion, however, a strong case can be made for the narrator himself as protagonist. It should be pointed out to students that the story takes place in a complex time frame—a frame that is itself ripe for questions and discussion—and its subject matter is filtered through the consciousness of the narrator. It is he who, after all, both relates the story and, finally, surmises the reason for the old man's death; the reader does not know for sure what precipitated it. In addition, the narrator's strong identification with Yi Changhwan's father, in his own dreams and yearning for the North, brings up what may be the central question of the piece: what, if anything, has the narrator, while experiencing a similar internal conflict, learned about himself from the old man's fate?

Works with which this selection might profitably be read include such seemingly diverse selections as Naguib Mahfouz's Zaabalawi, Fadwa Tuqan's "In the Aging City," Yehuda Amichai's "Jerusalem," and T. S. Eliot's "The Waste Land." In fact, the story works well with any literary work treating the longings, conflicts, and tensions in the human psyche produced by a clash of cultural paradigms and the disintegration of deeply held values and beliefs.

For informative and accessible treatments of Sonu Hwi, see Peter H. Lee's work, especially Flowers of Fire (Honolulu, 1986), Modern Korean Literature (Honolulu, 1990), and Korean Literature: Topics and Themes (Tucson,1965).

Questions for Study and Discussion:

1. At the end of the story the reader is asked to believe the narrator's "weird idea" of the old man's fate—that is, he saw his own wizened reflection in the water and dove in after it. This, however, does not really provide any closure to the tale, for, as the narrator tells it, it can be interpreted two ways: either the old man recognized the reflection as being his own, or, not being in full control of his faculties, he mistook the reflection for that of his father. What would be the significance to the story of both of these surmises?

2. Why do you think Sonu Hwi ultimately leaves the old man's fate to conjecture, both on the part of the reader and that of the narrator?

John Milton
Paradise Lost

This great Renaissance epic is so closely linked with the Genesis story of Adam and Eve in the Hebrew scriptures that the two really need to be read together. In such a way Milton's perspective on the original sin and its motivations can be clearly distinguished. His description of the Garden of Eden and indeed the whole prelapsarian world is interesting to contrast with that in Genesis. Paradise Lost is also usefully compared with Dante's Divine Comedy as a grand vision of the Christian cosmos in ways suggested in our headnote in the anthology. Other literary traditions also present heroic struggles between humans and the supernatural. Some interesting examples are the Epic of Gilgamesh, The Odyssey, The Bacchae, the Bhagavad-Gītā, and the struggle of Bao-yu with his spiritual destiny in The Dream of the Red Chamber.

    The grace, heroic tone, and enormous power of Milton's epic depend upon his masterful use of the iambic pentameter line perfected more than half a century earlier by Christopher Marlowe and William Shakespeare for dramatic purposes. Students need to understand precisely how iambic pentameter works, with the strong five-beat, unrhymed line of iambic feet. Milton usually varies the meter so that few lines are perfectly regular, but the iambic pentameter pattern beats in the background to give meaning to the deviations from its rhythm. Spending time on scanning several examples, and perhaps asking students to produce iambic pentameter lines of their own, give important training in understanding the underlying mnemonic and emotive intensity of rhythm, repetition, and order in poetry from all literatures. Any good handbook of literary terms can be consulted in brushing up on names and qualities of the metrical units often substituted for individual iambs, for example the spondee of two accented syllables used for hortatory or emphatic beginnings of lines as in "Sing, Heav'nly Muse" in line 6 of Book I. The grand tone of the opening twenty-six lines can be contrasted with the thunderous effects of Satan's fall from heaven in Book I, or the sensuous beauty of the description of Adam and Eve in Book IV.

    Milton's use of epic devices like the Homeric catalog and extended simile can be pointed out in Book I, and students can discuss the heroic qualities Milton associates with Satan in his hopeless determination to defeat God. Because Milton's exploration of authority, obedience to God, and the rebellious will to power are subtle, and because his reasoning on these matters is so different from present day American assumptions about individual freedom, it is important to look closely at the ways he structures Satan's self-justifications and the arguments he uses to rouse his fallen army. God's explanation of the divine position to his son Jesus in our selection from Book III stands in authoritative contrast to Satan's fallacious claims. It is useful to point out that Milton has already promised to let his audience know God's motivations ("to justify the ways of God to men"), and thus for dramatic purposes must arrange some situation where the almighty will explain himself. This is hardly a situation we expect in most religious contexts, in which the deity is mysterious and self-sufficient, not owing any being an explanation of the workings or purposes of the cosmos or divine will. Students can be asked to closely examine the differences between Satanic and divine logic.

    The beautiful descriptions of Adam and Eve and the garden of paradise can be analyzed and contrasted with the much simpler descriptions in Genesis. Students might try to decide what values Milton expresses through his aesthetic emphases here. Also attention should be paid to the poetic devices he uses in these descriptions, from the manipulation of the blank verse line, to descriptive adjectives and verbs, to imagery. Satan's anguished response to the innocent beauty he encounters in this scene is a very moving dramatic and psychological moment to discuss, for here he realizes what he has lost and betrays a sympathetic sensitivity to the virtues and blessings that are forever beyond his grasp. But this reaction melts into the vindictive determination to destroy all that he cannot have. Eve's questioning of God's rules that follows this passage is also interesting to examine, because Milton gives her many of the secular humanist philosophical questions that he himself had raised in works like the famous essay "Areopagitica," and yet intends here in the epic to show them as dangerously willful. Milton's hymn to wedded love that ends Book IV can be compared to The Song of Songs as divinely sanctioned erotic poetry; the Hebrew text was surely in Milton's mind when he wrote Paradise Lost.

Book IX is the famous seduction episode in which the splendid serpent beguiles the innocent mother of mankind into disobeying God's command. Its drama and complexity are as powerful as any epic scene from Homer or Virgil, though much more closely focused on the subtleties of psychological experience and on theological reasoning than anything one would find among the ancient poets. Students can be asked to describe how Milton sets up the scene for maximum effect, how he describes Satan's appeal, and what motivates Eve to take the bait he offers. Perhaps equally interesting is Adam's decision to join Eve in disobedience. After working through the temptation and Fall, students should try to decide what exactly has been lost and how Milton explains the ironic benefits of the disaster—the so-called "Fortunate Fall" that enabled God to extend grace to humans by sending his son to redeem them.

An excellent scholarly resource for answering questions about literary allusions and traditional interpretations of Paradise Lost is Douglas Bush's edition of The Complete Poetical Works (Boston, 1965). A good recent edition of Paradise Lost that includes a selection of criticism is Scott Elledge's revised Norton Critical Edition (New York, 1993). A. N. Wilson's The Life of John Milton (New York, 1983) is a readable, intelligent biography.

Questions for Study and Discussion:

1. What purpose does Milton define in his famous opening invocation to the muse?

2. Can you see why some have argued that Satan is the real hero of Paradise Lost? What qualities of his character and actions in Book I could create that impression?

3. How would you describe God's reasoning in forbidding the fruit of the tree of knowledge to Adam and Eve? Where in our text is it explained, and by whom? Does Adam and Eve's conversation in Book IV reveal much about their relationship?

4. What is Satan's response when he first sees Adam and Eve? Why? Pay close attention to how his mood changes.

5. In the great temptation scene of Book IX, does the serpent make legitimate arguments in favor of eating from the tree of knowledge? Make a list of his main claims, and decide how valid or false you think each is, and why. What arguments win Eve over, and how do they work upon her thinking? Why does Adam decide to share Eve's fate?

6. What is Adam and Eve's situation at the end of Paradise Lost?

Alexander Pope
Eloisa to Abelard

This poem would very profitably be read in the light of the letters of Abelard from the Middle Ages, as well as our selection from the Heroides, which depicts Dido's lament for her lover, Aeneas, who has abandoned her. Given the brilliance of Pope's poetic artistry, this poem might also be included in a section on poetry—its scansion, how it sounds, how it creates meaning—that could include the Japanese haiku, Sappho, Horace, Emily Dickinson, and Szymborska, to name just a few of the poets included here. Since Pope is known as a classically-inspired writer, this could be included among other selections in a unit on the classical (that is, Greco-Roman) tradition. The teacher might also include this among other works that focus on romantic love, using Petrarch, Cao Xueqin (who dramatizes the impossibility of a consummated love between his protagonists Bao Yu and Lin Dai Yu), and Milton in his representation of Adam and Eve in Paradise Lost.

    Students should be encouraged to see how the poem vacillates between the religious and the erotic, and how Pope's couplet is particularly adept at expressing this vacillation. Students should read passages aloud and learn how to read rhyming couplets effectively. They might even memorize some couplets; indeed, we strongly recommend this as a way to more fully appreciate the poetry.

    Students might consult the Life of Pope (London, 1854) by Samuel Johnson. They should also see Pope's biography by Maynard Mack (New York, 1985). On Pope and women, see Valerie Rumbold, Women's Place in Pope's World (Cambridge, 1989).

Questions for Study and Discussion:

1. How do Pope's couplets, with their antithesis and balance, express Eloisa's conflicting emotions?

2. Find some examples of phrases used by Eloisa that refer both to religious and erotic experience. Why does Pope make this ambiguity a part of his poetry?

3. How does Pope's imagery enforce his view of Eloisa's suffering?

Jane Austen
Pride and Prejudice

    Pairing this selection with that by Rousseau brings out the contrast between her text's anti-romanticism and his romantic sensibility. The emotionalism—the Cult of Feeling—he helped introduce is countered by the economy of Austen's language and, in Pride and Prejudice, by the balance sought and ultimately achieved between Elizabeth Bennet and Fitzwilliam Darcy. One would do well to remember that an early draft of the novel, written in the middle 1790s, was called "First Impressions"—a title taken directly from the lexicon of sentimental fiction, referring to faith in one's immediate feelings. Ideally, discussion of both these texts—that by Austen and that by Rousseau—would follow study of Pope's "Eloisa to Abelard," where pithy wit and metrical balance are preeminent virtues, signaling the tradition that informs Austen's writing. Considering Elizabeth Bennet, students are able to see how she upsets the lockstep decorum reflected in Pope's heroic couplets, particularly in her brash ramble to Netherfield in Chapter VII, but rejects the devil-may-care impulsiveness of her sister, Lydia, whose actions may stand in for the passion and exhibitionism championed by Rousseau. More broadly, the Austen selection can by discussed in a unit on courtship and love (perhaps beginning with the excerpt from "The Courtship of Inanna and Dumuzi"), or of women in society (including, among many other possibilities, Salwa Bakr's story, "That Beautiful Undiscovered Voice").

    E. Clerihew Bentley wrote in one of his funny little poems that "The novels of Jane Austen / Are the ones to get lost in," praising the vivid impression of a real world they create. The difficulty for many students, however, is of getting lost in a negative rather than a pleasurable sense, finding themselves unable to connect the precisely observed world of the novels with the one they know. Certain information needs to be provided students. For example, the implications of the Bennet estate having been entailed to "a distant [male] relation" is of central importance for understanding the extraordinary emphasis upon courtship and marriage felt everywhere in the novel. Recognizing that a prospect of homelessness and poverty lies behind Mrs. Bennet's urgent matchmaking tempers what otherwise appears an unaccountable mania or mere foolishness. Mrs. Bennet *is* foolish, but students can be challenged to discover the factors which make her so. Similarly, students may need to have explained to them the class structures in the novel—the significance of Sir William Lucas's position as a titled former tradesman, for example, or of the Bennet's position as the principal family of Longbourne living in an entailed estate.

    Much can be intuited, of course, from careful reading of Austen's language. Because the novel is subtle and ironic, such close reading is particularly well rewarded. The famous first sentence, renowned for its irony—"It is a truth universally acknowledged, that a single man in possession of a good fortune, must be in want of a wife"—brings the key terms "possession" and "wife" into play, indicating the direction of its main plot—that is, the relationship of Elizabeth and Darcy—with "good fortune" functioning as a more ambiguous signifier. Figuring out what "good fortune" means is one of the main challenges of the novel, for its characters and its readers alike. One good way to help students interpret the nuances of Austen's irony—helping them detect and make sense of the extreme economy of the observation that Mr. Hurst "merely looked the gentleman," for example, or that "Mr. Darcy is all politeness"—is by having them read key passages aloud. If, as many teachers believe, no greater barrier to students' understanding of Austen exists than the nuances of her tone, then reading aloud is a valuable teaching practice. Similarly, although many of the social relationships in the novel, meticulously and relentlessly defined in terms of class, may initially seem remote to students, verbally performing such attentive readings will help make them, too, intelligible. Hearing an effective reading of Mrs. Bennet's supposition that Darcy, to choose one example, has snubbed a neighbor at the Netherfield ball because "he had heard somehow that [she] does not keep a carriage, and had to come to the ball in a hack chaise," students can—while never having seen nor perhaps even heard of a hack chaise—grasp more readily the point of the comparison.

    Once attuned to Austen's tone, students have little difficulty responding to the main area of critical interest in the novel: the representation of women, with women from Mrs. Bennet, to Elizabeth and her sisters, to Charlotte Lucas providing distinct images of femininity. Intimately connected with this is the question of marriage, in relation to which all of these women (with the possible exception of Lydia and her mother) stake out different positions. One of the primary pleasures of the text is weighing these positions against one another for the insights they reveal into Austen's culture and our own.

    Criticism of Austen is abundant. Some of the best recent sources are <u>Approaches to Teaching Austen's Pride and Prejudice</u> (New York, 1993), edited by Marcia McClintock Folson, and Laura Mooneyham White's collection of <u>Critical Essays on Jane Austen</u> (New York, 1998), which together provide a good overview of the main currents of twentieth century Austen criticism. Jane Austen's Letters (Oxford, 1995) is interesting for the insights it gives into Austen's preoccupations and relationships with members of her family, as is David Noake's Jane Austen: A Life (New York, 1997), which portrays an Austen strikingly at odds with the traditional image of a saintly literary spinster.

Questions for Study and Discussion:

1. Pride and Prejudice is obviously a novel much concerned with the position of women in society. If Jane Bennet represents a proto-Victorian feminine ideal—a woman who is pliant, resolutely cheerful, self-effacing and physically beautiful—in what ways does this selection scrutinize and critique this ideal?

2. Mrs. Bennet is the most obvious butt of the opening chapters of the novel, relentlessly exposing herself to the ridicule of others. Because she is so ruthlessly exposed, however, she draws attention away from (in some instances subtler) criticism of other characters, particularly her husband. What are the deficiencies of the adult male characters—Bennet, Bingley, Hurst, and Darcy—in this part of the novel? What does Austen seem to be getting at by bringing these shortcomings to light?

3. How would you summarize Elizabeth Bennet's and Fitzwilliam Darcy's defects, and with what evidence?

4. The selection from Pride and Prejudice sets up a love story with ironic, comical accents. If a convention of romantic comedy is that obstacles lie in the path of lovers proceeding—maddeningly, circuitously—toward a happy ending, what are the main obstacles to a union of Elizabeth and Darcy? How are they articulated and by whom?

James Joyce
"Araby," "Eveline," Ulysses, Finnegans Wake

Possibilities for teaching the Joyce texts are probably as diverse as the range of stylistic maneuvers they present to readers. One approach is to consider them in a unit on modern experimental literature, with readings from Baudelaire, Kafka, Woolf, Beckett, Borges, Eliot, García Márquez, Rushdie, Mahfouz, Tuqan, or Thiep. Alternatively, the focus might be on the allusions to "exotic," far-off lands in the Dubliners stories and in the episode from Ulysses—allusions which are central to all three texts—and how they participate in or critique a Western tradition of exoticizing foreignness. Good pairings would include Catullus's "Aurelius and Furius, comrades sworn," selections from Abu 'Abdallah Ibu Battutah's and Marco Polo's respective travel narratives, The Song of Songs, The Thousand and One Nights, and examples of Provençal poetry. A clear advantage of teaching the "Calypso" episode from Ulysses in a world literature context is having for comparison the original from which Joyce drew inspiration and after which Leopold Bloom's day is ostensibly modeled, and this presents a further teaching possibility. Students generally like being able to identify Homeric parallels, and the "Calypso" episode provides several opportunities, in addition to highlighting the ironic, anti-heroic variations Joyce is working upon his classical precursor. The chapter from Ulysses might, following this line of inquiry, be included in a unit on epics and mock epics, in which it and

Cervantes's Don Quixote are read alongside "How Basat Killed Goggle-eye, O My Khan!," The Prose Edda, "Canto General: The Heights of Macchu Picchu," and Paradise Lost.

Perhaps the most startling realization for students new to Joyce is that all of the texts in this selection were indeed written by the same man. The "Calypso" episode from Ulysses is demanding, with its streams of language running through Leopold Bloom's mind, its allusive and elliptical wordplay, and its dearth of traditional readerly landmarks, yet it seems almost straightforward in comparison to the free-flowing neologisms and lexical rivulets that make up Finnegans Wake. By contrast to both of these, the two stories from Dubliners appear not only plain but downright—and misleadingly—simple. Because of the differences in technique, each of these prose selections calls for different reading and discussion strategies.

Unlike the other two texts, the challenge with the Dubliners stories is to help students see what is so remarkable about them. To a certain extent, this means recovering the historical moment in which Joyce's realism, like Ibsen's and Chekhov's, was shocking. Shabbiness and conformity are central to these stories, and discussion might begin by identifying where and how such shabbiness and conformity are felt in "Araby" and "Eveline." Without a sense of the culturally stultifying, the urge to escape is incomprehensible. Describing this desire for escape, students can be challenged to address the complex use Joyce makes of his characters' fantasies of distant lands, for Araby casts a spell similar to that which is produced by Frank's "stories of the terrible Patagonians," and both are overlaid by authorial irony. Probing this irony—asking, for instance, what "an Eastern enchantment" has to do with Mangan's sister, or how seriously we are meant to take Frank's sailors' tale of "terrible Patagonians"—students become attuned to other subtleties, such as Joyce's playing upon the word "blind" and related images in "Araby" and the patterned repetition of images of dust, death, and decay in "Eveline."

For the Ulysses episode, the question of where and how best to begin discussion is further complicated by its being a narrative that spins out by the dozens allusions to characters and events beyond its frame. One good place to center discussion is in Bloom's reverie of an easy and abundant East, which shades into a darker musing on Jewish history and homeland, and ends with the assertion "Well, I am here now. Yes, I am here now" and the poignant affirmation, "Yes, yes." This passage, besides prefiguring the well known words with which the novel ends, helps students make sense of the episode as a whole by focusing on its opposed poles: appetite and death. Eating sustains life and defecating ensures appetite; like the "vigorous hips" of the servant girl he eyes, the "bedwarmed flesh" of the wife he thinks longingly of, and the incipient sexuality of his daughter that worries him, they are fundamentally connected to the cycle of life. The movement of Bloom's thoughts—to and away from sensual reverie—is thus a movement between the antitheses of desire and loss. (This is, one recalls, an episode which begins with a description of Bloom's hearty appetite and ends with the tolling of bells for the dead Dignam.) Provided this toehold, students are more apt to see Joyce's description of Bloom's thoughts and actions as less simply prurient, scatological, and bizarre—as they may otherwise have seemed—and more complexly representative of human experience.

Although the "Calypso"episode is far easier to understand than others in Ulysses (and all of Finnegans Wake!), it does present certain challenges of a more basic nature. Students will, for example, be struck by Joyce's technique of compression, with which he approximates the flow of Bloom's thoughts. It is useful to explain how this technique works: by elision—"Cup of tea soon. Good. Mouth dry"—where parts of speech are omitted, and by the compounding of conventionally separate words, as in "liverslices," "shameclosing," "nothandle." The semantic and tonal range of Joyce's language, with puns featuring prominently and words such as "gelid," "scapulars," "dunam," and "naggin" interspersed alongside more accessible language, is a further challenge for first-time readers. All of these features combine to require extraordinarily alert readers greater than usual acts of attention; in the act of paying attention, readers are, in turn, drawn nearer to understanding a text that is about the scrutiny of—the paying attention to—a perfectly ordinary individual.

The critical literature on Joyce is voluminous, with book-length studies focusing on Joyce and a truly dazzling array of subjects. For readers new to Joyce, the most valuable resources are those that help identify characters and allusions and interpret action, particularly for the later writing. Of these, Ulysses Annotated: Notes for James Joyce's Ulysses, by Don Gifford (Berkeley, 1988) is excellent and The New Bloomsday Book: A Guide through Joyce's Ulysses (London, 1988) is quite good. Hugh Kenner's Ulysses (Baltimore, 1987) is another valuable tool and, for the "Calypso" episode alone, can be usefully supplemented by Adaline Glasheen's essay in James Joyce's Ulysses: Critical Essays by Clive Hart and David Hayman (Berkeley, 1974). There are collections of critical essays, in separate volumes devoted to each of the major texts, in the Critical Essays on Modern British Literature series, edited by Zack Bowen, and a good, new volume in the Columbia Critical Guides series: James Joyce: Ulysses/A Portrait of the Artist as a Young Man, edited by John Coyle (New York, 1999). Also of value is James Joyce from A to Z: The Essential Reference to the Life and Work, by A. Nicholas Fargnoli and Michael Patrick Gillespie (New York, 1995), a resource that lives up to its billing, providing readers with an alphabetical listing of characters, allusions, summaries, and other references for all of Joyce's writing. Richard Ellmann's James Joyce (Oxford, 1982) is the standard biographical work.

Questions for Study and Discussion:

1. Discuss the emphasis on "blindness" and vision in "Araby."

2. If Dubliners is at least partly a critique of Joyce's hometown, what specific aspects of the city are being critiqued in the two stories from that book?

3. Although one's first impression may be that "Calypso" lacks the features with which readers identify and follow a narrative, with increased familiarity one sees that Joyce has included useful interpretative markers. What are some of these "markers"—these clues and hermeneutic aids—that assist comprehension and how do they function?

4. The first page of Finnegans Wake gives a sense of Joyce's ambition for this avant-garde literary project. How would you characterize the goals of such a project? To what texts in The World of Literature does it seem to be a reaction?

Virginia Woolf
To the Lighthouse

As one of the greatest modernist writers in the European tradition, Virginia Woolf naturally belongs alongside Marcel Proust and James Joyce. All three were exploring the interior life of relatively ordinary people, demonstrating the amazing richness and nuance of daily consciousness. Woolf also stands in a venerable tradition of women writers whose existence and power she was one of the first to define. Thinking of Lady Murasaki Shikibu, the world's first woman novelist, we can see that Woolf had remarkable predecessors as long as a thousand years ago, who also captured the social and cultural conditions of women and men living together in a major civilization. The Sumerian goddess Inanna, together with Greek goddesses Athena, Hecate, and Demeter, provide archetypes of the feminine against which Mrs. Ramsay of <u>To the Lighthouse</u> can be measured and discussed. But she can also be seen to inherit long centuries of European women's struggle and accomplishment by being taught with Marie de France, Christine de Pizan, Madame de Sévigné, the great novelist Jane Austen, and poet Emily Dickinson. Virginia Woolf is one of the few writers in world literature to examine the domestic world of women's work as equally worthy of attention to that of the more public spheres in which most literature by men is set. Woolf's view of Mrs. Ramsay's centrality to her world and her accomplishments should be seen as a revolutionary contribution to notions of human value, and it complements James Joyce's portrait of the very ordinary hero Leopold Bloom who begins his day making breakfast for his wife.

Point of view is very complex in this selection from <u>To the Lighthouse</u>, and students at all levels need to be guided through the shifts from Mrs. Ramsay's opening promise to her son James, to James's blissful imaginings, to the rage his father's dismissal of his mother's plan arouses, and on to the various views of Mrs. Ramsay provided by Lily Briscoe, William Bankes, and Charles Tansley. An indistinct, anonymous narrative presence hovers over these characters and intervenes between them, weaving in and out in subtle ways that are hard to disentangle from the thoughts of the individuals. The basic situation of Mrs. Ramsay knitting the stocking for the lighthouse keeper's boy and measuring it against James's leg, is interrupted by memories of the past and by the musings of her guests as they watch her, and by her husband's insistent claims that the weather will not be good enough for a trip to the lighthouse. Mrs. Ramsay's own inner thoughts are glimpsed from time to time, and through them we learn that in spite of her beauty and serenity she has a sense of terrors seething just under the pleasant surface of life. It is a major task to help students understand the complexity of this portrait of a Victorian mother who is the creative center of her large family. Also, attention should be paid to the gender dynamics Woolf is depicting in the differences between Mrs. Ramsay's view of the world and that of her husband and his disciple Charles Tansley. Lily Briscoe, a single woman painter, stands in clear contrast to Mrs. Ramsay's domestic role; Lily represents the possibility of independent life for women that was just dawning at the beginning of the twentieth century. The obstacles she faces are dramatized in Tansley's insistence that "women can't paint; women can't write," projections of his desperate need to have someone to look down on in order to counter his own fear of failure.

The most valuable single guide for reading <u>To the Lighthouse</u> is Erich Auerbach's chapter, "The Brown Stocking," in <u>Mimesis</u> (Princeton, 1946. Pp. 525-553), his classic study of narrative technique. This careful reading of the opening sections of Woolf's novel explains what revolutionary manipulations of time and perspective are accomplished here, and it guides the reader through the complex movement of point of view. The best biography of Virginia Woolf, setting her work within the context of English intellectual life and her fellow modernists, is Hermione Lee's <u>Virginia Woolf</u> (London and New York, 1996). Other helpful studies of her fiction include Maria Di Battista's <u>Virginia Woolf's Major Novels: The Fables of Anon</u> (Yale, 1980), Lyndall Gordon's <u>Virginia Woolf: A Writer's Life</u> (New York, 1984), and Gillian Beer's <u>Virginia Woolf: The Common Ground</u> (Minneapolis, 1996). <u>Virginia Woolf and the Languages of Patriarchy</u> (Bloomington, 1987) by Jane Marcus is a major study of Woolf's feminism, and Alex Zwerdling explores Woolf's political activism in <u>Virginia Woolf and the Real World</u> (Berkeley, 1986).

Questions for Study and Discussion:

1. Think about the opening portrait of mother and son in this novel, and try to determine why Virginia Woolf focuses her novel here. What does Mrs. Ramsay's promise of a trip to the lighthouse mean to her son, and why is James so violent about his father's intervention in this conversation? What descriptive details help us understand what is at stake here?

2. Who is Charles Tansley, and what is his relationship to Mr. Ramsay? A whole satiric portrait of a segment of society is being presented through his character, and it has much to do with the contrasting values held by Mr. Ramsay and Mrs. Ramsay.

3. In the memory of Mrs. Ramsay's trip into town with Charles Tansley, what is the meaning of his attitude toward her? Does it change? And what does she think of him?

4. Mr. Bankes muses about both Mrs. Ramsay and her husband. Does he think their marriage is a success? Are the values underlying his view of Mr. Ramsay's work and his attitude toward Mrs. Ramsay consistent? That is, does Mr. Bankes evaluate Mr. and Mrs. Ramsay with the same expectations and standards? What is the significance of the ways he thinks about them?

5. What kind of person is Mr. Ramsay? His actions, as well as the behavior and views of friends and family, define his character.

6. What do we learn from Lily Briscoe? Look especially at the way she thinks about her painting, and the way she thinks about Mr. Ramsay's work. Why does she think of a table in a pear tree in connection with Mr. Ramsay's philosophy about "subject and object and the nature of reality"?

Samuel Beckett
Happy Days

As suggested in our general introduction, this play might be read alongside the other dramas included in this anthology from Greece, India, China, and Japan, as well as from England. Since our heroine seems to be awaiting a transfiguring event that never occurs, it would be interesting to teach this play in conjunction with our selections that present just such a transfiguring event—an event which, in sharp contrast to Beckett's dramatic narrative, has a deeply religious meaning, such as in Exodus or the selections from the New Testament.

Since the work will often be taught in the context of the modern period, students should be encouraged to ask what makes this work representative of Western modernity. They should also try to imagine how the work might be staged.

There are many secondary works that might be consulted, including <u>Samuel Beckett: A Study of his Novels</u> (Seattle, 1970) by Eugene Webb.

Questions for Study and Discussion:

1. The essence of drama is usually action, but in this play virtually nothing happens. What is the significance of this?

2. Winnie's situation seems pretty hopeless, and she has easy access to a revolver. Why (besides the fact that the play would likely end) doesn't she just do away with herself?

3. Say something about Beckett's use of language and his humor.

4. What is peculiarly modern about this play?

5. What is the significance of Winnie's parasol catching fire?

Madame de Sévigné
Letters

Mme de Sévigné lived in the golden age of French literature. She numbered among her close friends the novelist Mme de La Fayette and the epigrammatist La Rochefoucauld. She loved plays, especially those of her contemporaries, the tragedies of Racine and the comedies of Molière, whose Tartuffe was her favorite play. As a perceptive chronicler of court and aristocratic life, Mme de Sévigné offers revealing comparisons to Izumi Shikibu in medieval Japan, Murasaki Shikibu's Tale of Genji, and the later Chinese novel, The Dream of the Red Chamber (1792), by Cao Xuequin. Her attitudes stand in stark contrast to the romantic, self-absorbed musings of her later countryman, Jean-Jacques Rousseau, illustrating the change from a rationalist, ironic Enlightenment mentality to the passionate revolutionary sentiments of one of the initiators of the European Romantic movement.

Although she wrote only letters, it is easy to see that her talent might have been put to other uses. Consider how her anecdotes and character sketches might have been treated by contemporary writers:

1) tragic stories that Racine might have staged, or
2) satiric portraits that Moliere might have used, or
3) stories that Mme de La Fayette might have put into one of her novels, or
4) observations on human behavior that La Rochefoucauld might have published in his collection of epigrams.

As the letters frequently reveal, religion was very important to Mme de Sevigne. Her grandmother, who founded a religious order, was later canonized as a saint, and Mme de Sevigne was herself very devout. Compare her religious views to those of earlier writers in the Christian tradition and to those of writers outside that tradition. Compare her views on death specifically to those of her contemporary, the Japanese writer Bashō.

Questions for Study and Discussion:

1. Why is Mme de Sévigné considered a great writer? What qualities set her prose beyond ordinary letter writing?

2. Mme de Sévigné did not write her letters for publication. What was her motive in writing letters? How did she shape them for their recipients?

3. What do the letters reveal about her relationships with her correspondents and others?

4. What do the letters tell you about the status of a noble woman in seventeenth-century France?

5. What values does Mme de Sévigné seem to find most important in her life? Does her aristocratic status make her life exotic or her concerns distinctly different from those of ordinary people today?

6. How does Mme de Sévigné manage to paint a vivid picture of her world for her reader?

Jean-Jacques Rousseau
The Confessions

Though an original, Rousseau was deeply influenced by Montaigne and the vogue of the "memoir novel" of the eighteenth century. The Confessions can thus usefully be read in connection with Montaigne's writing, as well as in a unit on autobiography and the literature of self. St. Augustine's Confessions is the obvious great precursor; Dostoyevsky's Notes from Underground, Proust's In Search of Lost Time, and the poetry of Whitman and Neruda are important descendants.

Whereas other examples of Rousseau's writing—the political philosophy especially—are easy for students to admire, the very intimacy of his Confessions can be off-putting. On the one hand, Rousseau's extravagance and self-absorption encourage facile, dismissive labels: he is said to be delusional, narcissistic, masochistic, hypersensitive, and (particularly once one has read to the end of his Confessions) paranoid. On the other hand, students raised in a confessional culture find him disappointingly tame: a confessor, "the dark and miry maze of [whose] confessions" seems merely banal. The challenge is to establish the novel aspect of Rousseau's project, to help students see in his Confessions a revolutionary broadside against the prevailing version of Enlightenment thinking. One strategy which works well is to concentrate on Rousseau's account of his earliest education, where he describes reading aloud with his father until dawn. Reading this passage carefully, students can begin to get a sense of the outline for Romanticism it contains, with its emphasis on a "sensitive heart" and the primacy of passion and intuition over reason and analysis. ("I had grasped nothing; I had sensed everything.") Other passages—for example, the description of Rousseau's loss of "pure happiness" at Bossey—may work as well as this one; the important thing is for students to grasp the opposition between feeling and thinking that is at stake and, using this opposition as a guide, to begin to make sense of other, more elusive, aspects of Rousseau's writing.

By far the larger part of book-length criticism of Rousseau is written in French. However, Peter France's Rousseau: Confessions (Cambridge,1987) is useful, as is Huntington Williams's Rousseau and Romantic Autobiography (Oxford, 1983). Autobiography: Essays Theoretical and Critical (Princeton, 1980), edited by James Olney, provides a good discussion of Rousseau in context of the autobiographical mode.

Questions for Study and Discussion:

1. To whom is Rousseau confessing in this selection from his famous book? What are his principal confessions?

2. This selection is concerned with Rousseau's childhood. Why do you think this relatively uneventful period of the author's life receives such emphasis?

3. Why do you think Rousseau includes evidence of his sexual tastes in his Confessions?

4. In what ways is Rousseau successful in creating "a [self-]portrait in every way true to nature"? In what ways is he unsuccessful in this endeavor? Do you think an absolutely true account of oneself is ever possible?

5. Rousseau's confessions seem to alternate between boasts and regrets. Why do you think he adopts such a strategy? Which do you find more persuasive, the moments of pride or the moments of remorse? Why?

Charles Baudelaire
The Flowers of Evil

For students who are not already totally jaded by cinematic violence and depravity, Baudelaire raises the wonderful question of morality in art; beyond that, he makes us ask what poetry and beauty are, if these are beautiful poems. These are the issues most likely to stimulate discussion in class, though it should not be forgotten that Baudelaire is also one of the most useful examples in the anthology of the modern lyric, useful for illustrating issues like voice, subjectivity and persona.

His poems display craft, subtlety of expression, perfect rhythms of language and thought—but the subject matter is often disgusting, and the attraction is to our dark side. They can be presented as an aspect of European Romanticism, along with Rousseau (whom many students also find awful as a person), Hölderlin, and Dostoyevsky (whose Underground Man is also awful); but Baudelaire represents the Romantic and fin-de-siecle cults of urban decadence in the nineteenth century, quite the opposite of Rousseau's Romanticism of nature. One can compare his decadence with ancient decadence, as in the Latin poems of Catullus, or in the middle period in the Provençal poems, the Arabic poems of Hafiz, or those of the Chinese Song poets. (Actually, the poet in the anthology nearest to him in these terms is Petrarch, though his wretched excesses can only be matched by Chaucer's Pardoner.)

It is hard to think of non-European texts that quite capture Baudelaire's flavor, but as a representative of modern, despairing subjectivity, he can be usefully taught in contrast to Eastern and Western texts of all periods. What makes Baudelaire Baudelaire, in large part, is his presentation of himself as guilty, unfulfilled, desirous, despairing, passive, neurotic, with some sort of gap in him that aches for love as it forces him to wallow in self-loathing. Students are likely to know the type from popular culture. Having given up on civilization, he "represents art as divorced from society. No laws are recognized except aesthetic ones" (Paglia). Having given up on himself, he adopts a languorous passivity in the hands of women, whom he often portrays as cold, emotionless vampires.

Baudelaire's poems are more shocking to students than the familiar stories of Poe, who influenced Baudelaire; whereas students are accustomed to the idea of horror fiction, they bring into the classroom a more refined sense of what poetry is and does, or should be and should do. Baudelaire is famously attractive to teenage boys, who may discover in him some of their more lurid fantasies. Girls are more likely to find him repellently misogynistic. Classroom discussion should be lively.

The first poem, "To the Reader," is probably Baudelaire's most famous. Its images are over-the-top attempts to shock the reader. It is a memorable picture of the unconscious mind swimming with forbidden, barely repressed thoughts and desires. The poet hopes to force us to recognize these hidden evils in ourselves. The final stanza, which identifies the worst of our inner horrors as Boredom—l'Ennui—captures in a stroke the spirit of decadence. Since Baudelaire, boredom has become part of our cultural landscape: our newspapers and movies teem with stories of meaningless, banal evil, evil as a response to boredom, the search for a thrill. But Baudelaire's evil is largely aesthetic posturing, a rejection of society, an exaggerated embrace of death and decay.

If students begin with the question of Baudelaire's artistry and morality, however, they will find plenty of contradictions in the poems to prevent them from making hasty generalizations. Ask them to locate the most shocking moments in the poems, and also the most elevated and beautiful. "Elevation" and "Correspondences" illustrate this relatively positive side, though all the poems are a mix to one degree or another. In these two, poetry provides a means of escape from the sickly world—but an escape into what? What is the "fire that fills and fuels Emptiness"? The poet's "forest of symbols" is a memorable combination of sounds, scents, and colors—mostly scents (which is memorable because so rare in poetry); but what is Nature's temple? Note that both of these poems are sonnets in the Petrarchan form.

"The Head of Hair" ("La Chevelure") is an extraordinarily sensuous love poem, though typically Baudelaire pays no attention to his partner as a person. Students who can read the poem in French might report on how different it is even from Howard's fine translation. In his lover's long dark hair the poet discovers continents, jungles, oceans, ships and harbors, finally even the sky itself. Her hair is the occasion and the means for a swooning, sensuous escape from the sickness of the city into romanticized fantasies of travel—more fantasy than adventure, obviously, more an attempt to drown than to see the world.

"Vampire" is a hymn to addiction—to sex, drugs, or what? America's town malls are filled with teenagers affecting this Gothic pose, with white faces, lurid make-up and black clothes. What is the psychological attraction? "Spleen II," like "To the Reader," displays the contents of the poet's mind with almost comical method. A near-sonnet, students should spot the successive similes of the chest-of-drawers, graveyard, and closet, with all their pull-out and pop-up monsters. As with the first poem, one suspects the excesses of the imagery are a pose, stylized and artificial, rather than a more directly lyrical cry from the heart. This is the posture of decadence, an urban affectation, the pose of the corrupt dandy, like Andy Warhol. Paglia calls it "ennui hip." Students may be more aware of the rock music version of it. . .

An exciting discussion of Baudelaire which is extremely useful for those looking for classroom raps can be found in Camille Paglia's Sexual Personae, though she does not discuss these poems in particular. She is good on decadence, which she calls "a disease of the western eye, . . . an intensification of the voyeurism latent in all art."

Questions for Study and Discussion:

1. What do you make of the exaggerated imagery of "To the Reader"? Why does he call the reader "my twin"? How is Boredom the foulest of the mind's demons?

2. How serious is the claim of transcendence in "Elevation"? What is "the fire that fills and fuels Emptiness"?

3. In "Correspondences," what is "Nature's temple"? How are sounds, scents, and colors symbols? Symbols of what?

4. How is the poet's lover described in "The Head of Hair"? Is his fantasy a version of the transcendence of "Elevation," or the forest of symbols in "Correspondences"?

5. Try to describe the sexual addiction in "Vampire." What is the psychological attraction of this Gothic image? Find examples of this exaggerated pose in current popular culture. Do they help you understand Baudelaire better?

6. Itemize the similes and metaphors in "Souvenirs." How serious is Baudelaire's claim in this poem and "To the Reader" that he is so totally corrupt?

7. Why does Baudelaire so agressively reject morality in his art? Is his poetry immoral?

Marcel Proust
In Search of Lost Time

Like Rousseau's Confessions, In Search of Lost Time begins with a much older man's vivid recollections of his early life as, inspired by the taste of cake and warm tea, he relives the "far distant days" of his childhood. Since it is partly the actual memories of Marcel Proust that Marcel the narrator remembers and Proust records, In Search of Lost Time is even more closely linked to Rousseau, and from him to the whole corpus of autobiographical literature—from Rousseau and Henry Adams and Ben Franklin to Goethe, Mill, Stendhal, Robert Graves, Brendan Behan, Christopher Isherwood and many others—which extends to the present. (Given this connection, it is intriguing to note that the volume of Rousseau that Marcel was to have been given for his birthday at Combray is rejected by his father.) This selection may, for this reason, be usefully compared to examples of autobiography from various cultures contained in this anthology. (For the remembrances of another old man that contrast strikingly with those of Marcel in Swann's Way, students may want to compare Usāmah Ibn Munqidh's twelfth-century Book of Reflections. Doing so inevitably raises questions about the qualities of the "hero" in

Proust's book and, indeed, in much twentieth-century literature.) In Search of Lost Time is also, of course, a masterpiece of modernist literature and can be compared to the writing of Virginia Woolf, James Joyce, Franz Kafka and others. A further thematic connection is suggested by the description of the quivering leaf of the chestnut tree (p. 2027), which, along with many other descriptions in the Combray section, recalls Bashō in the acuteness of its observation of nature.

One of the main attractions of Proust's writing is the long, languorous, and highly nuanced prose line he employs. This and the narrator's intense love for his mother are very likely the biggest obstacles to enjoyment of this text by students new to it. Reading Proust takes patience. The beginning of this selection seems to many students unbelievably slow to develop, and it is crucial that students be helped to see what is at stake here: namely, that consciousness itself is what is being traced and recorded. The description of Marcel's mother's reading (p. 2034) is useful as an analogy for the kind of writing Proust sets out to produce, with his prose "breathing . . . a kind of emotional life and continuity" all its own; grasping this helps students adjust to the demands (and pleasures) of the text.

It is useful to pick out some of the objects upon which Proust focuses in this selection as the basis for early discussion of the text. The magic lantern (p. 2010) is a particularly compelling one, for it suggests the complex relationship between the senses and experience itself that is a main theme of the text. As Proust writes: "Perhaps the immobility of the things that surround us is forced upon them by our conviction that they are themselves and not anything else, by the immobility of our conceptions of them" (p. 2007). Students will notice that the magic lantern changes the appearance of objects in the world, and is analogous to the action imagination has upon perception. The implications of this malleability is a more radical flux, to the point where "none of us can be said to constitute a material whole"; rather, our "personality is a creation of the thoughts of other people" (p. 2017). Focusing on these passages gives rise to discussion of consciousness, and the way Proust investigates its mediating effects upon experience in art.

Scholarly and general resources for Proust and his writing are abundant. Some of the most useful for readers new to this author are Philip Thohy's Marcel Proust (New York, 1988) and Barbara J. Bucknall Marcel Proust Revisited (New York, 1992). The former offers a good, brief overview, whereas the latter is particularly useful as an introduction and guide to Swann's Way (see chapter 2). Angelo Caranfa's Proust: The Creative Silence (London, 1990) has a series of essays comparing various aspects of Proust's writing to that of other writers and non-literary artists; students considering Proust in a unit on autobiography will appreciate Caranfa's chapter on Proust and Augustine. The Selected Letters, in two volumes edited by Philip Kolb (New York, 1983/89), are a further useful resource for insights into Proust's highly autobiographical writing, besides giving students a chance to read amusing and elegantly crafted letters. There are, in addition to these resources, several biographies which students and teachers may want to consult.

Questions for Study and Discussion:

1. Why does Proust focus so intently on physical sensation—smells, colors, sounds, etc.—in this narrative?

2. Opening the text almost at random, one finds unusually long, languorous sentences. How does such a prose style contribute to the overall effect of the selection?

3. Why is the magic lantern a particularly appropriate object for attention? (See page 2010.)

4. Try writing a Proustian parody of the sentence on page 2015 that begins "And yet, as soon as I heard her 'Bathilde! . . . .'" What are its main features? For contrast, now try to recast this same sentence as succinctly as possible, using the spare, precise style that Pound and other modernist writers championed. What insights does this exercise provide about the writing of both of these modernists?

5. Marcel frequently draws from the lexicon of religion to describe his contact with his mother. Why do you suppose this is?

Friedrich Hölderlin
"Patmos"

As the headnote to this selection explains, Pindar's is the great classical model for Hölderlin's poetry. Like the former's ode to a victorious athlete which appears in this anthology, Hölderlin's poem celebrates a victory—in this instance, a victory of faith. One writer with whom Hölderlin can profitably be compared is, of course, Milton, whose Paradise Lost seeks to "justify the ways of God to men," much as "Patmos" insists that "all things are good." Like Milton, Hölderlin was also deeply indebted to classical Western writers. Alternatively, Hölderlin's poem might be read alongside other European Romantic writing, like that of Rousseau, or alongside their nineteenth- and twentieth-century descendants, Whitman and Neruda. Hölderlin, it may be recalled, began but never finished a poem called "Rousseau"; like Rousseau, he loathed the materialism and rationalism of the Enlightenment world view. (For the theme of resistance to the instrumentalization of life, one could also compare "Patmos" to Dostoyevsky's Notes from Underground.) Like Hölderlin, both Neruda and Whitman write in the tradition of the Romantic poet-prophet, albeit rather differently than does Hölderlin in "Patmos." Tracing the similarities and differences between their uses of this key Romantic trope (i.e., the self-representation of the visionary poet) is useful for understanding the poetry. A further comparison is suggested by the line "give us innocent water" in stanza 1, which finds an echo in Eliot's "The Waste Land." Comparing the natural imagery of the Romantic and the modernist poems is revealing.

The introduction to Hölderlin in the anthology notes his "impassioned search for the divine"—a search which resulted in "traces" of the heavenly presence. One good way to begin to come to grips with the poem is by having students locate some of these "traces"—some of the places in the poem where Hölderlin seems to come closest to making the divine present in the world of the poem. Students might be directed to the lines about John the Baptist—"the attentive man / Saw the face of the God exactly" (79-80)—as an analogy for the work of the reader in recognizing God in the poem.

This is not a poem that is immediately accessible, and students will probably need to be guided through its narrative. A strategy that works well in the classroom is, once the poem has been read carefully two or three times, to have students write in single sentences the main idea of each stanza. This has the advantage of helping students locate the places where the poem loses them, as well as where its meaning seems more clear.

Although most of the critical literature on Hölderlin is either in German or is more than fifty years old, the quality of recent English language scholarship is quite high. David

Constantine's Hölderlin (Oxford, 1988) is an excellent critical introduction to the writer, whereas Richard Unger's Friedrich Hölderlin (Boston,1984) is more compact but still useful. Hölderlin: The Poetics of Being (Detroit, 1991) is a fascinating study of the poetry for more advanced students. Hölderlin and Pindar (The Hague, 1962), while a bit stilted, remains an informative study of the two poets.

Questions for Study and Discussion:

1. As the headnote to this selection explains, Hölderlin derived from his study of Pindar the aim of revealing traces of the divine in the world. Where do you see such traces in "Patmos"?

2. After the dramatic visionary stanzas of the beginning of the poem, Hölderlin evokes the island of Patmos with noticeably understated, unpretentious images: it is a "poorer house" than Cypress, and is characterized by the "hot noonday copse" and "the field's / Flat surface" (stanza 5). How does this description serve the main purpose of the poem?

3. What is the "wisdom" that is achieved in stanza 8? Why do you think Hölderlin uses the phrase "Abysses of wisdom" to describe it? (As you formulate your answer, be sure to consider the mountain imagery that fills stanza 1 and reappears elsewhere in the poem.)

4. Paraphrase lines 160-61, "For the work of gods, too, is like our own, / Not all things at once does the Highest intend," as though you were presenting the idea they contain to an intelligent but uncomprehending friend. What is Hölderlin trying to say here? How do these lines help explain the parable of the sower's grain that precedes them?

5. Hölderlin is clearly trying to fuse ancient Greek and Christian elements in this poem—most notably in his choice of subject, the Greek island of Patmos where Saint John is said to have beheld the divine, but also in the poem's allusions to a Charon-like boatman (50), heroes (105, 206), a demigod (146), Christ (166, 205), sacrifices (217), and other overt and implicit references. Why do you think the poet chooses to attempt this fusion? How successful is he in achieving it?

Rainer Maria Rilke
Duino Elegies

Teaching Rilke's Duino Elegies to a group of college students is not an easy task. Rilke's work is mysterious and elusive. His poetry springs from the depths of a soul that is struggling to find some place, some sure ground, in a world where he feels profoundly, perhaps hopelessly, alienated (the poet W. H. Auden, who was in some ways influenced by Rilke, once referred to the latter as "The Santa Claus of loneliness"). Most college students will not identify with these struggles readily. Moreover, one easily becomes lost as one works through Rilke's poetry. The best approach to the two selections from Duino Elegies, we think, is to explain from the outset that the student should not try to reduce these difficult poems to some simple (or, for that matter, even complex) philosophical statement. Such reductionist reading, where poetry is regarded simply as encoded philosophy, should always be resisted, and this is particularly so in the case of Rilke, who, as the Russian poet Marina Tsvetayeva put it, is "poetry itself." Instead, students can be encouraged to summarize or explain the imagery or the "meaning" of any combination of lines they feel that they understand. Different students will seize onto quite different segments of the poems, and a sequence of readings will begin to build up. With some stimulation and guidance from the teacher, a more general interpretation of the poems will begin to take shape. However, the teacher should again emphasize that the poem is always more, always somehow different, than these readings. What we are suggesting, is that Rilke, as much as any of the poets in the anthology, permits a discussion of what poetry is—particularly what poetry is during the early part of this century when the work of Sigmund Freud and others encouraged one to plumb the depths of his or her consciousness.

But who are the "angels" who seem to play such a prominent role in these two elegies? As the "Second Elegy" says through an allusion, they are not the companionable angels like the one who accompanied Tobias in the account of the book of Tobit in the Apocrypha: "The boy and the angel left the house together, and the dog came out with him and accompanied them" (note that here we encounter a very un-Rilkean world where angels, humans, and animals are completely at home with one another! See Tobit 6.1). Instead, Rilke's angels are "terrifying." Rilke once explained to a friend that his angels are terrible because they are invisible, and we humans cling so tenaciously to the visible world. In a sense, then, they seem to represent death—killing us with "serene scorn" (p. 2045). In Rilke's world, however, we are also alienated from the visible world, including the world of animals, where we are "not comfortable." The "Elegies," on a certain level, are about being haunted, but not being haunted so much by ghosts or phantasms like those of Tagore's "Hungry Stones," but by our own deepest musings.

Even the best students (and, at times, teachers) will resist Rilke. It is easy to accuse him of being self-indulgent, of taking himself far too seriously, of falling into a type of preciousness that is worlds away from a poet: like, for example, Symborska (see pp. 2088-2096); and reading about Rilke's life, to be sure, will do nothing to alter this impression. He is almost a caricature of the solitary and eccentric artist (he occasionally walked around Paris in a black cloak, clutching an iris) who spends his time probing his own most tortured and sometimes tangled thoughts. In a letter written to a young poet, Rilke said that to be a poet one musts "Go into yourself." If either students or teachers do have an essentially negative reaction to Rilke, it is wise to express these and then to ask what has happened to the world of poetry, in fact the world of literature, since the time Rilke wrote to provoke our mixed reactions to his work. But, in the end, what assures Rilke a spot in any list of the world's great poets, is the fact that he emerges from his musings, however self-indulgent they might be, with an astounding verbal power that one can appreciate even in translation.

The "Introduction" of the poet in Robert Hass and Stephen Mitchell's translation of Rilke's poetry is very interesting and useful. See The Selected Poetry of Rainer Maria Rilke, edited and translated by Stephen Mitchell (New York, 1982), pp. xi-xliv. A new biography is that of Ralph Freedman, Life of a Poet: Rainer Maria Rilke (New York, 1996). Students who are interested in Rilke's views on poetry should consult his fascinating Letters to a Young Poet, translated by M. D. Herter, (New York, 1934).

Questions for Study and Discussion:

1. What do you think Rilke means when he speaks in line 13 of the "First Elegy" of "our translated world?"

2. In both of the elegies included here, Rilke speaks of love. How effective do you think love is, in Rilke's view, as a means of overcoming our estrangement and making us feel at home?

3. Death is described in the "First Elegy" as "strange." Why?

4. Why is it that the Attic steles ("Second Elegy," line 66) seem to be so attractive, and why can't we find anything so "pure, contained, narrow, human" in our own existence?

Franz Kafka
"A Country Doctor" and "An Imperial Message"

How could Kafka fail to stimulate thought and discussion in the classroom? And yet recent reports suggest that popular youth culture is now so Kafkaesque that some students actually find him boring. One hopes it isn't true, or that good teaching can overcome this feeling. Kafka's surreal depiction of everyday life as a nightmare has always been morbidly appealing to the young, like horror movies. The two pieces in the anthology make an effective teaching unit along with Dostoevsky's <u>Notes from the Underground</u>, Beckett's play <u>Happy Days</u>, and the stories of Borges and García Márquez, who were both influenced by Kafka; of the many Asian possibilities, there are the Japanese writers Kawabata and Abe, the Vietnamese Nguyen Huy Thiep, and the Indian Salman Rushdie. Kafka exerted a strong influence on "magical realism," which has become a popular narrative style in many emerging post-colonial literatures in the East and West.

In <u>The Country Doctor</u> one cannot miss the narrative style of dreams and nightmares. It is one of the best examples of literary narrative in the dream style, and offers an opportunity for students to think about how the unconscious mind perceives the world, and patterns it in narratives when we sleep. If there is a "natural" form of narrative that our minds use all the time, one might suggest, it is reasonable to think it might play some part in the way we write and read stories when awake. One needn't be a Freudian to make this point: the connection between dreams and myths, made popular by Joseph Campbell, is an effective classroom point. Many students are ready to see myth and folklore, which have inexplicably universal aspects and elements, as resembling dream-narratives in some ways. Myths are in some sense the dreams of whole societies.

One could begin the discussion of this story by asking students to itemize elements in it that seem particularly dreamlike, like the sudden opening, the travel that takes place instantly, the sudden discovery of the wound, the narrator's nakedness, etc. Realism and narrative coherence are obviously not to the point, so what is? Where does meaning come from in such a story, or does it have a meaning at all? It is like asking if our dreams have meaning, and many students resist this idea. And yet it should not be hard to get a class to see that the story creates moods, emotional states, and might be said to explore them. Further, when there are so few rational elements in the story to hold on to, they should grasp at the chance to find meaning in symbols.

As far as emotions go, the predominant one in this story is guilt. How is guilt expressed in this case? The narrator's inability to perform his duty, his sense of failure, his impotence in the face of the stableman's insolence and violence, his failure to protect Rosa the maid, his mis-diagnosis, the accusing family of the sick boy, the village elders, teacher and schoolchildren who threaten and then strip him, his nakedness, etc. And what is guilt? Not just the fact that one has done something wrong, but the <u>feeling</u> that one has done something wrong, or the fear that one might do something wrong, or simply a sense of personal worthlessness or impotence. These are reasonable lines of discussion in class in response to the story.

As for symbolism, if the story is symbolic, what does it mean? How do we interpret symbols? If students accede to the idea that it seems symbolic, we might ask them what is it symbolic of, and what are its symbolic elements? Have them find particular symbols and try to explain their meanings: the stableman (why is he an unnamed stranger?), the two horses (why are they named Brother and Sister? Isn't their exit from the barn peculiar?), the worm-infested wound (why is called a "blossom"?), the chorus of authority figures, the narrator's nakedness, his incoherent explanation of the boy's wound (the axe getting closer), the fur coat, and many other details. One can turn the questions around: Why would Kafka have left the stableman unnamed? Would anything be lost if the horses were named Trigger and Lightning? What does it add to our response that the wound is called a blossom? (Does "blossom" evoke Rosa in our minds?) I would not try actually to explicate the story's symbols to students, but let them wrestle with the possibilities. Stress that their interpretations do not have to be logical, rational, or consistent. And it's all right if they leave with a sense that the story's meaning is opaque; the discussion will at least have fixed the story in their minds, and they can think about issues like guilt and symbolism on their own.

This issue of symbolism may be more manageable with the tiny parable, "An Imperial Message." Who is the Emperor? The class will probably come pretty quickly to the suspicion that he represents God, or at least some ultimate source of meaning in life. What message is he sending for us? Perhaps it is the meaning of life, or perhaps it is our salvation—though perhaps it is more important simply that he cares enough for us ("you, of all people") to send a message, and the real message is that he exists. We will never receive the message, however; we wait our entire lives for it, imagining it, even after the Emperor has died—for he does die in the course of the short parable.

There is a spooky sense in reading the parable that the Emperor who is trying to send us a message is also Kafka himself, who is of course now dead; and perhaps he is also the messenger who cannot reach us in time. All we know is that we can never know what he wanted to tell us.

We, of course, are the ones waiting for the message that will never come; but symbolism being what it is, we can also identify with the dying king, whose wish to send a message is frustrated; and we are also the messenger, who finds it impossible to achieve even the clearest mission in this world because of the immense confusion surrounding him. Our own wishes for communication and successful action are destined to failure.

What does it all mean? That God is dead, but we still wait for some comforting word from Him that will never come? This anxious waiting, this impossible hope for understanding, the impossibility of communication, the frustration of action, taken together seem to be Kafka's estimation of the human condition.

Questions for Study and Discussion:

1. Make a list of the features of "The Country Doctor" that make it resemble a dream or nightmare.

2. The predominant emotion in the story seems to be guilt. How is guilt expressed in the narrative? What is guilt? What could the narrator (the dreamer?) be feeling so guilty about?

3. Is the story symbolic? What are some of its symbols? Account for the names of the stableman, the maid, and the horses. What do you make of the wound, the fur coat?

4. In "An Imperial Message," who is the Emperor, the messenger, the narrator? What is the message? What is the meaning of the parable?

Fyodor Dostoyevsky
Notes from Underground

The obvious companion piece for Notes from Underground is Rousseau's Confessions, since Rousseau's book is specifically cited—and scathingly if fleetingly critiqued—at the end of the selection reprinted here. Like Rousseau, the narrator of Notes feels a compulsion to explain, and by explaining, perhaps to understand. He thus sets out to confess the "abominable things" he has done, which is wholly in keeping with the "vile and despicable" tale Rousseau records against himself. The chief difference, however, is that whereas Rousseau was convinced that, baring all, he was getting at the truth of himself, Dostoyevsky's Underground Man harbors no such illusion. The Underground Man, who rages against reason even as he engages in reasoned discourse, is consistent in his contradictions: he doesn't believe in the possibility of an absolutely truthful self-accounting, but persists in writing one anyway. In thus questioning self-awareness as the cornerstone of all knowledge, showing how it seems always to be tinged or tainted by subjectivity, the Underground Man appears as the precursor to the many modern writers for whom existence itself is a disturbing puzzle. When, at the end of Part XI, the Underground Man decides that "[i]t was on account of the wet snow . . . that I recalled the incident that I can't get rid of now. And so, let this be a story on account of the wet snow," he anticipates Proust, whose In Search of Lost Time takes a similarly arbitrary-seeming recollection—a memory of childhood evoked by a madeleine cake dipped in lemon tea—as the basis for a grand analysis of his own subjectivity. Other writers to whom Dostoyevsky can be compared include Beckett, Nabokov, and Burroughs, all of whom feature hyper-analytical figures at the margins of society (only the first of which is included in this anthology, unfortunately).

Notes from Underground stands as a precursor to the modern psychological novel. It is also an experimental work. Students will be quick to point out—and perhaps be disturbed by—the "lies" the Underground Man writes, sensing a violation of an implicit contract between writer and reader. In his button-holing, cantankerous, outraged, darkly funny and deeply disturbing persona, the Underground Man is out to upset precisely such "rules" of social intercourse. Students can begin to engage the text by listing the various contradictions they detect in their reading of Notes and, having aired them, trying to decide what rhetorical strategy they might serve.

It is useful for students to know that Dostoyevsky's rejection of an Enlightenment faith in reason has a specific context: questions of human motivation were hotly contested among mid-nineteenth-century Russian intellectuals, most notably in Nikolay Chernyshevsky's What is to be Done? (1863), which posits enlightened self-interest as the basis for human action (that is, a theory grounded in scientific determinism). Dostoyevsky's Notes is, in part, a rejection of this totalizing and ultimately callous explanation of society. He ridicules the idea "that man makes mischief only because he does not know his own true interests," considering it an absurd fallacy to believe "that if he were enlightened . . . man would immediately stop making mischief, and would immediately become nice and noble." As he assembles his "notes," the Underground Man returns repeatedly to certain key terms: desire (irrational wanting, or what he memorably calls "all the itches") and reason (the schema, the logarithm, the system). In his formulation, irrational desire—caprices, liking what is not good for one—short-circuits reason and allows for a more fully human existence. Grasping this, students will see why he rails against theories of human behavior derived "from statistical figures and scientific-economic formulas," dismissing them as "mere logistics." The speaker's rhetorical strategies, evident in such phrases as "I lied about myself earlier" and "it's all the same to me," underscore his argument, trying to get around reason, as do his frequent—and frequently bad—jokes.

A line of inquiry which students consistently find interesting is the idea that reason, taken to its conclusion, leads to violence: the Underground Man's contention that the logic of civilization ultimately produces "the most refined blood-letters." In this, Dostoyevsky anticipates twentieth-century critics who, like Max Horkheimer and Theodor Adorno, critique Enlightenment rationality as the basis of the most efficient totalitarian systems. Students frequently begin to warm to the narrator of Notes as they see that he is not so much opposed to reason as he is horrified by the unreflective certainties of people who think themselves reasonable.

Richard Peace's Dostoyevsky: An Examination of the Major Novels (London, 1971) has a short, useful chapter on the early writing, including Notes From Underground. Robin Feuer Miller's "Dostoyevsky and Rousseau: The Morality of Confession Reconsidered," in Dostoyevsky: New Perspectives (Robert Louis Jackson, ed., Englewood Cliffs, NJ, 1984), pairs these writers to explore the complexities of the confessional mode. William J. Leatherbarrow provides a good, brief discussion of Notes, and Peter Conradi's introductory chapter to Fyodor Dostoevsky (New York, 1988) usefully places Dostoyevsky in his historical milieu.

Questions for Study and Discussion:

1. Describe the main point of each of the eleven sections in this selection.

2. Why are "men of action" targets of the Underground Man's diatribe? How would you characterize them?

3. How would you describe the "wall" of which the Underground Man writes? What is its function?

4. In Part VIII, the narrator asserts that "Reason knows only what it has managed to learn . . . ." This may well be the premise that drives the Underground Man's critique of reason, but what does it mean? Why is it significant?

5. Dostoyevsky satirizes faith in systems with which, as he puts it, "[a]ll human actions . . . will be computed according to . . . laws, mathematically, like logarithmic tables, up to 108,000 and entered on the calendar" (2069). In what ways do we have more or less faith in such systems today?

6. Is the Underground Man just being silly when he insists that "two times two makes five is sometimes a most delightful little thing" (2075)? What is the point of this assertion?

7. As the headnote states, Dostoyevsky's later writing embraces a redemptively Christian understanding of life. Do you see any harbingers of such a view in this selection?

Anna Akhmatova
Poems

Requiem, considered one of Akhmatova's greatest poems, records the suffering endured by women who stood in long lines outside Stalin's prisons in the 1930s waiting and hoping for news of their sons, husbands, brothers, lovers, and friends. The women in Akhmatova's poem experience the suffering both of not knowing and of knowing the fate of their loved ones. The ten central sections constitute an emotional drama of suffering, a chronology of grief and loss that moves from the first line in part 1, "They took you away at dawn," to the crucifixion scene in part 10 where the narrator's son is executed. Students will likely notice the movement from defiance to resignation to fear and horror, to despair, to a longing for death or even madness and finally to a conclusion in number 10 constructed out of heavily intertextual references to Christ's crucifixion. The first stanza in number 10 cites Christ's words to his father and mother; the second stanza references Mary Magdalene's sorrow, the paralyzing grief of St. John, and the unspeakable losses of "the silent Mother." But by referencing the crucifixion, Akhmatova also builds into the loss a possibility of hope, a possibility that the sacrifice and suffering might be redemptive.

The drama of the central section is framed by prefatory materials at the beginning and by epilogues at the end. Like an epic poet preserving the struggles of a nation in language, Akhmatova responds to a woman who asks, "Can you describe this?" And her response is the poem which is an affirmation that can function as an answer to the horrors of Stalin's purges. For the suffering and for the millions who died in the Gulags, the poem is a commitment to remember. In this way, it is fruitfully compared with Irena Klepfisz's poem, Bashert. Akhmatova's poem, although inspired by her own personal agonies, weaves "a wide mantle" for all who suffered during the Terror. She conceives of the poem as a requiem, a funeral song "through which a hundred million scream." While we might interpret the choral qualities of the poem simply, it is also useful to be aware of some of its less well-known references. These echoes lend the poem a more complex choral quality. In the Russian original, for example, the quotations from the crucifixion in number 10 echo the language of the Church Slavonic Bible. Elsewhere, the poet sprinkles allusions to Euripides, Dante, Shakespeare, Tyutchev, Pushkin, and other Russian writers. Pushkin's 1827 poem about a failed political uprising is quoted in Akhmatova's dedication: "But the prison bolts hold firm, / And behind them lie the 'prisoners' burrows.'" Pushkin's line is "Past the sombre bolts, / As my free voice reaches you / In your convicts' burrows." Ironic borrowings from state-promoted literature can also be heard in the poem. From Vasily Lebedev-Kumach's well-known patriotic song in praise of Stalin's regime and ideology (Song of the Motherland), Akhmatova borrows two lines: "For someone a fresh breeze blows, / For someone the sunset luxuriates." (Lebedev-Kumach wrote: "A spring wind is blowing across the country, / With every day life is more joyous.") For a careful reading of the emotional stages in Requiem, interested students and teachers can refer to A. Haight, Anna Akhmatova: A Poetic Pilgrimage (New York, 1976). For a close reading of the poem's intertexuality, see S. Amert, In a Shattered Mirror: The Later Poetry of Anna Akhmatova (Stanford, 1992).

Akhmatova claimed that her poem, "Dante," expressed her ideas about art. On one level, the poem describes the exiled Italian renaissance poet, Dante, and his refusal to return to Florence under the degrading conditions set down by the city. Dante was, however, the focus of study for Akhmatova and many other poets in her circle. The persecution of Dante becomes an allegory whereby Akhmatova can deplore the Soviet state's attacks on artists. The epigraph, "Il mio bel San Giovanni" comes from the Inferno XIX, 18 and refers to the principal cathedral of

Florence, a symbol not only of Dante's longing but also of spirit over state or aesthetic sensibility over political tyranny. Her lines "To the one who, leaving, did not look back, / To him I sing this song" applauds Dante (and by implication, the persecuted and executed artists of Akhmatova's circle) for not succumbing to the state's demands. With an allusion perhaps to the ancient Greek myth of Eurydice who looked back at hell and was, thus, drawn back into it, Akhamatova weaves a poem praising the artistic resistance to an oppressive political regime.

Questions for Study and Discussion:

1. Examine the ten central poems of Requiem closely, noting the different psychological stances the poet/narrator assumes. Describe the changes you see occurring in the narrator. What techniques does the poet use to help us understand that we are hearing a crescendo of despair?

2. Although most of the central poems in Requiem are written in the first person, number 2 and number 4 include material written in third and second person. What effects do these shifts in person have?

3. Have students locate a copy of Dante's Inferno and examine Canto XIX to discover further the ways this allusion helps Akhmatova condemn the poets who sold their talents to create Stalinist literature in her poem "Dante."

4. What various representations of the state can be found in these few selections from Akhmatova? Do you sense any nostalgia? If so, for what? What seems to give life meaning in these few poems?

Wislawa Szymborska
Poems

Szymborska's contemporary lyrics clearly participate in the modernist European poetic style of spareness, understatement, and oblique commentary that requires reader involvement to unravel. Although she may not be familiar with Asian poetry, her work compares in interesting ways to Bashō's haiku poems. More obvious links can be made with Emily Dickinson's riddling and humorous little poems, Pablo Neruda's Book of Questions, and the Elizabeth Bishop poems in our selection. Her poem "Water" has interesting parallels to Langston Hughes's "The Negro Speaks of Rivers" (not in our anthology).

Each of Szymborska's poems speaks for itself if carefully read, and students can seek the metaphorical trick or puzzle that animates each poem. Her simple word choice and ironic use of detail are also worthy of attention as each poem is closely examined. "Water" draws together many illustrations of the omnipresence, dynamic movement and transformation, utter necessity for life, and historical resonance of water, all imagined by the poet's contemplation of a drop of water on her index finger. This simple image allows a meditation on the complex unification of life and the elements of our world. "Conversation with a Stone" has a humorously dialogic approach to a supposedly inert object which would not have been out of place coming from Emily Dickinson's pen. Szymborska uses the dialogue between the human speaker and the stone to gradually reveal the limitations of humanity's relentless search to connect with and understand every aspect of the physical world, and also to suggest that there are other realities and consciousnesses besides our own. "Theatre Impressions, " like most of the selected poems, develops one trope in complex ways to provide wry commentary on our desire for a realm beyond the suffering and incompleteness of mortal existence. By conjuring up a sixth act for tragedies, in which pain is soothed, loss restored, and ironic vengeance taken on conventional winners, Szymborska teases the reader with the possibility of the "miraculous return of all those lost without a trace," but then turns the tables at the end with her paradoxical notion of the emotional uplift brought by the curtain's fall, and the surprise hand that strangles her. Such gallows humor also dominates "The Century's Decline," with its argument that "good and strong / are still two different men" and the final notion that "the most pressing questions / are naive ones." "Seen from Above" appears at first to congratulate humans on their superiority to other creatures but ends ambiguously, with an arrogant statement that undermines itself as it throws the humble beauty of the dead beetle into relief. "Our Ancestors' Short Lives" similarly seems to differentiate the experience of ancient humans from our own but ends asserting their similarity. Finally, "Nothing's a Gift" turns a simple accounting metaphor into a powerful commentary on entropy, and the way our living is a process of self-loss.

Some recent assessments of Szymborska's work are Krzysztof Karasek's "Mozartian Joy: The Poetry of Wislawa Szymborska" in The Mature Laurel: Essays on Modern Polish Poetry, ed. Adam Czerniawski (Chester Springs, PA, 1991) and Bogdana Carpenter's "Wislawa Szymborska and the Importance of the Unimportant," World Literature Today Vol 71 (Winter 1997) 8-12. A popular response to her Nobel Prize appeared in Publisher's Weekly, Vol. 244 (April 7, 1997) 68-69.

Questions for Study and Discussion:

1. What kinds of imaginary exercises does Szymborska perform on the drop of water she sees on her hand? Why does she speak both of naming water in every tongue and also keeping silent?

2. What kind of character or personality does the stone reveal in "Conversation with a Stone," and what human inadequacy is revealed in the conversation?

3. Go through "Theatre Impressions" and make a list of the changes that occur in the imagined sixth act of the tragedy. What do these events and revelations tell us about the purpose of tragedy, or the dissatisfactions left behind in the audience after the traditional end of the play? What is the unseen hand at the end, and what is its relation to the rest of the poem?

4. What is the relationship between "Seen from Above" and "Our Ancestors' Short Lives"? Look closely at the attitude with which each begins, and compare that with the poem's ending.

5. What does the word "decline" finally mean by the end of "The Century's Decline"?

6. What kind of debts are the subject of "Nothing's a Gift"? How does Szymborska use the metaphor of accounting to explore the intrinsic destruction at the heart of life, and what does the soul have to do with the final accounting?

The Popul Vuh

Teachers can help students orient themselves to a cultural world as unfamiliar as that of the Maya, by providing a bit of historical background from the sources listed below. However, the selections we have included are themselves revealing if closely examined. The nature of Mayan deities is quite different from those of classical Greece and Rome, or from India or Mesopotamia. Supernatural forms of important Central American animals are some of the first gods. Students will find these deities and their functions puzzling but fresh and amusing. Discussing the tone of the creation story, and why humor seems to coexist with the most solemn cosmic events can be a productive way into the narrative's underlying assumptions about the world. The dynamism of the cosmos during the creation process, and the enmeshment of divine powers in it, are intriguing to contrast with more familiar creation traditions such as the Greek, Hebrew, and Indic. Teachers can move students through the various stages of the creation story, asking them to decide what is at stake at each stage, and what problem causes the destruction of early efforts. Seven Macaw appears at the end of our creation selection, puffing himself up arrogantly and thus setting himself up for eventual defeat in a section we have not included.

The story of the birth of the divine twins Hunahpu and Xbalanque is a more or less self-contained part of the longer narrative that climaxes with their defeat of the lords of death. The twins' mother becomes pregnant in a strange underworld adventure that can be discussed for its possible symbolic significance, with the spittle from the bone of dead One Hunahpu representing the living force of the tree where it is lodged. The spirit of this dead hero seems to have been transmitted into the tree, and his vitality transmitted through the spit—or sap—which lands in Blood Woman's hand and impregnates her. Strong connections between the human and plant worlds are suggested here. Blood Woman's predicament reveals a different kind of kinship system than those familiar to us from European and Asian societies, and students can try to infer what its outlines or at least its values and problems may be. The story of the hero twins' early years and defeat of their unkind elder brothers can be treated somewhat as a fairytale might be, but its allegorical possibilities should be discussed.

As suggested above, fruitful comparisons and contrasts may be made between Popol Vuh and other creation traditions such as Vedic hymns of creation, the Hebrew story of Genesis, the Japanese Kojiki, and Greek Theogony, as well as Ovid's Roman version in the Metamorphoses. The Mayan work can also be linked to stories such as the Indian Ramayana and the Chinese story of Monkey, or Journey to the West, which also dramatize trickster figures as semi-divine characters central to important cultural stories.

Dennis Tedlock's translation of the Popol Vuh (New York, 1986) includes an extensive introductory essay and extremely helpful notes. For basic background information about the Mayans and their history, Michael Coe's The Maya (London, 1984) is informative but not overwhelming. Useful maps of Mayan settlement, and illustrations of art, hieroglyphs, architecture, and the layout of urban centers and ceremonial sites are provided, as well as an account of the rise and fall of the civilization. A Forest of Kings (New York, 1990) is a longer introductory study of Mayan civilization.

Questions for Study and Discussion:

1. What kind of deities do the Mayans worship? What do they tell us about attitudes toward the natural world?

2. Why does the Maker, Modeler, mother-father of life have to keep trying again and again? Does this sense of the divine suggest imperfection, or does it express a different kind of world view than we are familiar with?

3. What is the tone of the Popul Vuh? What kind of a culture is suggested by it?

4. What do we learn about Mayan values and customs from the creation story?

5. Do we learn about the inner feelings of the characters in the story of the birth of the Hero Twins? What kind of person is their mother, and what are her relationships with her father and her mother-in-law? How does the story illustrate kinship relations among the Maya?

6. What traits do the Hero Twins exemplify? How do they differ from their older brothers? What kind of dramatic tension moves their story forward?

Jorge Luis Borges
Stories and Other Writing

Borges is so intelligent and so witty that many students will be left in the dust while their teachers swoon in admiration or laugh themselves silly. He is a writer's writer, a master artist. The longest of these three pieces (only six pages), is definitely not teen-age literature; but good students of any age can find in it a welcome glimpse of postmodernism's comic heart. In the syllabus, Borges can be read along with the magical realists he inspired, like García Márquez in the West, Abe in Japan, and Rushdie in India; and he should be taught along with Kafka, who is one of his chief inspirations. In addition, "Pierre Menard" can naturally be linked with Cervantes's Don Quixote. The delightfully ironic one-page parable "Borges and I" is an effective companion to Kafka's one-page "An Imperial Message"; and the little poem about reading Beowulf might be marginally more meaningful to those who have read that poem. Most of all, however, Borges should be taught as a South American postmodernist with a unique voice, a writer who sees life as a mirrored, labyrinthine funhouse where truth seems to be everywhere but can never be held on to. Many students have grown up in this labyrinth, and Borges can be a beneficial reminder to them that postmodern uncertainty and disorientation needn't always be desperate, amoral or tragic, but can be comic, warm, and life-affirming too.

"Pierre Menard, Author of the Quixote" is first of all a parody of literary criticism, a fictional book review as vacuous, precious, pedantic, pretentious, and absurd as the book it pretends to be reviewing. Thus it is an ironic exaggeration of the follies of modern intellectual life, where common sense is discarded for nonsense, and erudition substitutes for truth. One is reminded of Monty Python—but don't expect most students to get the point. The opening list of Menard's "visible" works is a catalogue of lunatic one-liners that can be revealed as delightful—for example, "A technical article on the possibility of enriching the game of chess by means of eliminating one of the rooks' pawns. Menard proposes, recommends, disputes, and ends by rejecting this innovation." This is only one of several examples of Menard's "resigned or ironic habit of propounding ideas which were the strict reverse of those he preferred." Are intellectuals really this weird? (Of course not!)

One might ask students to hunt through these six pages for particularly inspired lunatic assertions, like "the fragmentary Don Quixote of Menard is more subtle than that of Cervantes," or "He resolved to outstrip that vanity which awaits all the woes of mankind; he undertook a task that was complex in the extreme and futile from the outset." Ask them also to ferret out what they think might be the point of it all. The clearest statement of it is probably, "There is no intellectual exercise which is not ultimately useless," which undermines all pretentiousness.

We might also ask, though, whether beyond all the satire and absurdity there may in fact be something in Menard's project, and in the concluding proposition that literary history might better be read backwards. Menard is after all a parody of a modern reader, as well as a scholar. Quixote meant one thing in the seventeenth century, and another thing today. Students have asked me, "If a playwright today could write Shakespearian plays as well as Shakespeare, would the plays be great like Shakespeare's, or only imitative and anachronistic?" The question comes from students who have learned to write, say, good Shakespearean sonnets, but who realize that that doesn't qualify them as original. One of the questions "Menard" poses is: What is originality in art? Another is: How does a modern reader read an ancient work without distorting and falsifying its meaning by anachronistic interpretation?

As challenging as "Pierre Menard" is, the tiny "Borges and I" does not take a sophisticated intellectual to appreciate it. It is a classic illustration of a common and important conundrum. Who am I? Am I the person I know directly, or am I the person others claim to know from reading what I write? Artists, movie stars and comedians—anyone famous—knows this split in an exaggerated way. "This isn't really me! You don't know the real me!" Every rock group sings songs about it, and English professors sing about it too, since we always warn against confusing a work's narrative or lyric voice (the persona) with the author's. Here Borges wonders about that author named Borges. He says autobiographically that he has tried to escape the other Borges by changing his styles—his early stories were indeed about slum-gangsters, and his later ones about time and infinity—but of course one can never escape. Ironically, "I recognize myself less in his books than in those of others or than in the laborious tuning of a guitar."

Ask students if they can identify with this feeling when they write. How authentic is the voice in your writing? Lead them into thinking about alienation from oneself, and the otherness and objectification of the self in language. The true postmodernist might suggest there is no genuine, authentic, personal Borges, only the projection of his supposed "self" in writing—famously, "there is nothing outside the text." The surprising final line of this little meditation captures the mystery of the writer's self-knowledge perfectly.

The "Poem Written in a Copy of Beowulf" is not really about Beowulf, but about the futile struggle to learn another language late in life. This impossible project becomes, in the poem, an example of human longing, generally. Our passion for starting what we cannot finish captures the paradox of the human condition (compare Kafka's "Imperial Message"), and seems to imply an unspoken belief that there must be something beyond death, even though we know better. The memorable charm of the poem is the simile of language-learning, of studying and forgetting, studying and forgetting, for life, especially in old age: "My life in the same way weaves and unweaves its weary history." Is the poem depressing, or life-affirming? Note that the poem is a sonnet, and for all its casual and conversational tone it has a traditional rhyme-scheme, even in translation. The half-rhymes are almost inaudible at first, until one reaches the final couplet and then re-reads.

Questions for Study and Discussion:

1. "Pierre Menard" is a satire, a parody. What is being satirized, and what is being parodied? Is Borges himself the "author"? How can you tell?

2. Make a list of the most outrageous assertions in "Pierre Menard". Which are by Menard himself, and which by the author? How would you describe the tone of the essay?

3. Is there a serious point being made in "Pierre Menard"? Find statements that reflect the belief of Borges himself. Could there be a point in Menard's claims?

4. What statement is Borges making about art or writing in "Borges and I"? Does his point apply to people like us? What version of you do others percieve in your writing?

5. What does the "Poem Written in a Copy of Beowulf" have to do with "Beowulf", if anything? Paraphrase the sonnet, one short sentence per stanza, and try to restate its theme. Does it state Borges's faith in immortality, or simply his resignation to death? Try to relate the poem to the problem of "Borges and I" (a subtle assignment).

Pablo Neruda
"The Heights of Macchu Picchu," "The Word," The Book of Questions

Of the many possible pairings of authors in this anthology, none is more exact and compelling than that between Pablo Neruda and Walt Whitman, the latter having had a pronounced influence upon the former. Indeed, in many ways, the poetry of Neruda is a twentieth-century elaboration upon Whitman's nineteenth-century innovations—a literary legacy Neruda proudly acknowledged. Both poets use speakers who are, somewhat paradoxically, earthy yet also possessed of a quasi-mystical, god-like perspective. Both poets are passionately committed to celebrating the common people and their respective lands. Both favor techniques of repetition and accretion, and frequent allusion to nature. Both favor a poetics grounded in the long, unrhymed, and hypnotic line. Furthermore, both poets wrote modern American epics. For all of these reasons, introducing Neruda alongside Whitman is a good way to begin discussion of the poetry, and an excellent way to highlight its main features.

Since the selection from Neruda's Canto General is an epic, it makes sense to read it alongside other epic narratives, such as the selections from The Book of Dede Korkut, The Aeneid, the Prose Edda, or the Shāh-nāmah. Paired with the Whitman text, Neruda's poem can be read for its exquisite renderings of the natural world, and both can be compared to natural imagery in the haiku and the travel diary of Matsuo Bashō. It can also usefully be considered in context of creation narratives, such as Hesiod's Theogony and the selections from the Rig Veda and Genesis. Another good possibility for introducing Neruda's writing is as part of a unit on the literature of suffering, remembrance, and consolation, incorporating texts by Master Wŏlmyŏng, Wislawa Szymborska, Anna Akmatova, Irena Klepfisz, Zhang Heng, and Yamanoue Okura.

Along with Salvador Allende (the slain democratic leader), Pablo Neruda is one of the folk heroes of modern Chile. Neruda's former home in Isla Negra (since sealed by military authorities) has become a shrine for admirers of his poetry—particularly for lovers, who cover its fence with messages of affection and gratitude. This fact is significant, because it helps us recall that Neruda was as much a poet of erotic love as he was a politically engaged writer of commemorative odes and epic poetry. One approach to the selection from Neruda is to challenge students to locate images, of which there are many in "The Heights of Macchu Picchu," which reflect this other profound impulse in his poetry. Tracing its sensual imagery will help attune new readers to the characteristic tone of Neruda's poetry, which is intensely emotive and impassioned.

As discussion of the poem moves from an impression of its tone to formal considerations, students should be helped to see how form and content combine to powerful effect. Stanza nine, where subject and technique are perhaps most strikingly merged, is an ideal point at which to focus attention in this relatively long poem. Students will notice how Neruda creates a tower of nouns in imitation of the edifice he is describing. This noun pile is at once an invocation, willing the described structure into existence in imagination, and the "frayed," "frozen" syllables—the literal words—that are the poet's materials. (In "The Word," it will be recalled, Neruda calls language "the wavelength which connects us / with the dead man and the dawn"—the medium, that is, of history and human connection.) Elsewhere in "Macchu Picchu," the repetition of words evokes the repetitive actions of the slave-laborers, whose entire lives went into the building.

Moving outward from stanza nine, students can begin to make sense of more abstract, difficult images. This is, as students will gather, an intensely intuitive poem—one whose massed and juxtaposed images function differently than in most other epics. (The selection from The Book of Questions is illuminating here, for it suggests Neruda's method of arriving at images that are at once unassuming and, because of skillful juxtaposition, also vividly and startlingly complex. Thus, Neruda is able to take ordinary, everyday words—"air," "corn," "moon," and "sand" are some of his favorites—and make them seem strikingly renewed.)

Most of the critical work on Neruda is in Spanish, although there are some English language resources. Alexander Coleman's essay "The Ghost of Whitman in Neruda and Borges," in Walt Whitman of Mickle Street, edited by Geoffrey M. Sill (Knoxville, TN, 1994), is useful for the links between these two great American poets. As Neruda's incantatory lines make clear, he wants us to hear as we read. Another good resource, therefore, is Neruda's reading of "Macchu Picchu" and other poems on the Cædmon recording (New York, 1995). Despite the language barrier, this rendering lets listeners hear the slow, upward straining of the beginning of the sixth stanza and again at stanza eight. (As with other texts in this anthology, students may want to know how much is lost in translation, and this gives them one index by which to judge. Intent listeners, whether or not they know Spanish, will hear the chiming within lines upon which Neruda frequently relies in "Macchu Picchu." Thus, line 30 which, in the original, reads "y taladra metal palpitante en sus manos," lets listeners hear clearly the heavily stressed a's which imitate what they describe.)

Questions for Study and Discussion:

1. Comment on the series of questions Neruda poses in stanza 10 of "The Heights of Macchu Picchu," beginning with "Macchu Picchu, did you put / stone upon stone and, at the base, tatters?" What is the poet getting at with these questions?

2. Why is the poet-speaker like "an / empty net" at the beginning of the epic poem? How is this a useful figure for a poet setting out to write an epic?

3. Discuss the form of the poem. Why are there extended parentheses in the first two stanzas? Why does the form shift dramatically at stanza nine? Why are certain lines set off by themselves?

4. How does reading "The Word" help you understand Neruda's project in the long poem that precedes it?

5. In the excerpts from The Book of Questions, what are lines about Hitler (numbers LXX and LXXI) doing in a sequence remarkable for its charming naivete and whimsical insouciance?

Gabriel García Márquez
"The Handsomest Drowned Man in the World"

This story works well with other examples of Magical Realism in the anthology, most of them produced by writers who must live a double cultural life. This technique, first used by García Márquez, has proved an excellent vehicle for presenting the complex cultural realities of developing countries caught between traditional institutions and modern EuroAmerican cultural pressures from outside. Toni Morrison's Sula utilizes a kind of gothic exaggeration for symbolic purposes as her American predecessor William Faulkner did before her, but the fantastic behavior of Shadrack's hands in our selection from her novel shares the quality of quiet acceptance of the gigantic and preternatural in everyday life that García Márquez achieves in "The Handsomest Drowned Man in the World." Other stories to be compared with García Márquez's are Ángela Hernández's "How to Gather the Shadows of Flowers" and Salwa Bakr's "That Beautiful Undiscovered Voice."

García Márquez's use of apparently supernatural events that are accepted as normal can be contrasted with the tone and effects of ancient mythic traditions like those presented in Homer's Odyssey or the Mayan Popul Vuh, and with more modern works like Wu Cheng'en's Monkey or Cervantes's Don Quixote. Of course the most obvious influence on García Márquez is Jonathan Swift's Gulliver's Travels, with its long episode describing Gulliver's adventures as a giant among the Lilliputians. In García Márquez's hands, however, the trope of the giant among the midgets is not used to satirize the smallness of human society, but rather to suggest the marvelous effect of mysterious visitation.

The simple language and flat description used in "The Handsomest Drowned Man in the World" contrast oddly with the enormous size of the body that washes up beside the bleak little village that seems so lacking in character. García Márquez's technique could be seen as a reversal of the mock heroic strategies used in Don Quixote. Students can be asked to try to define the effect the body has on the villagers, partly by closely examining the descriptions of how the body is lovingly brought into town and cared for, and partly by contrasting the appearance of the village before and after this strange visitation. Attention to particular detail will go as far as any other interrogative technique in illuminating the story's subtle effects, especially if it is paid to the way the villagers' behavior changes through the story.

Among many recent studies Raymond L. Williams's Gabriel García Márquez (Boston, 1984) offers a good introduction to the life and works. For a variety of critical approaches, see Critical Essays on Gabriel García Márquez, edited by George R. McMurray (Boston, 1987) and

Critical Perspectives on Gabriel García Márquez, edited by Bradley A. Shaw and Nora Vera-Godwin (Lincoln, Nebraska, 1986).

Questions for Study and Discussion:

1. What kind of place is the setting for this story? Look closely at the details García Márquez chooses to use in describing it, and try to decide what effect he wants to create. When you get to the end of the story, contrast the appearance of the village to its initial look.

2. Why do the village women decide that the drowned stranger's name is Esteban? What kinds of desires do they project upon him, and how do their feelings change?

3. What is it about his face that leaves the village men as well as the women breathless?

4. How and why does Esteban change the villagers' behavior after the funeral? What might he represent in our own lives?

Ángela Hernández
"How to Gather the Shadows of the Flowers"

The plight of Faride in this story of surreal retreat into poetry echoes the theme of the abandoned or betrayed woman that is common in world literature because of women's social dependence upon men in so many cultures. However, such situations stand in stark contrast to the archaic portraits of independent goddesses in the Sumerian hymns to Inanna and the Homeric "Hymn to Demeter." Interesting connections can be made between the gender relations implied in the ancient portraits of goddesses and later depictions of conventional limitations for women's lives, and Hernández's story can be set in this historical context. Early examples of women writing of dependence and loss in relations with men are the medieval Japanese journals of Izumi Shikibu and Murasaki Shikibu's great novel, The Tale of Genji, as well as the letters of the medieval French nun Heloise to her former lover Abelard. Later works which offer comparisons are Cao Xueqin's Dream of the Red Chamber, in which Dai-yu wastes away and dies because her love for Bao-yu is thwarted, and Korean poet Hŏ Nansŏrhŏn's "A Woman's Sorrow." But the 15th century Indian bhakti poet Mirabai finds escape from the limitations of the traditional wifely role in her devotional poetry to the god Krishna. A modern story close to Hernández's metaphoric use of art as reflection of women's unexpressed talents and emotions is Salwa Bakr's "That Beautiful Undiscovered Voice." Women characters who rebel against conventional restrictions are Jane Austen's Elizabeth Bennet of Pride and Prejudice, Virginia Woolf's artist Lily Briscoe in To the Lighthouse, and Louise Erdrich's "Saint Marie." Their strategies for self-fulfilment offer illuminating contrasts to the entrapment depicted in "How to Gather the Shadows of Flowers."

One easy way to help students get a handle on this unusual story is to ask them to identify the different voices or perspectives from which it is told. The most obvious distinctive voices are the poems of Faride and the italicized passages of the anonymous outside reporter who is a friend of Faride's brother José. The other three voices are those of a sister, the mother, and Faride herself. Examining the interweaving of these voices helps to sort out the several attitudes toward Faride's situation, but it might be useful also to discuss why Hernández decided to use so many instead of a more straightforward narrative to dramatize the psychological withdrawal of a young woman abandoned by her husband. The symbolism of flowers and gardens is obviously central to Faride's psychological situation, and thus close attention to it and to interpretations of her poems can reveal possible ways of defining the changes which gradually lead to her death. Hernández's use of surreal imagery and Faride's strange sleeping habits can be linked to Marquez's "Magic Realism" and also to Toni Morrison's treatment of Shadrack in Sula. Students should try to figure out whether Hernández is suggesting the existence of some parallel universe or supernatural realm where Faride finds solace for her distress.

Because Hernández writes in Spanish and is part of a literary community that is newly reaching the awareness of Euro-American readers, commentary on her work is not readily available. One useful background study, however, is Ileana Roderiguez's House/Garden/Nation: Space, Gender and Ethnicity in Post-Colonial Latin American Literatures, translated by Robert Carr and Ileana Roderiguez (Durham, NC, 1994).

Questions for Study and Discussion:

1. Why does this story begin with a poem? How does the author capture our attention in the opening paragraphs? Where exactly do we see the central problem of Faride's life coming clear?

2. How many different voices are operating in this story? What distinguishing features do they have? Are some more reliable than others?

3. What kind of person is Faride, and what happens to her? How does her psychological state change and develop?

4. What do Faride's narratives and poems reveal? Does she have access to another world, or is she merely hallucinating? Is her poetry good?

5. Why does Faride die, and what is the ultimate point of the story?

Walt Whitman
"Memories of President Lincoln: When Lilacs Last in the Dooryard Bloom'd"

This famous elegy, in which Whitman grieves for the slain president, works particularly well when introduced alongside other, older texts of mourning. Gilgamesh's lament for Enkidu is a good starting point, and one that has the additional advantage of providing a context for the sensual love of comrades which is such an important feature of the poetry in Leaves of Grass. Pericles's oration (Book II of Thucydides's The Peloponnesian War) is another excellent companion piece, its exaltation of duty in battle as a civic virtue giving rise to discussion of patriotism and loss. By contrast, the account of the death and return of Jesus of Nazareth in The New Testament provides another emphasis and a different kind of solace. The "Lament for a Brother," by al-Khansā', is a further possibility—one that shares a direct, thematic connection with Whitman's poem—while Rilke's Duino Elegies have a more oblique, but productive, connection. Among contemporary texts, Anna Akhmatova's Requiem and Irena Klepfisz's Bashert are two that work well with the Whitman poem. A good alternative strategy is that hinted at in the introduction: focusing on the metaphysical elements in the poetry—evidence of Whitman's role as poet-priest—and the many places comparable elements appear in other sections of The World of Literature.

In subject and sensibility this is, emphatically, an American poem—a fact that fairly leaps off the page in a world literature course. Whitman set himself purposefully against European models of poetry, dubbing himself "the begetter of a new offspring out of literature," and creating a rugged persona—a new voice "[o]f pure American breed, large and lusty"—to match his poetic ambition. The persona and the self-promotion are themselves as American as the poems in Leaves of Grass. Describing the poem's "Americanness" is a good way for students to begin. From there, any number of possible approaches to exploring "When Lilacs Last in the Dooryard Bloom'd" are available. Broad lines of inquiry might include the daring of Whitman's opening up of the poetic line—an expansive line for an expansive subject—and how "free verse" mirrors a democratic vision; the incantatory, cataloguing, "cinematic," egocentric, sensitive, inquisitive, and exhilarating voice of the speaker, and its creation of an archetypal American everyman; or, alternatively, the way the poem moves from grief to acceptance.

Teachers are pleased to find that this selection has a cumulative force that still communicates strongly to students, even if its strategies and some of its symbols go unrecognized. Whitman may have become—or been turned into—the Good Grey Poet, but he is also a bohemian radical, iconoclast, and precursor of literary modernism, and it is perhaps this element in him and his poetry to which students are drawn. To help understand the techniques Whitman is using in this poem, discussion might well begin with the thrush's song at its core, where students generally have the easiest time understanding each word and line. The reconciliation with death sung by the thrush makes intelligible the broader reconciliations—notably of North and South—which the poem seeks to effect. Just as Whitman had personal knowledge of the event at the core of the poem (his friend and companion, Peter Doyle, was inside Ford's Theater when Lincoln was shot), it is useful to recall that, in addition to his work tending the wounded of both armies, his brother George was a Union soldier, whereas his friend, Doyle, fought for the Confederacy. Reconciliation, as a result, was not an abstract idea for Whitman. The journey of Lincoln's coffin becomes the occasion for capturing the epic sweep Whitman wants in his poem, with large, natural cycles serving as reminders of regenerative healing. Provided this background, students can better understand the choice of the three key symbols—lilac, star, and bird (all of them mediated by the poet-speaker)—and judge the extent to which they achieve the twin goals of memorialization and reconciliation that Whitman has set for himself.

Two manageable and accessible introductions to Whitman's life and writing are Joann P. Krieg's A Whitman Chronology (Iowa City, 1998) and James E. Miller Jr.'s Walt Whitman (in the Twayne's United States Authors series, Boston, 1990). Krieg's book steers a middle course between the scanty and the superabundant, giving a select day-by-day account of the poet's life, culling from the momentous and the ordinary in it. Miller's book, for its part, fills out the picture of the poet which is implied by Krieg's useful outline. For Whitman's critical reputation, Walt Whitman: The Contemporary Reviews (New York, 1996), edited by Kenneth Price, is a record of the poet's reception in his own time. Walt Whitman and the World, edited by Gay Wilson Allen and Ed Folsom (Iowa City, 1995), is valuable for bringing together a series of essays devoted to Whitman's international reputation and critical reception in other parts of the world. For recent criticism, Ezra Greenspan's The Cambridge Companion to Walt Whitman has ten thoughtful essays and a useful introduction.

Questions for Study and Discussion:

1. Compare Whitman's elegy with twentieth-century texts of mourning. What differences do you notice?

2. How does this poem fulfil the basic aim of the elegy, that of moving an audience from grief to acceptance? How well does it succeed?

3. Why is Lincoln's death significant? How effective is Whitman in making of the event an occasion for more general mourning and reconciliation?

4. Why does the poet focus on lilacs in a dooryard? Wouldn't the poem be better served by a first line like, say, "When our noble leader, Lincoln, breathed his last"?

Emily Dickinson
Poems

The striking thing about Emily Dickinson's poetry is its fresh, daringly modern tone and riddling use of language. Thus she can be read with more recent poets who use oblique, allusive techniques, poets like Wislawa Szymborska and Elizabeth Bishop, as well as with Pablo Neruda's Book of Questions. Although she apparently did not know the Japanese tradition in poetry, she writes verse that shares many qualities of economy and lightness of touch with the court poets of the Heian period. And like Bashō's haiku masterpieces, Dickinson's poems say a great deal in few words, are often focused on ordinary natural scenes, and have a wry, riddling way of making their point. Dickinson's vision was essentially religious, though unconventionally so, and thus she shares Bashō's concern with the spiritual realm that coexists with the familiar world of everyday life. Her poetry can be interestingly related to the Psalms of the Hebrew Bible, because of course she knew the Old Testament well. Hers is a witty, questioning relationship with the patriarchal deity, however.

The most traditional way to read Dickinson is as a contrast and complement to Walt Whitman. Together they established new ways of writing American poetry that would define the practice of most twentieth-century poetry in the United States. Dickinson's compact, intense messages in the familiar form of hymn meter work very well for students raised in the Protestant tradition of hymn singing, and demonstrations of how they can be sung can be a vivid way of dramatizing their form. In order to communicate her indirect way of making her points, one can start a discussion of our selection of poems with "Tell All the Truth but tell it slant," because there the poet explains the dazzling power of truth that must be approached from around its edges rather than directly. Other riddling poems that show her playfulness and intellectual ingenuity are "The Brain—is wider than the Sky" (632) and "A narrow Fellow in the Grass" (986).

Poems can be grouped by subject, with 465 and 712 discussed as two quite different treatments of death. "I heard a Fly buzz—when I died" (465) is a famous example of the intimate terror Dickinson often captures when she confronts the inevitable experience that awaits us and that she witnessed often in a world where the domestic setting was the place where most people died. The tiny sound of the fly's buzz focuses the tension of the scene almost humorously but also with a grotesque power, as the speaker's consciousness is blotted out. "Because I could not stop for Death," (712) in contrast, uses a graceful courtship metaphor for the final journey to the grave, passing along the road where ordinary scenes of life are bid farewell. "The Soul selects her own Society" (303) and "Much Madness is divinest Sense" (435) communicate in paradoxical terms Dickinson's intense sense of privacy and individuality. Her spirituality is clear in poems like "This World is not Conclusion" (501) and "These are the days when Birds come back" (130). The second of these compares the Christian sacrament of communion, with its bread and wine representing the body and blood of Jesus, to the poignant beauty of autumn through the awed vision of a child of God. This little poem is intellectually quite complex, because it begins with the suggestion of fraudulent weather, "a blue and gold mistake," which turns into the sacred revelation of the beauty of the dying year. Students may reasonably be puzzled by what kind of belief is meant at the end of the third stanza, and what tone is achieved by the end of the poem.

For background on Dickinson's life, the definitive biography is Richard B. Sewall's The Life of Emily Dickinson (New York, 1974). David Porter examines her poetics in Dickinson: The Modern Idiom (Cambridge, Mass., 1981), and Judith Farr assesses her contribution in The Passion of Emily Dickinson (Cambridge, Mass., 1992). A variety of recent approaches to Dickinson's life and work can be found in The Emily Dickinson Handbook, edited by Gudrun Grabner, Roland Hagenbuchle, and Cristanne Miller (Amherst, Mass., 1998).

Questions for Study and Discussion:

1. What kind of a person emerges from these poems? Choose three different poems and examine the persona or sense of voice conveyed by each. How is the effect created in each case, and what might its purpose be for the poem's meaning?

2. How is religious imagery used in "These are the days when Birds come back" (130)? Notice how puns on religious terms are used. How do the birds function to introduced the poem's subject? What time of year is Dickinson describing, and why?

3. How does Dickinson define "Madness" in "Much Madness is divinest Sense," and who can determine where sense and madness diverge ?

4. In "This World is not Conclusion," identify the ways the poet defines the invisible world beyond ordinary reality. What experiences and sensations does she use as analogous to the unseen realm? What is the "Tooth" that nibbles at the soul?

5. How does Dickinson develop the point of view of "I heard a Fly buzz—when I died"? Who is speaking, and what kind of storm might be meant at the end of the first stanza? What is the function of the fly for the speaker, and why is its buzz blue and stumbling?

6. Why is death described as a courtly gentleman in "Because I could not stop for Death"? What are the stages of the journey in the strange carriage, and why does the poet describe the grave as a house?

7. Identify the different comparisons Dickinson gathers up to describe the "narrow Fellow in the Grass." What is the tone of the poem, and what is gained from the riddling approach?

Ezra Pound
Poems

As we mention in the introduction, the first two selections from Pound are translations from the Chinese poet Li Bai. The third is inspired by Chinese poetry and Japanese haiku. We recommend that these selections of Pound be taught in conjunction with these Chinese and Japanese poems and that students look into how Pound's drawing on these Asian traditions changed the nature of modernist lyric in English. Canto I can be taught in relation to epic poetry—for example, alongside Hymns to Innana, Gilgamesh, Homer, Virgil, or Dante—as well as in the context of modernism.

Pound had a marvelous ear, so the students should be encouraged to read the poems aloud. Pound himself has recorded at least two of these, which are available on Cædmon records. It would be good to discuss Pound's meter, especially in the first Canto. Students should know that Pound is here drawing on the line of Old English poetry, with its strong pause in the middle of the line, its alliteration, and its accentual (rather than accentual-syllabic) verse. In other words, what matters in the Anglo-Saxon line and in the lines of this Canto are the stresses; the number of syllables is variable.

Students should be aware that Pound, at the time he was "translating" the first two poems in our selection, did not know any Chinese. He was relying upon notes by Ernest Fenelosa of Japanese translations of the Chinese.

Hugh Kenner's The Pound Era (Berkeley, 1971) remains an important gloss on Pound and his poetry; it is wide-ranging and authoritative. Donald Davie's Ezra Pound: Poet as Sculpture (New York, 1964) is also very useful. A very good recent book that looks at Pound's use of Chinese and Japanese poetry is Orientalism and Modernism: The Legacy of China in Pound and Williams (Durham, NC, 1995) by Zhaoming Qian.

Questions for Study and Discussion:

1. How do depictions of the natural world, in the first three poems, create a sustaining mood?

2. What is the relation between Pound's modernism and his use of poetic models from China and Japan?

3. Comment on the use of juxtaposition in the third and fourth selections.

4. What is Pound saying about the poet/artist in Canto I?

5. What is the principle of Pound's poetic line in Canto I?

T. S. Eliot
"The Waste Land"

Working very meticulously through the sections of "The Waste Land" included in the anthology will reward students with the sense of encountering and gradually understanding an extremely difficult text. It is important for them to know that the selection in the anthology is not the complete poem, and some students may want to explore the whole text more thoroughly. One might begin by reading the poem in class with the students, helping them to understand the tissue of quotations that make up the poem. Students will be amazed to discover the borrowings that constitute so much of the poem. Then, gradually moving from an understanding of where the lines and images come from to a sense of individual stanzas to a sense of the sections, teachers might encourage students to slowly construct a sense of the poem's main meanings. Reading the poem aloud also reinforces its multi-vocal nature and the fact that the sounds and rhythms of the poem are very carefully crafted to further meanings. Students could even be asked to read and reread the poem aloud, entertaining possible ways of reading the sections.

Beginning with a close reading of the poem in class <u>before</u> students attempt to read on their own is another useful strategy. Students can be challenged to move through the selections line-by-line, identifying paradoxes and tensions and their own associations with the poetic material. The first section, entitled "Burial of the Dead," would seem to be funereal, and yet its first line ends with the word "breeding." And where April's showers are sweet in the first line of Chaucer's <u>Canterbury Tales</u>, Eliot's April "is the cruellest month." Being stirred awake is, in the Waste Land, painful. The poem is also a tissue of memories—cultural ones and apparently individual ones. The voice in 13-17 recalling a childhood visit to an aristocratic cousin remembers a time when she felt frightened but alive: "In the mountains, there you feel free." But the adult voice framing that memory, the one who runs into a relative or friend, the one who stops in the Hofgarten and drinks coffee and visits quietly for an hour is much more stolid: "I read, much of the night, and go south in the winter" (see lines 8-12 and 18). Students will need to be encouraged to see and hear these and other fragments as meaningful elements in the poem. Eliot refused to give "The Waste Land" a precise narrative framework or exact chronology; instead, he asks his readers to fill in the spaces between scenes, to construct an understanding of the contrasts and echoes found throughout the text. It is a poem that demands active readers; that is, it is a poem that demands that readers wake up out of their complacence and respond to the text by working to make meaning. Still, students will probably need help with the foreign languages and with the many quotations—quotations ranging from Dante to Baudelaire, Shakespeare to mythology—which it contains. They may also need help with the echoes of early twentieth-century popular songs and important English landmarks. Annotations of these various references are available in any good critical edition of "the Waste Land," particularly those found in Norton editions of the poem. These are supplemented productively by Lois Cuddy and David Hirsch, editors, in <u>Critical Essays on T. S. Eliot's "The Waste Land"</u> (1991).

Questions for Study and Discussion:

1. Find all the images and scenes that seem to depict death, sluggishness, or moral turpitude; then make a list of all the images and scenes that seem to depict life, activity, moral or spiritual hope. Do some of these dominate some parts of the poem? Does this help us understand the meanings in the poem? How so?

2. What does Eliot accomplish by weaving together all these quotations and voices from other times, places, cultures, and writers? Does he accomplish something that could not be accomplished by any other means?

3. The poem consists of several scenarios and dialogues between people. Identify where these occur, who speaks, who listens, and what seems to be the literal meaning of the exchange.

4. Do the titles of the individual sections help us construct an interpretation of the poem?

5. Identify the paradoxes and tensions found within each section of the poem. Do these tensions provide any clues as to the poem's meanings?

6. The use of the fragment is fundamental to Eliot's vision of the world in "The Waste Land." Do all these fragments pull meaning apart? Do they accumulate and create something greater than any one fragment? Is there any unity resolving the fragments into something? Or do the fragments confirm non-meaning and disintegration?

William Faulkner
"That Evening Sun"

The despair of Nancy, the black servant of Faulkner's decadent white Compson family, is an extreme example of the plight of women whose sexuality is exploited in societies controlled by men. Her situation as the mistress of a white deacon in the Baptist Church is different from women's entrapment in other stories in our selection because of the peculiar circumstances of life in the segregated Deep South of the United States, but Nancy shares with many women around the world problems of powerlessness and an inability to legitimately voice their pain. Dai-yu's grief-stricken death in Dream of the Red Chamber is a passive response to hopeless love. Hŏ Nansŏrhŏn's poem "A Woman's Sorrow" expresses the grief of an abandoned wife, as does Ángela Hernández's story "How to Gather the Shadows of Flowers." Heloise's letters to Abelard voice her sorrows within a patriarchal religious ideology that defines women's very being as corrupt. Faulkner's Nancy, by contrast, is trapped in a situation where her chief exploiter kicks out her teeth when she complains, and her disgruntled husband stalks and eventually kills her. Salwa Bakr's "That Beautiful Undiscovered Voice" uses magical realism to present a metaphor for the potential of women that is lost in the blankness and trivia of domestic service, while Ōba Minako's "The Three Crabs" depicts infidelity and interracial minglings that do not take on a tragic import but merely define dissatisfied marital relationships in an alienated society. The only work of fiction in our anthology that comes close to defining the terror of racial oppression like that revealed in Faulkner's story is Toni Morrison's Sula, in which Shadrack, the shell-shocked survivor of World War I, embodies in his prophetic madness the suffering of his whole African-American community.

Point of view is crucial to this story, so that Quentin Compson's age and level of understanding need to be determined at the beginning. The opening paragraphs create a nostalgic childhood memory of the sleepy little county seat of Jefferson, Mississippi, before the era of paved streets and electricity. This dreamy picture contains several ironic foreshadowings such as the comparison of the bundles of clothes carried by the washerwomen to bales of cotton or references to Nancy's sad face and missing teeth. But primarily it sets an idyllic scene that almost immediately erodes through the gradual revelation of what lies beneath the placid surface of village life. Narrative voice here seems to be that of an adult remembering, but once we are plunged into the dramatic immediacy of the story, told primarily through dialogue with only brief narrative links, we have been returned to the minds of the Compson children who are baffled by Nancy's strange behavior. Students can be asked to identify suspenseful moments created by the children's baffled questions—"Off what vine?" "Talking what way?" "Are you drunk, Nancy?" Also, attention to the family's dynamics is revealing, with particular interest lying in the

relationship between the parents, Mr. and Mrs. Compson, who offer a less violent parallel to the problems between Jesus and Nancy. Working with students to unravel the mystery of Nancy's behavior is certain to open the story's terrible center to understanding. And attention to the title's
relation to the blues song of that name can focus students' sense of the story's pervasive irony.

The one-volume edition of Joseph Blotner's <u>Faulkner: A Biography</u> (New York, 1984), is the definitive study of the life and work. Joel Williamson's more recent <u>William Faulkner and Southern History</u> (New York, 1993) represents a dramatic breakthrough in revealing the African-American side of Faulkner's lineage that corresponds to the mixed McCaslin family in his fiction. Williamson's book is also the most intelligent treatment of the crucial historical context of Faulkner's work. Edmund Volpe's <u>A Reader's Guide to William Faulkner</u> (New York, 1964) can provide a basic introduction to the fictional Yoknapatawpha County where Faulkner's writing is set, and to the characters who people it.

<u>Questions for Study and Discussion</u>:

1. What do the opening paragraphs tell us about the theme of the story, and how does the tone of description change as we move into the present? Identify sinister clues to problems under the surface of the world described in the first paragraph.

2. Who is telling this story, and why? Point of view is a matter of narrative craft that makes a crucial difference here, particularly given Faulkner's highly sensitive subject matter. Can you guess why several magazines turned the story down when he first submitted it, and even its eventual editor H. L. Mencken was uneasy about printing it in his magazine, The American Mercury?

3. How do we come to know the personalities of the Compson children?

4. Why is Mrs. Compson so querulous? What is the relationship between Mr. and Mrs. Compson, and is it at all pertinent to the focal marriage of the story, that of Nancy and Jesus?

5. What is the matter with Nancy, and what specifically reveals her problems? Are we supposed to sympathize with her or condemn her? How does the author shape our response? (In other writings, Faulkner's Compson characters refer to Nancy's murder by her husband.)

6. Why did Faulkner name Nancy's husband Jesus?

Elizabeth Bishop
Poems

Like the great Chilean poet, Pablo Neruda, who was her contemporary, Elizabeth Bishop uses the language of ordinary life for her poetry. Bishop lived a good part of her adult life in Brazil, thus sharing the postcolonial Latin cultural environment of South America with Neruda. However, these poets can be usefully contrasted in the ways they conceive the world and communicate their ideas. Bishop's work is muted, understated, and oblique, while Neruda's imagination fuses the grandeur of Chile's landscape and human passions with the sweep of history and the powerful fecundity of nature. Bishop shares the instinct for privacy with her American predecessor Emily Dickinson, and similarly focuses her contemplations upon homely domestic details and situations. Reading Bishop side by side with T.S. Eliot makes clear the difference between his scholarly, difficult Modernism and Bishop's more accessible uses of allusion and oblique treatment of painful subjects. Another poet who can be fruitfully read beside Bishop is Polish poet Wislawa Szymborska. Both write with wry humor and use apparently ordinary settings to explore large issues.

Working with students to unravel the tightly-packed meanings of Bishop's poems can be an exciting experience. At first the poems may seem to be completely flat, but if students are asked to question the use of words that seem oddly out of place, they will begin to open the surprising images and ideas that transform the apparently ordinary subjects about which she writes. In "The Fish," for instance, key words that seem to declare that the poem simply describes a large, ugly fish soon are thrown into question by comparisons of the fish's skin to wallpaper or his flesh to feathers, and his bladder to "a big peony." Looking back from these surprising comparisons to the poem's opening, one sees that the word "tremendous" has gained a strange significance, as has the string of adjectives, "battered and venerable and homely." Contrasting objective details such as barnacles and sea-lice with the poet's responses and her references to domestic objects (wallpaper, tinfoil) begins to open the poem up to a sense of wonder at the heroic old fish. Gradually, as military terms alternate with acutely observed details of the fish's appearance, we are prepared for the final glory seen ironically in the puddle of oil in the boat's bilge that seems to celebrate the old fish's nobility and leads the poet to release him.

"At the Fishhouses" begins with a clear description of a New England fishing harbor and seems to promise little more than an elegantly rendered evocation of place. However, the short middle stanza moves the scene down into the water via a long ramp, and in doing so moves the poem into the deeper metaphysical significance that has been gathering in the background from the beginning. If students look closely at how the scene is built up in the poem's first half, and then look for words like "mortal" and references to Christianity that begin the final section, they will begin to see that the seal who appears and seems to communicate with the speaker is really gesturing towards an enormous mysterious reality beneath the surface of appearances.

"The Armadillo" also opens out from a seemingly simple beginning, this time to deal with the terrible question of what humans do to other animals. Students can be asked to identify where the paper "fire balloons" begin to take on larger than literal meanings, and what specific techniques Bishop uses to indicate the change. Attention should also be called to the two halves of the poem: first the general description, and then the specific crash of one "egg of fire" and its consequences.

"In the Waiting Room" is one of Bishop's best known poems. Students will begin to make sense of the poem if they look closely at details, think about the cry the little girl hears, and then focus on the emotional crisis that is linked to what she sees in The National Geographic Magazine.

A fresh, immediate sense of Elizabeth Bishop's mind and views on poetry is provided by the recent Conversations with Elizabeth Bishop, edited by George Monteiro (Jackson, Miss., 1996). This is a collection of interviews with the poet that reveals her sense of humor, her no-nonsense view of her poetry, and her deep personal modesty. For at least a decade after Bishop's death in 1979, friends carefully protected her privacy by not speaking about her personal life or allowing access to letters and other memorabilia. In recent years, however, these materials have become available so that it is possible to have a much fuller view of her life and work. Two well-informed recent studies are Victoria Harrison's Elizabeth Bishop's Poetics of Intimacy (New York, 1993) and Marilyn May Lombardi's The Body and the Song: Elizabeth Bishop's Poetics (Carbondale, 1995).

Questions for Study and Discussion:

1. Make a list of the specific comparisons Bishop uses in "The Fish." What connotations do they bring to the poem? What kinds of adjectives does she use for the fish? Do they suggest a pattern of meaning? What does the poet learn by looking at his eyes, and what makes her let him go? How does the rainbow work?

2. In "At the Fishhouses" what changes between the first and second halves of the poem? Why does the poet repeat "Cold dark deep and absolutely clear" in the last section, and what does the seal communicate? Look for religious imagery throughout the poem, and try to determine what the poet achieves by referring to Martin Luther's hymn "A Mighty Fortress is our God" and Christmas.

3. What is the relationship between the first and second half of "The Armadillo," and where has the poet taken us by the end of the poem? Why is it named for the armadillo, when the poem seems to be more concerned with the fire balloons?

4. What literally happens to the little girl who narrates "In the Waiting Room"? Why did Bishop choose to describe the volcano pictured in The National Geographic? What is the turning point of the poem, and what has the speaker learned. Why does the poem end so flatly?

Toni Morrison
Sula

From its first sentence, Sula is about dispossession from and belonging to community. In this section of the novel, it is shell-shocked Shadrack who, like the nightshade and blackberry vines (the choice of plants not being incidental) torn from their roots, is deprived of his senses, left "with no past, no language, no tribe"—only to be gathered, gradually, into "the fabric of life up in the Bottom of Medallion, Ohio." Left "permanently astonished" by World War One and convinced that his own appendages are monstrous, Shadrack joins the ranks of famous casualties of the twentieth-century, Virginia Woolf's Septimus Smith and Franz Kafka's Gregor Samsa among them. Sula can be taught in a unit on such extreme mental states, with pairings drawn from Abe Kōbō's and Dostoyevsky's stories, Eliot's poem, Beckett's play and, among older texts, Shakespeare's King Lear. Alternatively, the Morrison selection can be considered in terms of the experience of diaspora and cultural disruption, discussed with poems by Anna Akhmatova, Fadwa Tuqan, Yehuda Amichai, Irena Klepfisz, and Leopold Sédar Senghor; stories by Louise Erdrich, Sonu Hwi, and Ding Ling; and the play by Wole Soyinka.

Although there are many currents to be brought to the surface in discussion of this section of Morrison's novel, two are crucial. Morrison's depiction of Medallion's black neighborhood is, significantly, elegiac. It has already passed before it is presented to readers: it is a place where "there was once a neighborhood." Although Morrison writes that "perhaps it is just as well" that suburbs erase the old neighborhood, this is a ruse: Medallion, as its name implies, is commemorative, and Sula is that act of remembering against effacement. The elegiac tones of Morrison's description seep into and temper the "shucking, knee-slapping, wet-eyed laughter" that partly characterizes life in the black community. At the same time, it is clear that "laughter was part of the pain" of the place, and it is this subtle mixture which is central to Morrison's rendering of black life in segregated America.

The other strand to which attention should be drawn is the text's movement between order and disorder—a movement in which "freedom" is not identical with either term (perhaps because, in the context of a segregated society, it can never signify fully). Students can trace the play of "order" and "disorder" in this selection, seeing the joyful disorder of "a bit of cakewalk, a bit of black bottom, a bit of 'messing around'" in the Bottom (the very name of which disorders intuition, with "the Bottom" on high, the valley below). They can recognize in the "shouts and explosions" of December, 1917 the disordering event that forever rattles Shadrack's senses, as well as "the neat balance of the triangles" of food that Morrison describes Shadrack being served as he convalesces, and "the cropped shrubbery, the edged lawns, the undeviating sidewalks" with which he is confronted upon his release from the hospital. Shadrack's disordered stumbling (mistaken for drunkenness) gets him into trouble in the "pretty, quietly regulated downtown" into which he zigzags; his invention—National Suicide Day—is his mad effort to impose order on the rest of the year, making it "safe" as well as "free." In making room for Shadrack's madness, "absorb[ing] it into their thoughts, into their language, into their lives," Morrison is making a point about the nature of black culture—its flexibility and resilience, its capaciousness and variety—and some of the strategies with which it negotiates the order and disorder that is its history.

Recent years have seen a flurry of exciting critical work on Toni Morrison's writing. Since 1995 alone, Jill Matus and Linden Peach have each published books titled Toni Morrison (New York, 1998 and London, 1995, respectively), Philip Page's Dangerous Freedom: Fusion and Fragmentation in Toni Morrison's Novels has appeared (Jackson, Miss., 1995), as have Toni Morrison's Fiction by Jan Furman (Columbia, SC, 1996), Toni Morrison's Fiction: Contemporary Criticism, edited by David L. Middleton (New York, 1997), Toni Morrison: Critical and Theoretical Approaches, edited by Nancy J. Peterson (Baltimore, 1997), and Unflinching Gaze: Morrison and Faulkner Re-envisioned, edited by Carol Kolmerten, et. al. (Jackson, Miss., 1997). All of these are valuable resources. Critical Essays on Toni Morrison, edited by Nellie Y. McKay (Boston, 1988) is another good, slightly older, source, with significant reviews of and essays on Morrison's writing, in addition to interviews. Philip M. Weinstein's What Else But Love?: The Ordeal of Race in Faulkner and Morrison (New York, 1996) is also valuable for the insightful connections it makes between these two major American authors, although Sula does not feature as prominently in it as do others of Morrison's novels. Students may also be directed to the substantial body of journal articles devoted to Morrison's writing.

Questions for Study and Discussion:

1. The opening section of Sula describes life in the Bottom of Medallion, Ohio. To what extent is this a description of resilience, adaptability, and triumph?

2. If Morrison is interested in definitions of African-American selfhood, then what kind of self—or lack thereof—is represented in Shadrack?

3. Discuss the significance of Shadrack seeing and taking pleasure in the sight of his black face in his jail cell.

4. If her writing is, as Toni Morrison contends, never simple entertainment, what more serious issues does this selection help uncover?

Irena Klepfisz
"Bashert"

Oscillating back and forth from liturgical and poetic sections to prose, this cross-genre text performs at the intersections of literary categories just as its narrator lives at a crossroads of nations, languages, historical moments, and selves. One way to begin working on this poem is to read the liturgical opening aloud. The repetition of the word "because" emphasizes the futility of finding reasons or understandable causes for something as horrific as genocide. Within the consolation of repetition is an unfathomable and shocking mystery of why and how millions of people could be murdered. Where we usually use the word "because" to point to reasons, to logical relationships, here the word emphasizes the irrational and the inexplicable fact of genocide and survival.

"Bashert" is organized in a roughly chronological fashion after its opening section. Jumping from memories and accounts of war-torn Poland in the 1940s to Chicago in 1964, the poem also rather powerfully juxtaposes the agony of European anti-semitism with the agony of American racism and classism. Having come from a world in which Jews were despised and annihilated, Klepfisz recognizes the people who are struggling to survive in the United States: the homeless, the latino, the poor, the non-white, welfare mothers and children, the elderly and so on. Aware that she is both individual and precious survivor of a nearly annihilated group, Klepfisz writes at the point of reciprocity, at the crossroads of self and other. The grief, demands, expectations, and sorrows of adult survivors of the concentration camps nearly overcome her in part 3 when, at fourteen on April 17, 1955, she commemorates the Holocaust in a darkened auditorium. She writes, "I am numb with terror at the spectacle around me. I fear these people with blue numbers on their arms, people who are disfigured and scarred, who have missing limbs and uneasy walks, people whose histories repel me . . . . They call out to me and I feel myself dissolving." At that moment, at that young age, she is claimed by the community precisely because she is young and she survived. Later, in the fourth section set in 1981, rather than being horrified at the bodies and sorrows of Jews who died or who survived the Holocaust, she embraces them: "Like these, my despised ancestors, I have become a keeper of accounts . . . . I know they can be revived again that I can trigger them again. That they awaken in me . . . ." The cross-genre text is both remembrance and elegy—remembrance and the record of a gradually transforming self who moves through extremes of place and time and situation to find a sense of self that can encompass the enormity of its own experience. It is a re-membering, a putting back together again what had been so scattered, so dispossessed, so "displaced."

"Bashert" can be read as an elegy alongside other elegies in the anthology. In contrast to the pervasive despair of Eliot's "The Waste Land," "Bashert" takes the fragments of a very real crisis and fragmentation of self and of people and weaves them into a more sure and life-affirming statement. The poem might be read alongside Akhmatova's <u>Requiem</u>, a poem that elegizes the experiences of women who survived Stalin's purges, another monumental holocaust in twentieth-century human history that brutally murdered millions.

Questions for Study and Discussion:

1. What happened to Irena Klepfisz's mother and father during World War II?

2. What happened to Elza? Why is she mentioned in Klepfisz's text?

3. What is "the Holocaust without smoke" that Klepfisz discusses toward the end of section 2?

4. Why is the narrator's thirtieth birthday so important? What does she mean when she claims that she lived at that time "almost equidistant from two continents?"

5. In the fourth section, dated 1981, the narrator takes the phrase "keeper of accounts" and makes it her own. Why does she do this? How does she do this? What does the phrase mean?

6. What happens to the sentences in the fourth section? Why do they begin to fragment, become randomly punctuated by white spaces?

7. Why do you think Klepfisz entitles her poem "Bashert"?

Louise Erdrich
"Saint Marie" (from Love Medicine)

At the heart of Marie Lazarre's story is a struggle for power: an adolescent girl's effort to define her own identity. That she is part Native American, that she leaves the reservation for the convent, and that she finds herself in mortal combat with a wily and fanatical nun are all factors which give her story its particular force, while making salient the story's connections to a larger drama of people at or near the margins, battling for survival. Struggles like Marie's—of marginalized figures in societies governed largely by patriarchal networks and institutions—are at the heart of any number of texts in The World of Literature. The biblical story of Ruth, for example, tells of a woman forced to choose between Moabite and Jewish cultures; her story, like the stories in Love Medicine, forms a "little whole" in a larger and more complex narrative. Christine de Pizan's The Book of the City of Ladies, which, like Erdrich's, draws upon legends and myths, is another text with which "Saint Marie" can be productively paired: at the center of both is a demand for inclusion. Erdrich's story can be considered in tandem with other stories of women in society, as well as in units on women writers, mainstream and marginal peoples, or narratives of everyday life. Likely pairings include texts by Salwa Bakr, Rajee Seth, Ding Ling, Sonu Hwi, Wislawa Szymborska, Toni Morrison, and Irena Klepfisz.

Students respond readily to this story of Marie's struggle with Sister Leopolda and her own dubious "sainthood." Erdrich's rendering is vivid and accessible—indeed, so much so that some readers, lulled by the clear conflict and engagingly naive first-person narrative voice, are tempted to conclude that this is an essentially artless tale—a grimly amusing anecdote, but not literature. This is partly a consequence of the association of oral traditions—upon which Love

Medicine draws—with children's stories. Erdrich's interweaving of motifs from the Hansel and Gretel folktale may reinforce this tendency to read uncritically. It is precisely here, in the interweaving, however, that much of the provocative richness of "Saint Marie" lies.

As the introduction to this selection points out, Louise Erdrich is of mixed German American and Chippewa Indian ancestry. This "double heritage" is a crucial strand of Marie's story, which centers on a meeting of tribal and Catholic religious traditions. Although Marie claims she "was privy to both worlds," her assertion is complicated by its being the recollection of a much older woman recalling the actions of a feisty adolescent—an adolescent, moreover, who, leaving the reservation, goes to the convent on the hill to prove her "whiteness." As students identify and explore Marie's conflicted motivation, they may also begin to sense the disparity between the powerful, recognizably "literary" moments of her narration (her sophisticated self-description, for example: "Veils of love which was only hate petrified by longing—that was me") and the equally powerful vernacular in which much of it is related. A similarly complex strand woven into the fabric of the story is Marie's comic turns of phrase, juxtaposed with the horrors of the abuse she endures at the convent. Discussion of "survivor's humor"—a key concept in much of Erdrich's writing—is a valuable focus in itself. Complex, too, is the moment of recognition with which the story ends: the sudden access of pity that floods the "joyous heat" of Marie's triumph over Sister Leopolda is, significantly, a double sensation, as is the meaning of the wounds/stigmata on her hands. Tracing these and other doublings and juxtapositions in "Saint Marie" is a good way to begin to come to grips with Erdrich's writing.

Although Erdrich is a major contemporary writer, she has not received the sustained, book-length criticism she no doubt will in the future. She has, however, been the subject of numerous interviews in which she critiques, explains, and sometimes defends, her writing. The single best source is <u>Conversations with Louise Erdrich and Michael Dorris</u>, edited by Allan Chavkin and Nancy Feyl Chavkin (Jackson, Miss., 1994), which includes many of Erdrich's interviews since the publication of <u>Love Medicine</u> in 1984. Other resources include Peter G. Beidler's "Three Student's Guides to Louise Erdrich's <u>Love Medicine</u>" (in <u>American Indian Culture and Research Journal</u>, Fall 1992, 167-74), which provides good, basic tools—family trees, lists of principal events in the lives of characters, study questions—for teaching the novel. Debra A. Burdick's "Louise Erdrich's <u>Love Medicine, The Beet Queen</u>, and <u>Tracks: An Annotated Survey of the Criticism through 1994</u>" (in <u>American Indian Culture and Research Journal</u>, Fall 1996, 137-66) summarizes the reception of these three novels in literary reviews.

<u>Questions for Study and Discussion</u>:

1. Describe Marie's motives in going to the convent.

2. Who is "the Dark One" in this story?

3. Is Sister Leopolda simply lying when she says she loves Marie?

4. Comment on the last sentences of the story ("Rise up! . . . this dust!"). What might they mean, given a careful reading of Marie's and Sister Leopolda's characters?